Cathy Carson
President
Ozona Woman's League
1986-88

Diamonds in the Desert

Mary Jo Mason

Ozona Woman's League
Ozona, Texas

The purpose of the Ozona Woman's League is helping to improve themselves and their community.

The calorie count totals listed herein were carefully calculated using the sources listed below. These totals are not intended to serve as absolute authority. Other recognized figures may be available.

"Nutri-Calc." Version IBM-PC/XT. Camoe Corporation. 1986.

Jean A. T. Pennington and Helen Nichols Church. *Food Values of Portions Commonly Used.* 14th Edition. New York: Harper & Row, 1985.

Copies of *Diamonds in the Desert* may be obtained from:

The Ozona Woman's League
Box 1552
Ozona, Texas 76943

or by mailing an order blank from the back of the book to the above address.

Proceeds from the sale of *Diamonds in the Desert* are returned to the community.

Art work by Mary Jo Mason

ISBN: 0-9618029-0-1
Ozona Woman's League
Library of Congress Card Catalog 87-090525
First Printing August 1987 – 5000 copies

Printed by Hart Graphics, Inc.
8000 Shoal Creek Blvd.
Austin, Texas 78758

OZONA: "THE BIGGEST LITTLE TOWN IN TEXAS"

Ozona is located in Southwest Texas on IH 10 midway between El Paso and Houston. It is the only town in Crockett County, which, at 3,000 square miles, is the sixth largest county in Texas. Ozona, still an unincorporated town, has a population of about 4,000. It marks the change between the Edwards Plateau region and the Trans-Pecos country of Texas. The arid area has an annual rainfall of 15 inches. The average temperature ranges from 95° in July to 38° in January.

Ozona is in the heart of the ranching district with sheep, goats, cattle, and horses being the prime agricultural products. Crockett County is a major sheep-producing county. Oil and natural gas also contribute to the economy. The town has long been noted for its large pecan trees which overhang the streets and the beautiful homes along the main streets of town. It earns its nickname of "The Biggest Little Town in Texas" from the friendliness of its citizens.

THE OZONA WOMAN'S LEAGUE

The Ozona Woman's League was organized in July 1960, by 38 young women who wanted the opportunity to broaden their lives by becoming involved in their community. They affiliated with the General Federation of Women's Clubs in 1961 and became a part of the Heart of Texas District. The goals of the organization have not changed since the beginning. They remain focused upon improvement of the community in several areas: civic, cultural, educational, and charitable. Some of the more noted projects embarked upon through the years include: constructing elementary school playground equipment, awarding college scholarships and loans, spearheading efforts to organize and establish both the County Public Library and the Youth Center, furnishing volunteers and supplies for numerous groups such as the Day Care Center, the Kindergarten Pre-Screening Clinic, the County Museum, the Hospital/Care Center, and the Drug Awareness Program.

Since its inception, the Ozona Woman's League has managed to finance itself entirely with only one fund-raising project a year, a pre-Thanksgiving bazaar. This bazaar has become quite well-known in the surrounding area of West Texas with its professional quality arts and crafts and its mouthwatering food section. Receipts from the Food Booth alone make up more than 50% of the Bazaar's sales. Local residents now send in requests for special orders in advance and plan their Thanksgiving dinners with help from the League cooks.

Members have always strived to help those at home by using the funds they raise to assist local needs. Many organizations and families in Crockett County have become recipients of the League's generosity through the years. Currently, membership stands at 45 active members and 7 sustaining members.

COOKBOOK SUPPORTERS

GOLD SPONSORS

Crockett County National Bank
Ozona Butane, Inc.
Ozona National Bank
South Texas Lumber Co.
Mrs. Rufus Ward
The Wardrobe, Pecos
Barn Door Restaurant, San Antonio
Mr. and Mrs. Bill Carson, Jr.
Mr. and Mrs. Buster Deaton

SILVER SPONSORS

Robert A. McCleskey, Midland

PATRONS

Emma Adams
Lockie Sue Bissett
Mike Burkholder
Fred H. Chandler
Geniece Childress
Mary Kinkaid Friend
Ruth White
Mr. and Mrs. J. B. Miller
Susan Pinkard, Marietta, GA
Holland Jewelry, Inc.,
  San Angelo, TX
Perry Hubbard
Harry Stuber, M.D.,
  Cookeville, TN
Thorntons Supermarket, Inc.
Melba Trobaugh, Midland
Mrs. W. C. Ward
Mr. and Mrs. Robert
  Pennington, Atlanta, GA
John L. Henderson,
  Conservation Contractor
Upham Insurance Agency

COOKBOOK COMMITTEE

Chairman—Lou Deaton

Sandy Baggett
Helen Bean
Tina Bean
Cathy Carson
Jeannine Henderson
Camille Jones
Barbara Malone

Mary Jo Mason
Susan McMullan
Shawn Mitchell
Carmen Sutton
Nancy Vannoy
Sherry Scott

OZONA WOMAN'S LEAGUE MEMBERS

Lee Allen
Paula Bailey
Cynthia Berry
Tammy Bunger
Marilyn Chalmers
Ann Childress
Becky Childress
Karen Childress
Sandra Childress
Susie Childress
Elizabeth Clark
Shelley Conner
Nancy Forehand
Sharon Forehand
Debbie Glasscock
Karen Huffman
Benny Gail Hunnicutt
Carol Hunnicutt
Patti May

Lorelei McMullan
Luann Pierce
Jane Richardson
Jodie Sessom
Susan Slaughter
Kay Stewart
Vicki Stokes
Elizabeth Upham
Lisa Wagoner
Lou Whitley
Belinda Wilkins
Laurie Hale
Sharman West
June Cameron
Janie Chandler
Darla Jones
Mae Lay
Jann Miller
Sammye Pierce

ACKNOWLEDGEMENTS

A project of this magnitude involves a large number of people. Without their help, it would have been impossible to produce a cookbook of this size. The Ozona Woman's League is grateful to the following people for their invaluable assistance:

Cookbook name—Shawn Mitchell
Cover design and artwork—Mary Jo Mason
Computer typist—Corie Lane
Computer assistance—Lane Scott
Calorie count—Rachel Hall, County Extension Agent
Production—Nan Mulvaney and Hart Graphics, Inc.
Supplies—Mr. and Mrs. Mike Burkholder of Pecos
Tasting sales—Ozona National Bank and Crockett County
　　　　　　　National Bank
Publicity—*The Ozona Stockman* and KYXX-FM
Fund-Raising—Mary Margaret Scott and Ellen Weinacht of
　　　　　　　Pecos, Gary Buck Mitchell, and Richard Berry

A special thank-you goes to the people of Ozona and Crockett County for their support and encouragement of club projects through the years. League members worked tirelessly for 1½ years preparing the book. Their husbands and families endured the triple-testing of recipes and the hours of committee work in order to help them fulfill a dream. In addition, former club members also contributed to the success by submitting recipes as well. It is with honor that the Ozona Woman's League presents *DIAMONDS IN THE DESERT*.

TABLE OF CONTENTS

Menus

Draw — usually a dry creek bed until it rains.

MENUS

BRUNCH
Darla Jones

*Poached Eggs Supreme
Smoked Sausage Links
Fresh Fruit
Coffee   *Cocoa

BRUNCH
Cathy Carson

Bloody Mary
*Montezuma's Quiche
Fresh Fruit in Season
*Rumaki
Biscuits with Assorted Preserves
*Nut Bread Sandwiches
Coffee   Tea

Cook your favorite nut bread or quick
bread in miniature loaf pans. Slice and
butter to make small sandwiches. These
are great for teas or coffees, too.

COUNTRY DINNER
Sandy Baggett

Apple and Pecan Salad
*Baked Country Ham
*Sweet Potato Casserole
English Peas
*Biscuits and Honey
*Peach Cobbler

THANKSGIVING FEAST
Mary Jo Mason

Roast Turkey
*Cornbread Dressing with Oysters
Giblet Gravy
*Fancy Sweet Potatoes
*Cranberry Salad
Broccoli with Herbed Butter Sauce
Dinner Rolls
*Ambrosia
*Apple Pie   *Pecan Pie

BREAKFAST
Becky Childress

Fresh Fruit with Poppyseed Dressing
*Sausage Casserole
Juice   Coffee

CHRISTMAS OPEN HOUSE
Cathy Carson
Lou Deaton

*Daiquiris   *Eggnog
*Miniature Meat Pies
Turkey and Ham, Cubed
Assorted Cheese, Cubed
Assorted Crackers
*Strawberry Cheese Ball
*Pineapple Cheese Ball
*Rotel Dip   *Shrimp Dip
Assorted Chips
*Christmas Candy
(Fudge, Divinity, and Pralines)

COMPANY DINNER
Lou Deaton

*Shrimp Victoria
Rice   Asparagus
Congealed Salad
Lemon Meringue Pie

COMPANY DINNER
Sandy Baggett

Artichoke Dip with Melba Rounds
Tossed Green Salad with Vinaigrette
*Beef Tenderloin
Green Beans
Parsley Potatoes
*Sour Cream Biscuits
*Creamy Cheesecake with Blueberries

Serve cheesecake on chilled plates.

FAMILY DINNER
Mary Jo Mason

*Chicken Breasts
with Green Peppercorn Sauce
Rice
Steamed Broccoli with Lemon Butter
Honey Glazed Carrots
*Strawberry Pie
or
*Frozen Lime Cream Pie

FAMILY MEAL
Lou Deaton

*Fried Venison Backstrap
Gravy and Biscuits
Mashed Potatoes
*German Squash
Tomato and Lettuce Salad
*Peach Cobbler

*Recipes included. Consult the index.

FAMILY DINNER
Cathy Carson

*Baked Ham with Strawberry Sauce
*Daisy's Potato Salad
Or
Au Gratin Potatoes
*LaVaun's Beans
Steamed Zucchini
Iced Tea

My mother always served this dinner on my first night home from being away, varying the potato dish according to the weather. Serve potato salad in the Spring or Summer and au gratin potatoes in the Winter or Fall. It is still my favorite meal, but very fattening for one who is no longer a teenager. Either the potatoes or the beans can be omitted for persons counting calories.

FAMILY DINNER
Lou Deaton

*Frijoles
Stewed Potatoes
Cabbage Slaw
Cornbread
Vinegar Cobbler

FAMILY MEAL
Lou Deaton

*Baked Goat Meat
Beans
*Sweet Rice
Sliced Tomatoes
Hot Rolls
*Bread Pudding and Vinegar Sauce

FAMILY SUPPER
Cathy Carson

*Mexican Spaghetti
*Pinto Beans
Green Salad
*Ranch or Italian Dressing
Flour Tortillas
*Pecan Pie
Iced Tea

This is my husband's and one of my brothers' favorite meals. In the early 1970's, I served this to my brother and a fraternity brother of his, whom I had never met until he came to the ranch deer hunting. He still thinks I'm a gourmet cook!

PICNIC
Benny Gail Hunnicutt

*Cornish Hens, cooked in foil
Iced Tea or Soft Drinks
Ritz Cracker and Peanut Butter Cookies

LUNCHEON
Barbara Malone

*Donna's Chicken Divan
Fruit Salad
Whole Wheat Dinner Rolls
*Oatmeal Cake

I call this an everyday luncheon that you can prepare ahead of time, except for dinner rolls. I use this when company's coming and I like this for the first meal so I can be free to spend time visiting with them.

BRIDESMAID'S LUNCHEON
Cathy Carson

*Mimosas
*Hawaiian Chicken
Parslied Rice
*Marinated Asparagus
*Orange Glazed Carrots
*Crescent Rolls
Iced Tea
Bride's Favorite Dessert

I like to ask the bride's mother for her daughter's favorite dessert. It helps make her day a little more special.

ITALIAN DINNER
Sandy Baggett

Tomato Slices, Mozzarella Slices and
Purple Onion Rings
with
Basil Vinaigrette
*Eggplant Parmiagana
French Bread and Butter
Strawberries and Cantaloupe Balls

MEXICAN BUFFET
Cathy Carson

Margaritas or Mexican Beer with Limes
*Tortilla Roll-Ups
*Avocado Dip with Tortilla Chips
*Green Enchiladas
*Enchilada Suisse
*Spanish Rice
Lettuce and Tomato Salad
Iced Tea   Sangria
*Brazo de Gitano
*Pralines

GOAT SHEARING DAY
Lorelei McMullan

*Enchilada Pie
*Baked Squash
Green Salad
*Pecan Pralines

Many times goat shearing falls on a cold, February day. An enchilada pie is an easy cold day meal. Goats are famous for hiding in canyons and under bluffs so cowboys are usually pretty hungry and tired after running over hills—lots of times leaving horses tied on top of rims and going afoot.

RUSSIAN DINNER PARTY
Sandy Baggett

Caviar with Melba Toast
Smoked Salmon Slices
with garnish of
Chopped Onions, Egg Yolks,
Egg Whites and Capers
**Beef Stroganoff over Buttered Noodles
Pumpernickel Loaf
with
Butter and Cream Cheese
*German Chocolage Cake
Chocolate Almond Coffee

Wines and Liqueurs:
Hors d'oeuvres—
Vodka Shots chilled over crushed ice
Appetizer—
Dry Chardonnay or White
Burgundy
Entree—
Red Burgundy, i.e. Nuits-Saint-
Georges 1978 or Jordan 1980
Dessert—
Liqueurs like Grand Marnier or
Chambourd Raspberry Liquer,
Cognac and Brandy

1. Serve caviar in small bowl over crushed ice.
2. Make melba toast by cutting off crust of white bread and cutting into bite-sized pieces with small cookie cutter. Lightly brush with butter and broil at 200° until very light brown.
3. For salmon garnish, hard boil eggs and serve salmon on a bed of leafy lettuce.
4. Soften butter and place in molds.
5. Serve after-dinner coffee in demitasse cups and saucers.
6. Play late 19th-century Russian music in the background.

*Recipes included. Consult the index.

RANCH DINNER
Sandy Baggett

Sliced Tomatoes and Onions
*Ranch Style Dressing
*Oven Baked Brisket
*Pinto Beans
*Nannie's Squash
Cornbread
*Baked Apple Crisp
Vanilla Ice Cream

Centerpiece: Crock pitcher with flowers
Linens: Plaid or bandana napkins and natural placemats

RANCH WORKDAY MEAL
Lorelei McMullan

*Baked Goat Meat
*Pinto Beans and Tortillas
Jello Salad
Zucchini Squash
*Chocolate Cake
Freshly Brewed Iced Tea

Cook beans in crock pot and bake goat meat in a slow oven. Bake cake and fix jello salad the night before. Cook zucchini and warm up tortillas when you get in from the pasture. Meals are such that I might leave at 6:30 on horseback and come in tired but have nearly all my meal hot and ready to eat.

LET'S SHEAR SHEEP!
Elizabeth Upham

*Barbecued Beef Brisket
*Frijole Beans with Pico De Gallo
*Marinated Vegetable Medley
*Garlic Cheese Grits
Hot Rolls
*Cobbler, The Easy Way

Appetizers

Sheep — producers of food and fiber, lamb and wool.

Mimosas

CALORIES: 139
CARBOHYDRATES: 16g

PROTEIN: 1g

chilled champagne

chilled orange juice

Fill champagne flute or wine glass half full with champagne. Add orange juice to fill. Garnish with fruit orange slices.

Cathy Carson

Champagne Punch

YIELD: 32 4 ounce servings
CALORIES: 51

CARBOHYDRATES: 9g

⅔ cup lemon juice
⅓ cup sugar
3 cups cranberry juice
ice or decorative ice ring

3 26 ounce bottles
champagne
1 28 ounce bottle of ginger ale

Chill all liquids. Stir lemon juice with sugar until dissolved. Mix in cranberry juice. Place ice or ice ring in punch bowl. Add fruit juices, champagne and ginger ale.

Cathy Carson

This recipe doubles or triples easily for a crowd.

Wine Punch

YIELD: 4 large servings
CALORIES: 333

CARBOHYDRATES: 25g

1 bottle dry white wine
1 cup dry Marsala wine
¼ cup Cognac or Brandy
¼ cup superfine sugar
ice cubes

½ cucumber, thinly sliced
lemon slices for garnish
1 cup sparkling mineral water or club soda

In a large pitcher, combine the first 4 ingredients. Add the ice cubes and stir until the sugar is dissolved. Stir in the cucumber and lemon slices. Add the sparkling water, stir again briefly and serve.

Camille Jones

Frozen Daiquiris

YIELD: 12
CALORIES: 82

CARBOHYDRATES: 9g

1 6 ounce can frozen limeade   ice
1 6 ounce can light rum

Place limeade in blender container. Add can of rum. Fill blender with ice. Process until slushy. Several recipes may be made and placed in freezable container and frozen. Remove from freezer 1 hour before serving.

Cathy Carson

Dub's Eggnog

YIELD: 6 quarts
CALORIES: 565
CARBOHYDRATES: 25g

FAT: 34g
PROTEIN: 5g

1 dozen egg yolks
1 pound powdered sugar
½ teaspoon salt
2 quarts whipping cream
1 quart milk

1 quart 101 proof bourbon
6 ounces light rum
6 egg whites
nutmeg

Beat the egg yolks well. Add the sugar and salt and beat well. Add the cream and milk, beating until smooth. Add the bourbon and rum, beating well. Chill for 3 hours. Beat the egg whites stiff. Fold into the chilled mixture. Chill 24 hours before serving. Use the nutmeg for garnish.

Lockie Sue Bissett

Easy Eggnog

YIELD: 12 servings
CALORIES: 414
CARBOHYDRATES: 21g

FAT: 30g
PROTEIN: 6g

1 quart commercial eggnog
1 pint vanilla ice cream, softened

½ pint whipping cream, whipped
½ cup rum
nutmeg

Pour the eggnog into a large bowl and add the rum and stir. Fold in the whipped cream. Add the ice cream. Serve cold with nutmeg for garnish.

Lou Deaton

Mamaw's Eggnog

YIELD: 16 cups
CALORIES: 267
CARBOHYDRATES: 16g

FAT: 17g
PROTEIN: 7g

6   eggs, separated
¾   cup sugar
1   pint whipping cream

2   quarts milk
bourbon to taste

Beat the egg yolks with ½ cup of the sugar. Add the cream and milk and beat well. Add the desired amount of bourbon. Beat the egg whites with remaining ¼ cup sugar until stiff. Fold the egg whites into the first mixture. Serve cold.

Karen Childress

Hot Apple Cider

YIELD: 8 cups
CALORIES: 134

CARBOHYDRATES: 34g

8   cups apple cider
3   tablespoons red-hot
    candies
1   cinnamon stick (optional)

1   teaspoon lemon juice
4-6 whole cloves (optional)

Mix all the ingredients together and heat to boiling. Remove from heat and strain if using cinnamon stick and cloves. Serve hot.

Sherry Scott

Spicy Percolator Punch

YIELD: 28 servings
CALORIES: 108

CARBOHYDRATES: 27g

2   quarts cranberry juice
2   quarts unsweetened
    pineapple juice
1   quart water
⅔   cup firmly packed brown
    sugar

1   tablespoon whole cloves
1   tablespoon whole allspice
4   cinnamon sticks
2   lemons, sliced and
    quartered

Combine the fruit juices and water in a 30 cup electric percolator. Place remaining ingredients in basket of percolator. Perk for 30 minutes or until pot stops.

Benny Gail Hunnicutt

Spiced Mocha Mix

YIELD: 2¼ cups mix
CALORIES: 133
CARBOHYDRATES: 27g

FAT: 1g
PROTEIN: 7g

2   cups sweetened cocoa mix
⅓   cup instant coffee (may use
    decaffeinated)

1   teaspoon cinnamon

Mix all ingredients thoroughly. Store in an airtight container. To serve, use 3 tablespoon of mix to ⅔ cup hot water in a cup or mug.

Barbara Malone

Spiced Tea

YIELD: 96 servings
CALORIES: 30g

CARBOHYDRATES: 7g

2   cups Tang drink mix
¼   cup lemon instant tea
¾   cup regular instant tea
3   cups sugar

1   heaping teaspoon
    cinnamon
1   tablespoon allspice

Mix all ingredients well and pour into an air tight container. To serve, use 3 teaspoons mix per cup of hot water.

Benny Gail Hunnicutt and Carmen Sutton

VARIATION: Increase Tang to 3 cups and decrease sugar to 2 cups.
Cathy Carson

Almond Tea

YIELD: 2 quarts
CALORIES: 98

CARBOHYDRATES: 25g

1   lemon
1   cup sugar
2   quarts water

2   cups strong tea
1   teaspoon almond extract
1   teaspoon vanilla

Boil water, add juice of the lemon, sugar, tea, almond extract and vanilla. Continue to boil for 5 minutes. Cool. Pour over ice and add a sprig of mint in each glass.

Cynthia Berry

Good on a hot afternoon!

Chocolate Mocha Punch

YIELD: 2 gallons or 70 to 75 punch cups FAT: 4g
CALORIES: 99   PROTEIN: 2g
CARBOHYDRATES: 13g

1   16 ounce can chocolate   1   cup sugar
    syrup   1   quart boiling water
1   2 ounce jar instant coffee   ½   gallon vanilla ice cream
1   teaspoon vanilla   milk

Mix all the above ingredients, except the ice cream and milk in a
gallon jar. Add enough water to fill jar, refrigerate until ready to
use. Pour equal amounts of syrup mixture and milk over vanilla
ice cream in a punch bowl.

                                                    Nancy Vannoy

*Coffee mixture will keep indefinitely in refrigerator when not mixed
with milk or ice cream.*

Pineapple Banana Slush

YIELD: 6 quarts   CARBOHYDRATES: 57g
CALORIES: 224

4   cups sugar   12 ounces frozen orange juice
6   cups water   5   bananas
46 ounces pineapple juice   3   bottles ginger ale

Dissolve sugar in water, add pineapple and orange juice and
mashed bananas. Freeze-stir when partially frozen. Serve partially thawed with ginger ale poured over it and slush is formed.
Remove frozen mixture from freezer 3 hours before serving.
                                            Katharine Russell

*VARIATION: Use 2 16 ounce frozen orange juice
            1 16 ounce frozen pineapple juice
            1 16 ounce frozen lemonade.*

                                                    Nancy Vannoy

Frozen Fruit Punch

YIELD: 25 cups
CALORIES: 161

CARBOHYDRATES: 41g
PROTEIN: 5g

2   cups sugar
4   cups water
½   cup reconstituted lemon
    juice
1   teaspoon vanilla
¼   teaspoon almond extract

48 ounces pineapple juice
48 ounces pineapple-
    grapefruit juice
48 ounces HI-C Orange Drink
1   quart 7-UP

Dissolve sugar in boiling water. Mix with other ingredients and freeze. Remove from freezer a couple of hours before serving. When ready to serve, add 1 quart 7-UP.

Nancy Vannoy

This is a wonderful slushy punch.

Children's Punch

YIELD: 1 gallon
CALORIES: 71

CARBOHYDRATES: 18g

1   quart pineapple juice
1   quart orange juice

1   quart lemonade
1   34 ounce bottle of ginger
    ale

Combine first 3 ingredients. Gently add chilled ginger ale just before serving. Serve over crushed ice.

Carmen Sutton

Easy Punch

YIELD: 20 to 24 servings
CALORIES: 57

CARBOHYDRATES: 15g

1   large can Hawaiian Punch   3   cans Squirt
3   cans Sprite

Freeze canned punch just overnight or it won't come out of the can. Place in punch bowl and pour canned drinks over it. As it melts, it is ready to serve. This is a slushy type punch.

Elizabeth Clark

Good Punch

YIELD: 2 gallons
CALORIES: 246

CARBOHYDRATES: 62g

6 cups sugar
14 cups boiling water
6 teaspoons almond extract
8 teaspoons vanilla
2 large cans pineapple juice

1 large can frozen orange
   juice concentrate
1 large can frozen lemon
   juice concentrate

Combine all of the ingredients, blend well, chill and serve over ice.

Barbara Malone

Very quick to fix. Kids especially enjoy it as a summer refresher.

Jello Punch

YIELD: 20 servings
CALORIES: 53

CARBOHYDRATES: 13g
PROTEIN: 1g

1 3 ounce package jello, any
   flavor
1 quart pineapple juice

1 cup sugar
   juice of 3 lemons
2 tablespoons almond extract

Mix all the ingredients in a 1 gallon container. Fill to the top with water. Serve cold. Use only 5 lemons if doubling the recipe.

Benny Gail Hunnicutt

May be mixed the day before.

Kid's Delight

YIELD: 4 large or 6 small servings
CALORIES: 70

CARBOHYDRATES: 17g
PROTEIN: 1g

1 cup orange juice
2 cups strawberries, fresh or
   frozen

2 bananas
2 cups ice
   sugar to taste, optional

Place all ingredients in a food processor equipped with metal blades. Process until a thick, smooth slush. To thicken, add more ice, to thin, add more liquid.

Jane Richardson

Great afternoon treat or breakfast surprise.

Artichoke Dip

YIELD: 6 servings
CALORIES: 373
CARBOHYDRATES: 7g

FAT: 34g
PROTEIN: 9g

1   14 ounce can artichoke
    hearts, drained and sliced
1   4 ounce can chopped green
    chilies, drained

1   cup Hellman's mayonnaise
1   cup Parmesan cheese,
    grated
1   teaspoon artichoke juice

Mix together and pour into a small casserole or gratin dish. Bake in a 350 degree oven until bubbly, about 10 minutes. Serve hot with melba toast.

Sandy Baggett

Cheryl's Dip

YIELD: 2½ cups
CALORIES: 133
CARBOHYDRATES: 1

FAT: 13
PROTEIN: 3

32 ounces softened cream
    cheese
8   ounce jar picante
    sauce(Pace)

garlic salt to taste

Combine and mix well. Serve as dip or spread on flour tortillas, roll up, slice and serve with toothpicks as hors d'oeuvre.

Lockie Sue Bissett

Good with veggies or chips.

Hot Broccoli Dip

YIELD: 1 quart
CALORIES: 76
CARBOHYDRATES: 2g

FAT: 6g
PROTEIN: 3g

½ cup chopped onion
½ cup chopped celery
½ cup chopped mushrooms
3 tablespoons butter
1 10 ounce package frozen,
   chopped, cooked and
   drained broccoli

1 can cream of mushroom
   soup
1 6 ounce package garlic
   cheese

Saute onion, celery and mushrooms in butter until tender. Add to broccoli. Mix in mushroom soup and the cheese. Cook over low heat until cheese is melted and well blended. A squeeze of lemon juice aids broccoli in retaining its green color. Serve in a chafing dish with Tostados, Fritos or toast rounds. This can be prepared ahead of time but do not heat until the last minute. May also be frozen.

Sandy Baggett

Dill Dip

YIELD: 6 to 8 servings
CALORIES: 155 or 46 lo-cal
CARBOHYDRATES: 4g or 5g lo-cal

FAT: 14g or 3g lo-cal
PROTEIN: 1g lo-cal

1 cup mayonnaise or reduced
   calorie mayonnaise
1 cup sour cream or yogurt
3 tablespoons minced fresh
   parsley

3 tablespoons grated onion
3 tablespoons minced fresh
   dill
1 teaspoon seasoned salt

Blend ingredients together and chill. Can be made several days ahead. Serve with raw vegetables. For less calories use reduced calorie mayonnaise and yogurt.

Mary Jo Mason

Best made with fresh dill and parsley.

Hot Sausage Dip

CALORIES: 251
CARBOHYDRATES: 3g

FAT: 19g
PROTEIN: 17g

1 pound hot sausage
1 pound lean ground beef
1 onion
2 pounds Velveeta cheese

1 can Rotel tomatoes and green chilies
1 can mushroom soup

Saute the onion and add crumbled sausage and beef. Brown well and drain. Mix the cheese, tomatoes and soup. Heat until cheese melts. Add meat to cheese mixture. Stir and serve.

Jill Seahorn and Benny Gail Hunnicutt

Scrumptous Dip

CALORIES: 166
CARBOHYDRATES: 5g

FAT: 11g
PROTEIN: 11g

1 pound hamburger meat
½ onion, chopped
garlic
salt and pepper
1 teaspoon chili powder

1 can Rotel tomatoes and chilies
1 can yellow hominy, drained
1 pound American cheese or more

Brown meat with onion, garlic, salt and pepper. Add some flour to absorb grease if needed. Add 1 teaspoon chili powder. Add tomatoes, cheese and hominy. Heat until cheese is melted. Serve warm.

JoNel Stokes

Shrimp Dip

YIELD: 1 cup
CALORIES: 70
CARBOHYDRATES: 4g

FAT: 5g
PROTEIN: 3g

1 4½ ounce can shrimp, drained and chopped
¼ cup plus 2 tablespoons mayonnaise
3 tablespoons catsup

juice of 1 lemon
1 teaspoon minced onion
1 teaspoon garlic
paprika
parsley

Mix first 6 ingredients well. Sprinkle with paprika and garnish with the parsley. Serve with crackers and chips.

Cathy Carson

Seafood Dip

YIELD: 20 to 24 servings
CALORIES: 109
CARBOHYDRATES: 3g

FAT: 9g
PROTEIN: 5g

2-8 ounce packages cream
    cheese
½ teaspoon horseradish
3 tablespoons mayonnaise

½ medium onion, chopped
1 jar cocktail sauce
2 packages frozen crab or
    shrimp or combination

Mix first four ingredients and place in the bottom of a 9×11 serving dish. Top with a jar of cocktail sauce. Top that with crab, shrimp or a combination of both.   **Lou Deaton**
Delicious and very easy!

Spinach Dip

YIELD: 3 cups
CALORIES: 179
CARBOHYDRATES: 24g

FAT: 8g
PROTEIN: 2g

10 ounces frozen spinach,
    chopped
1 cup chopped water
    chestnuts
1 large onion, chopped

1 cup sour cream
1 cup mayonnaise
1 package Lipton's vegetable
    soup mix

Thaw spinach and dry well with paper towels, squeeze out all water. Mix with all other ingredients. Cover and chill overnight to soften instant soup.   **Carolyn Stuart Wilson**

Shawn's Fast Taco Sauce

YIELD: 8 cups
CALORIES: 10

CARBOHYDRATES: 2g

15 ounce can tomato sauce,
    with tidbits
15 ounce can tomato sauce,
    special
4 ounce can green chilies,
    chopped

salt, pepper and garlic powder
    to taste
2 to 3 tablespoons pickled
    jalapeno juice

Combine all of the ingredients in a sauce pan. Bring to a boil and reduce heat to simmer for 15 minutes. Refrigerate in covered container. Serve with chips, beans or eggs.
          Shawn Mitchell

This recipe can be doubled or tripled.

Layered Tex-Mex Dip

CALORIES: 222

CARBOHYDRATES: 13g

FAT: 17g

PROTEIN: 7g

3 medium ripe avocados
2 tablespoons lemon juice
½ teaspoon salt
¼ teaspoon pepper
1 cup sour cream
½ cup mayonnaise or salad dressing
1 package taco seasoning mix

2 cans bean dip
1 cup chopped green onions with tops
2 3½ ounce cans chopped ripe olives
2 cups chopped tomatoes
8 ounces cheddar cheese, grated

Peel, pit, and mash the avocados with the lemon juice, salt, and pepper. Combine the sour cream, mayonnaise and taco seasoning mix. Spread the bean dip in a large shallow platter or in a 9×13 inch casserole. Top with avocado mixture. Layer with taco sauce mixture. Sprinkle top with the onions, tomatoes and olives. Cover with the cheese. Serve chilled, or at room temperature with round tortilla chips.

Becky Childress and Nancy Vannoy

Chili Con Queso

YIELD: 24 or more servings-makes 1 quart

CALORIES: 86

CARBOHYDRATES: 3G

FAT: 6G

PROTEIN: 4G

1 large onion, finely chopped
1 tablespoon bacon drippings
2 10 ounce cans of Rotel tomatoes
juice from Rotel tomatoes

1 4 ounce can chopped green chilies
1 teaspoon salt
1 pound American cheese, grated
several dashes pepper

Saute onion in drippings until soft but not brown. Drain Rotel tomatoes reserving liquid. Coarsely chop tomatoes and chilies then add to onion. Add salt and pepper and simmer slowly about 15 minutes. Add cheese and stir over low heat until melted. Thin to desired consistency by adding reserved Rotel liquid, one tablespoon at a time. Serve from chafing dish with tortilla chips

Sandy Baggett

Old Jean's Tomato Dip

YIELD: 1 quart
CALORIES: 19
CARBOHYDRATES: 4g

FAT: 1g

2   medium onions
16 ounce can tomatoes, whole
    peeled
12 ounce can tomato paste
1   teaspoon ground cumin

1   teaspoon dry garlic, or 2
    cloves, minced
1   tablespoon salt
¼   cup lemon juice
1   jalapeno

Chop ingredients that require it and mix all together. Place in airtight container in refrigerator at least 6 hours before serving. More jalapeno may be added to suit taste.

Jean Read

Keeps 7–10 days in the refrigerator.

Normal Folks Pico de Gallo

YIELD: 1½ quarts
CALORIES: 111
CARBOHYDRATES: 7g

FAT: 9g
PROTEIN: 2g

2   medium onions
4   avocados, firm
4   tomatoes, firm
½   bunch cilantro
2   tablespoons olive oil

4   tablespoons lime juice
1-2 serrano peppers, seeded
3   banana peppers, seeded
salt to taste

Chop all ingredients finely by hand or in a food processor. Add oil and lime juice. Add more than 2 serranos if you like it really hot. Allow to set and season at least 6 hours. Serve with toasted tortilla chips, or on fajitas.

Jean Read

Will keep in the refrigerator for a week.

Rotel Dip

CALORIES: 70
CARBOHYDRATES: 2g

FAT: 6g
PROTEIN: 1g

1   10 ounce can Rotel
    tomatoes with green chilies

2   cups sour cream

Chop tomatoes and partially drain. Mix ingredients well. Serve chilled with assorted chips.

Cathy Carson

May add dash of cayenne pepper for spicy taste.

Fresh Hot Sauce

YIELD: 2 cups
CALORIES: 36

CARBOHYDRATES: 9g
PROTEIN: 2g

6 ripe tomatoes
4 serrano peppers or jalapenos
4 poblano peppers
3 large cloves garlic, chopped or ½ teaspoon garlic powder

1 teaspoon salt
¼ teaspoon pepper, freshly ground
¼ teaspoon honey
½ cup chopped green onions
¼ cup chopped fresh cilantro

Bring two quarts of water to a rapid boil. Add tomatoes and boil until skins split. Remove promptly and allow to cool 5 minutes. Peel tomatoes and cut into large chunks. Remove seeds and stems from peppers. Use rubber gloves to keep from irritating your fingers. Blend ½ of the tomatoes, garlic, salt, pepper, honey and hot peppers in a food processor or blender until mixture is finely chopped. The remainder of the ingredients will add texture to the sauce, so lightly blend the remaining tomatoes, green onions and cilantro. Store covered in the refrigerator until ready to serve. Serve as a dip with tortilla chips, over eggs or as an accompaniment to beef or vegetables.

Sandy Baggett

Hot Relish

YIELD: 5 cups
CALORIES: 90
CARBOHYDRATES: 6g

FAT: 7g
PROTEIN: 1g

½ pound fresh jalapeno peppers
2 large onions
2 green tomatoes
1 firm avocado

2 cloves garlic
salt and pepper to taste
½ cup salad oil
¼ cup white vinegar

Finely chop all ingredients by hand or using a food processor. Add oil and vinegar. Put in small containers and freeze. Refrigerate when opened. Will keep a long time.

Benny Gail Hunnicutt

Very, very hot!

Pleas' Hot Sauce

YIELD: 20
CALORIES: 25
CARBOHYDRATES: 5g

FAT: 1g

¼ teaspoon whole cumin
½ garlic clove or ¼ teaspoon garlic salt
8-10 Serrano peppers
¼ onion, ground

6 to 8 8 ounce cans tomato sauce
8 ounce can tomato juice or water

Grind cumin in a molcajete, then peppers, onion and garlic. (Could use blender or food processor.) Mix these ingredients with tomato sauce and juice, less sauce for hotter, more sauce for milder. Chill, serve as dip or hot sauce.

Sandra Childress

Men love it!

Pimiento Cheese Spread

YIELD: 2 dozen sandwiches
CALORIES: 183
CARBOHYDRATES: 1g

FAT: 16g
PROTEIN: 8g

2 pound box of Velveeta cheese
4 ounces pimientos

1 cup salad dressing or enough to spread easily

Grate the cheese on the large size grater. Add grated pimiento plus juice and the salad dressing and mix well. For smooth spread, let mixture sit at room temperature until cheese melts a little.

Lou Deaton

Good as a stuffing for celery, too.

Shrimp Spread

YIELD: 2 cups
CALORIES: 52
CARBOHYDRATES: 5g

FAT: 1g
PROTEIN: 6g

2   cans shrimp
½   cup bottled chili sauce
⅓   cup catsup
1   tablespoon lemon juice

1   tablespoon horseradish
1   to 2 teaspoons
    Worcestershire sauce

Drain and rinse shrimp. Mash shrimp in medium size bowl, add remaining ingredients. Store in covered container and chill. Serve with crackers. Can be mixed in a food processor.

Sherry Scott

Family favorite for 20 years

Wayne's Crab Spread

CALORIES: 176
CARBOHYDRATES: 22g

FAT: 7g
PROTEIN: 6g

8   ounces cream cheese,
    softened
6   ounces frozen crabmeat,
    thawed and drained
¼   cup finely chopped green
    onion with tops

1½ to 2 teaspoons capers,
    drained and finely
    chopped
Party rye bread slices or
    crackers or chips

Mix all ingredients and spread on small slices of rye bread, toasted or plain, or use on any cracker or chip.

Lockie Sue Bissett

Shrimp or Oyster Cocktail Sauce

YIELD: 6 servings
CALORIES: 36

CARBOHYDRATES: 9g
PROTEIN: 8g

6   tablespoons lemon juice
½   cup tomato ketchup
1   tablespoon horseradish
3   drops Tabasco sauce
⅛   teaspoon salt

½   teaspoon celery salt
½   teaspoon sugar
3   stalks celery, finely
    chopped
dash of ground cloves

Blend lemon juice with ketchup. Add remaining ingredients and stir well. Chill well before serving. Add more horseradish for more zip.

Karen Childress

Dip for Fruit

YIELD: 2 cups
CALORIES: 106
CARBOHYDRATES: 13g

FAT: 5g
PROTEIN: 1g

8   ounces cream cheese, softened
1   7 ounce jar marshmallow creme

1   tablespoon orange juice
1   teaspoon grated orange rind
or 1 tablespoon Grand Marnier

Thoroughly mix cream cheese and marshmallow creme. Add either of the flavorings. Use as a dip for fresh fruit.

Lockie Sue Bissett

This makes a great dessert, too.

Sour Cream Sauce for Fruit

YIELD: 1½ cups
CALORIES: 75
CARBOHYDRATES: 9g

FAT: 4g
PROTEIN: .5g

1   cup sour cream
½   cup brown sugar

1   teaspoon vanilla

Combine all ingredients and whip well with an electric mixer. Serve as a dip for fresh fruits or a sauce over fruit. You may also dice ½ cup fruit and mix in above ingredients when you whip to give dip color and taste.

Ann Childress

Great for a morning coffee or dessert course.

Cheese Ball

YIELD: 1 ball
CALORIES: 82
CARBOHYDRATES: 2g

FAT: 7g
PROTEIN: 3g

2   jars bacon spread
2   3 ounce packages cream cheese, softened
1   tablespoon parsley
1   tablespoon dried onion flakes

½   cup pecans, chopped (optional)
paprika (optional)

Mix first 5 ingredients together, mold and sprinkle with paprika or roll in pecans.

Debbie Glasscock and Susie Childress

Chili Cheese Ball

YIELD: 2 balls
CALORIES: 192
CARBOHYDRATES: 1g

FAT: 18g
PROTEIN: 8g

2 pounds Velveeta cheese,
   softened
2 8 ounce packages cream
   cheese, softened

1 cup chopped nuts
dash of salt
chili powder

Mix softened cheeses together well. Add nuts and salt. Shape into ball or roll. Roll in chili powder. May be frozen.

Patti May

Pineapple Cheese Ball

YIELD: 1 ball
CALORIES: 230
CARBOHYDRATES: 7g

FAT: 22g
PROTEIN: 4g

1 pound cream cheese,
   softened
8½ ounce can crushed
   pineapple, drained
2 cups chopped pecans

¼ cup chopped bell pepper
2 tablespoons chopped green
   onion
1 tablespoon seasoned salt

Beat the cheese until very soft. Add the remaining ingredients except 1 cup of pecans. Shape into a ball. Roll in the pecans. Refrigerate.

Carmen Sutton

Strawberry Cheese Ball

YIELD: 1 ball
CALORIES: 200
CARBOHYDRATES: 26g

FAT: 10g
PROTEIN: 2g

2 8 ounce packages cream
   cheese, softened
2 tablespoons red wine

½ cup pecans, chopped
1 18 ounce jar strawberry
   preserves, chilled

Combine softened cream cheese, wine and pecans. Mix and form into a ball. Cover and chill. When ready to serve, put cheese ball on serving platter. Pour preserves over cheese. Serve with assorted crackers.

Cathy Carson

A cheese ball with a difference.

Carol's Cheese Roll

YIELD: 1 roll
CALORIES: 170
CARBOHYDRATES: 2g

FAT: 15g
PROTEIN: 8g

2 pounds Velveeta cheese
1 pound cream cheese
6 bunches fresh green
onions, chopped

1 7 ounce can green chilies,
chopped
2 to 3 jalapeno peppers,
chopped

Bring Velveeta cheese and cream cheese to room temperature. Roll Velveeta cheese between 2 pieces of wax paper into a rectangle shape about ¼ inch thick. Spread softened cream cheese on Velveeta cheese. Top with onions, chilies and peppers. Roll jelly roll style. Refrigerate at least 1 hour before serving. Sprinkle with paprika and garnish with parsley if desired.

Carol Hunnicutt

This can be done in 2 small rolls by halving the recipe.

Cheese Ring

YIELD: 20 servings
CALORIES: 352
CARBOHYDRATES: 13g

FAT: 27g
PROTEIN: 12g

16 ounces extra sharp cheddar
cheese, grated
16 ounces medium cheddar
cheese, grated
1 small onion, grated

1 cup mayonnaise
1 teaspoon red pepper
1 cup pecans, chopped
parsley sprigs
strawberry preserves

Combine first 5 ingredients and mix well. Sprinkle about ¼ cup pecans in a oiled 7 cup ring mold and press cheese mixture into mold. Chill until firm. Unmold onto a platter and pat remaining pecans onto cheese ring. Garnish with parsley sprigs. Spoon strawberry preserves into the center and serve with crackers.

Lou Deaton

Cheese Ritz

CALORIES: 150
CARBOHYDRATES: 9g

FAT: 11g
PROTEIN: 4g

2   cups flour
1   cup margarine
2   cups sharp cheese, grated
2   cups Rice Krispies cereal

½   teaspoon Tabasco
¼   teaspoon cayenne pepper
½   teaspoon garlic salt

Combine all ingredients and mix by hand. Roll into small balls and place on ungreased cookie sheet. Press with a fork. Bake at 375 degrees for 8 to 10 minutes. Let cool for 5 minutes before removing from cookie sheet.

Barbara Malone

VARIATION: Omit Tabasco and substitute ½ teaspoon salt for the garlic salt.

Sherry Scott

Jean Read's Wafers

YIELD: 156 1½ inch wafers
CALORIES: 28
CARBOHYDRATES: 1g

FAT: 2g
PROTEIN: 1g

½   pound margarine
½   pound sharp cheddar
     cheese, grated
½   cup chopped pecans
2½ cups flour

¼   teaspoon red pepper
1   teaspoon salt
dash of garlic salt or garlic
     powder

Soften margarine and blend with grated cheese. Add flour, nuts and seasonings. Mix well. Roll into logs about 1½ inches in diameter on pieces of wax paper. Wrap wax paper around the logs and secure ends. Chill overnight. Cut slices ⅛ inch thick and bake 8 to 10 minutes on slightly greased (use Pam) cookie sheets at 350 degrees.

Lockie Sue Bissett

Easy and good.

Cheese Pecan Bites

YIELD: 6 dozen
CALORIES: 61g
CARBOHYDRATES: 3g

FAT: 5g
PROTEIN: 1g

2   cups flour
1   teaspoon salt
2   cups grated sharp cheddar
    cheese (8 ounces)

1   cup butter or margarine,
    softened
1¼ cups pecan halves

Combine flour and salt in mixing bowl. Add cheese and mix well. Cut in butter until mixture resembles coarse meal. Mix with hands until dough is smooth. Shape into a ball and roll to ¼ inch thick on a lightly floured surface. Cut into rounds with a 2 inch cookie cutter. Place rounds on a lightly greased baking sheet and place a pecan half in center of each round. Fold two opposite edges of dough to center of pecan overlapping edges slightly. Press gently to seal. Bake at 425 degrees for 10 minutes.

Lou Deaton

Great for a coffee.

Cheese Petit Fours

YIELD: 6 dozen
CALORIES: 109
CARBOHYDRATES: 9g

FAT: 7g
PROTEIN: 3g

3   loaves very thin sandwich
    bread
2   cups margarine
4   jars Kraft Old English
    cheese spread
1½ teaspoons Worcestershire
    sauce

1   teaspoon Tabasco sauce
1   teaspoon onion powder
cayenne pepper
and dill weed for topping

Cut crusts off of bread (3 slices at a time). Beat margarine, cheese spread, Worcestershire, tabasco and onion powder until consistency of 'icing'. Spread mixture between each layer of bread, 3 slices thick. Quarter and spread mixture on top. Sprinkle each with cayenne and dill weed. Freeze on cookie sheet, then put in plastic bags. Do not defrost. Bake at 350 degrees for 15 to 20 minutes.

Susan McMullan

Artichoke Squares

YIELD: 24 servings
CALORIES: 64
CARBOHYDRATES: 3g

FAT: 4g
PROTEIN: 4g

2 6 ounce jars marinated
   artichokes
1 onion, chopped
1 clove garlic, minced
4 eggs
¼ cup bread crumbs

dash tabasco
½ teaspoon oregano
salt and pepper
2 cups grated cheddar
   cheese, or ⅔ cup each
   Swiss, Parmesan, cheddar

Drain juice from 1 jar of artichokes into a skillet. Saute garlic in juice. Drain remaining jar and chop all of the artichokes. In a bowl beat the eggs and add the bread crumbs and seasonings. Stir in the onions, garlic, cheese and artichokes. Mix well. Bake in a 9×13 inch pan at 325 degrees for 30 minutes. Cut into squares and serve warm.

Shirley Kirby

VARIATION: Saute the garlic with the onion, substitute Monterey Jack cheese for cheddar or others listed. Use ¼ teaspoon dried, crushed oregano and add ¼ teaspoon dried, crushed basil and ⅛ teaspoon pepper. Add 2 tablespoons chopped green chilies to egg mixture and proceed as above.

Lou Deaton

Jalapeno Cheese Squares

YIELD: 60
CALORIES: 35

FAT: 3g
PROTEIN: 2g

2 or 3 jalapenos, seeded and
   chopped
1 pound sharp cheese, grated

6 eggs, beaten

Sprinkle peppers in well greased 9 inch square pan. Cover with cheese, add beaten eggs. Bake at 350 degrees for 30 minutes or until firm. Cool. Cut in squares to serve.

Tina Bean

Crabbies

YIELD: 48 pieces
CALORIES: 42
CARBOHYDRATES: 2g

FAT: 3g
PROTEIN: 1.5g

1 can crabmeat	dash salt
1 tablespoon mayonnaise	1 jar Old English cheese
6 tablespoons butter	spread
½ teaspoon garlic powder	6 English muffins

Blend first 6 ingredients together well. Cut muffins in half, spread mixture on them then cut into quarters. Place on a cookie sheet. Freeze at least ½ hour. Before serving, broil until golden brown and bubbly.

Sharon Forehand

May be made and frozen 2 weeks in advance.

Sausage on Rye

CALORIES: 176
CARBOHYDRATES: 14g

FAT: 10g
PROTEIN: 8g

1 pound hot sausage	1 large jar Cheez-Whiz
1 pound regular sausage	1 package small party rye
	bread

Brown sausage and drain. Add the Cheeze-Whiz and mix well. Spread on slice of bread. May be frozen at this point on cookie sheets and stored. When ready to use, place frozen on cookie sheets and bake at 350 degrees for 15 minutes or until bubbly.

Carol Hunnicutt

Lamb Dijon

CALORIES: 262

FAT: 17g
PROTEIN: 23g

1   butterflied leg of lamb

1   jar Dijon mustard

Remove the bone from leg of lamb. Trim away most of the fat and membrane. Score the lamb to make the thickness of the leg as even as possible. Spread one side with mustard and place under broiler. Broil, turn over and spread mustard on the other side. Broil to desired doneness approximately 10 minutes each side. Remove from broiler and let rest 5 to 10 minutes before cutting. Slice in small pieces and serve with bread or biscuits as an appetizer. We like jalapeno jelly and various mustards. Preferably sweet and hot.

Paula Bailey and Carmen Sutton

Crab Stuffed Mushrooms

YIELD: 10 to 12 servings
CALORIES: 70
CARBOHYDRATES: 4g

FAT: 4g
PROTEIN: 3g

3   dozen large whole fresh
    mushrooms
1   7½ ounce can crab meat,
    drained and flaked
1   tablespoon parsley,
    snipped
1   tablespoon pimientos,
    chopped

1   teaspoon capers, chopped
¼   teaspoon dry mustard
½   cup mayonnaise

Wash and dry mushrooms and remove stems. Combine crab, parsley, pimientos and capers. Blend dry mustard with mayonnaise and toss with crab. Fill each mushroom cap with 2 tablespoons of the mixture. Bake at 375 degrees for 8 to 10 minutes.

Darla Jones

Crab or Ham Miniature Pies

YIELD: 3-4 dozen
CALORIES: 64 crab 90 ham
CARBOHYDRATES: 5g

FAT: 4g - 6g
PROTEIN: 2g - 3g

CREAM CHEESE PASTRY

8   ounces cream cheese
½   cup margarine

2⅔ cups flour

Mix ingredients in food processor. Chill at least 1 hour. Roll out dough and cut into desired shape. Fill as desired. Seal and vent. Bake at 400 degrees for 12 minutes or until light brown. May be cooked for 6 minutes and cooled and frozen. Bake for 6 more minutes before serving. Brush dough with egg white before baking. When using ham filling, use unsalted margarine.

CRABMEAT FILLING

2   tablespoons minced onion
2   tablespoons butter
1   6½ ounce can crabmeat, drained, or shrimp or any fresh shellfish

2   tablespoons mushrooms, chopped
garlic powder to taste

Saute onion in butter, add crabmeat, mushrooms and garlic. Fill pastry for miniature pies.

HAM FILLING

½   pound ham, finely chopped
½   pound American cheese, grated

1   bell pepper, finely chopped
1   tablespoon Worcestershire Sauce

Mix all ingredients together well. Use as filling for miniature pies.

Cathy Carson

Use either filling with cream puff shells, too.

Egg Rolls

YIELD: 21
CALORIES: 146
CARBOHYDRATES: 1g

FAT: 5g
PROTEIN: 5g

2½ cups celery, chopped
½ pound bulk sausage
2 cups cooked chicken
1 cup bamboo shoots
½ cup water chestnuts
⅓ cup mushrooms
1 tablespoon dry sherry
2 teaspoons salt

½ teaspoon sugar
½ teaspoon MSG
½ teaspoon pepper
2 tablespoons peanut oil
1 tablespoon cornstarch
2 tablespoons chicken broth
2 packages egg roll wrappers
1 egg, beaten

Boil celery for 5 minutes, drain and press out water. Saute sausage in oil for 3 minutes. Blend cornstarch and chicken broth and set aside. Add remaining ingredients to the sausage. Saute for 5 minutes, stirring to mix. Add the cornstarch and broth mixture and stir until mixture thickens slightly. Transfer contents to a bowl and let cool. Place approximately ¼ cup of the mixture on an egg roll wrapper, fold the sides and one end in and roll. Dip egg roll in beaten egg and deep fry in peanut or vegetable oil. Oil may need to be changed half-way through frying. Do not overcook or they will be tough.

Paula Bailey

Tortilla Roll Ups

YIELD: 72 pieces per 1 dozen tortillas
CALORIES: 83
CARBOHYDRATES: 3g

FAT: 4g
PROTEIN: 4g

2 8 ounce packages softened cream cheese
1 8 ounce carton sour cream
1 7 ounce can chopped green chilies, drained

garlic powder and salt to taste
3 large packages flour tortillas
1 bottle picante sauce

Using mixmaster, mix cream cheese and sour cream, add plenty of garlic powder and a little salt. Fold in green chilies. Chill overnight, 1 hour before serving or you may spread them on morning of night to be served. Spread some mixture on each tortilla, roll it up. Wipe off excess. Place on cookie sheet and cover tightly with plastic wrap. Chill until serving time, Cut each tortilla roll into 1 inch slices and serve with picante sauce.

Susan McMullan

Quesadillas

YIELD: 8
CALORIES: 261
CARBOHYDRATES: 1g

FAT: 14g
PROTEIN: 7g

2   cups cheddar cheese
8-10 flour tortillas

¼   cup margarine
1   4-ounce can chopped green
    chilies

Grate cheese. Place 1 tablespoon margarine in skillet, melt. Place a tortilla in skillet for about 10 seconds and turn it over. Cover the tortilla with a thin layer of cheese and peppers. Place another tortilla on top and flip so that the last tortilla can heat for 10 seconds or until cheese melts. Cut in 4 or 5 pieces and serve while hot. Repeat until all tortillas are used.

Sandra Childress

Rumaki

YIELD: 40
CALORIES: 126
CARBOHYDRATES: 22g

FAT: 3g
PROTEIN: 4g

1   pound bacon, thinly sliced
1   8 ounce can water
    chestnuts, drained and cut
    in half
½   pound chicken livers
    (about 20) rinsed, drained
    and cut in half.

½   cup brown sugar
ground cloves to taste

Microwave bacon on high 1 minute, in the package, until easily separated. Divide bacon slices between 4 paper towel lined paper plates. Cover with paper towels. Microwave one plate at a time for 2½ minutes on high. Cut each slice in half. Sprinkle bacon strips with ground cloves and brown sugar. Place one chicken liver piece and one water chestnut piece at the end of each bacon strip. Roll up, securing with a toothpick. Cover with paper towel. Recipe may be refrigerated at this point. Microwave one plate at a time on high for 3 to 4 minutes rotating dish ½ turn after 1½ minutes. When microwaving from refrigerator temperature, increase time for each plate ½ to 1 minute.

Cathy Carson

Great to make ahead and finish in the microwave.

Beer-Boiled Shrimp

YIELD: 8 servings
CALORIES: 81

CARBOHYDRATES: 2g
PROTEIN: 13g

1   12 ounce can beer
4   whole cloves
2   cloves garlic, minced
1   bay leaf
1   teaspoon salt

½   teaspoon dried dillweed
¼   teaspoon pepper
1   pound fresh shrimp,
    cleaned

In wok, combine all ingredients except shrimp. Bring to a boil and boil 5 minutes. Add shrimp and return to boiling. Cook 3 to 5 minutes until shrimp turn pink. Drain, discard cloves and bay leaf. Serve hot with melted butter or cold with cocktail sauce.

Shirley Kirby

Bettye's Cocktail Weiners

YIELD: 120 bites
CALORIES: 34
CARBOHYDRATES: 1g

FAT: 2g
PROTEIN: 1g

2   to 3 tablespoons brown
    sugar
1   can beer

catsup, (same amount as beer)
2   packages weiners

Mix sugar, beer and catsup together in a saucepan and heat to boiling. Cut weiners into bite size pieces and heat in the sauce. Serve in a chafing dish with toothpicks.

Sherry Scott

Chicken Livers in Wine

CALORIES: 90
CARBOHYDRATES: 2g

FAT: 5g
PROTEIN: 7g

2   tablespoons butter or
    margarine
1   pound chicken livers
¼   cup dry sherry or Madeira
    wine

2   tablespoons snipped
    parsley
1   tablespoon lemon juice
¼   teaspoon salt
⅛   teaspoon pepper

Cut livers into bite size pieces, melt butter in skillet, stir in livers, cook uncovered over medium heat 4 to 5 minutes. Stirring, add wine, snipped parsley, lemon juice, salt and pepper. Serve on toast rounds or from chafing dish with toothpicks.

Benny Gail Hunnicutt

Louisiana Shrimp Boil

YIELD: 6 to 8 servings
CALORIES: 288
CARBOHYDRATES: 8g

FAT: 3g
PROTEIN: 57g

2 teaspoons salt
½ bell pepper, sliced
1 onion, chopped
1 celery rib, chopped
4 small hot red peppers
or 1 large dried red pepper,
   chopped

dash cayenne pepper
Tabasco sauce
1 lemon, sliced
1 package shrimp boil
3 to 4 pounds shrimp

To a large pot of boiling water, add first 8 ingredients and boil for 30 minutes. Then add shrimp boil package and shrimp. Boil frozen shrimp 3 to 5 minutes. Boil fresh shrimp in shell for 5 munutes. Don't overcook. Pour into colander, reserving liquid. Chill shrimp. If when served all are not eaten, you may return them to chilled liquid and refrigerate. They will keep for 6 to 7 days if so processed.

Sandy Baggett

Venison Meat Balls

YIELD: 450 meatballs
CALORIES: 18

FAT: 1g
PROTEIN: 1.6g

8 slices stale bread
¾ cup milk
4 pounds ground venison
2 pounds hot sausage
5 eggs, beaten
garlic salt
salt and pepper
½ cup finely chopped parsley

2 medium onions, chopped
4 ribs celery, chopped
oil
6 cans cream of mushroom
   soup
8 ounce jar Woody's Cookin
   Sauce

Soak bread slices in milk to soften. Mix all ingredients together with your hands, except the oil, soup and barbeque sauce. Roll into bite-size balls. Brown in a small amount of oil and remove to drain. Pour off fat. Mix soup and barbeque sauce together in remaining drippings. Pour over meat balls which have been placed in a large baking pan. Place in a 350 degree oven and simmer for about 1 hour. Cover with aluminum foil. Serve in a chafing dish with toothpicks.

Shawn Mitchell

Fantastic for parties. They are wonderful.

Dilly Bites

CALORIES: 101
CARBOHYDRATES: 7g

FAT: 8g
PROTEIN: 1g

¾ cup Wesson oil
2 tablespoons dill weed

2 ounce package Ranch
   dressing mix
24 ounces soup crackers

In a large bowl combine oil, dill weed and dressing mix until well blended. A wire whip works well. Add soup crackers and with your hands, blend the mix until the oil is absorbed. Store in airtight container.

Sue Arledge

A good snack or as croutons on soup or salad.

Roasted Pecans

CALORIES: 259
CARBOHYDRATES: 6g

FAT: 27g
PROTEIN: 3g

2 cups pecans
2 tablespoon vinegar
1 tablespoon sugar

¼ cup butter, melted
salt and garlic to taste

Shake pecans into vinegar and sugar. Roast in a 250 degree oven for 30 minutes or until crisp. Pour butter over pecans and toss. Add salt and garlic if desired.

Sammye Pierce

Sour Cream Mushrooms

CALORIES: 104
CARBOHYDRATES: 3g

FAT: 9g
PROTEIN: 1g

2 pounds mushrooms, sliced
1 green onion, finely
   chopped
2 teaspoons paprika
½ cup unsalted butter

½ teaspoon salt
¼ teaspoon cayenne
4 tablespoons flour
½ cup vermouth or sherry
2 cups sour cream

Saute the mushrooms, onions and paprika in the butter until tender. Season with the salt and cayenne. Add the flour and cook for 3 minutes. Add vermouth and sour cream. Bring almost to a boil. Remove from heat immediately, so as not to curdle the sour cream. Serve in cream puff shells or chafing dish with melba toast.

Camille Jones

Cheese Olive Surprises

YIELD: 3 dozen
CALORIES: 51
CARBOHYDRATES: 2g

FAT: 4g
PROTEIN: 1g

1 cup flour
½ teaspoon baking powder
1 cup cheddar cheese, grated

½ cup margarine
3 tablespoon cold water
1 7 ounce jar small stuffed olives, drained

Cut together first 5 ingredients with pastry blender or 2 knives. Knead until dough is formed. Pinch off dough and roll into 1 inch balls. Surround an olive with dough which you have flattened between thumb and fingers. Bake on ungreased cookie sheet at 400 degrees for 10 minutes. Serve hot. These may be made ahead and refrigerated or frozen. Let come to room temperature before baking.

Lou Deaton

These are an all time Christmas party favorite.

Olive-Cheese Nuggets

YIELD: 4 dozen
CALORIES: 28
CARBOHYDRATES: 1

FAT: 2
PROTEIN: 1

¼ pound mellow processed cheese
¼ cup margarine, softened

¾ cup flour, sifted
½ teaspoon paprika
48 small stuffed olives

Blend grated cheese with margarine, add flour and paprika mixture to cheese mixture to form a dough. Drain olives well on paper towels. Using hands, roll a small piece of dough into a ball and then flatten with thumb and wrap around olive. Place wrapped olives on a ungreased baking sheet. Bake at 400 degrees for about 12 to 15 minutes. Serve warm. Best kept chilled until baking time. Dough can be made in food processor.

Sherry Scott

Try olives stuffed with onions or almonds.

Jalapeno Eggs

YIELD: 8
CALORIES: 97
CARBOHYDRATES: 6g

FAT: 6g
PROTEIN: 7g

8	eggs		jalapenos
1	onion		pimientos (optional)
¾	cup white vinegar	¾	cup jalapeno juice

Place eggs in a 2 quart saucepan. Cover with water. Bring water to a rolling boil, and remove from heat. Let set for about 20-25 minutes. Slice onion and separate into rings. Slice pickled jalapenos. Peel eggs while hot, place in a wide mouth jar, alternating with jalapenos, onions and pimientos. Bring vinegar and jalapeno juice to a boil. Pour over eggs immediately. Cover and refrigerate, about 2 weeks. Remember to always have half jalapeno juice and half vinegar if you choose to fix more than 8 eggs. Work fast so eggs will stay hot, if allowed to get cold, the eggs will become tough when hot liquid is poured over them.

Jane Richardson

You may also add slices of raw cauliflower.

Spanish Olives

YIELD: 2 10 ounce jars
CALORIES: 95
CARBOHYDRATES: 1g

FAT: 10g

2	10 ounce jars green olives, with pits or stuffed, drained	3	cloves garlic, minced
½	cup salad oil	2	teaspoons oregano leaves, crushed
½	cup vinegar	2	large jalapenos, minced

Place all ingredients in a glass mixing bowl. Mix well and allow to marinate in refrigerator for at least 72 hours, spooning marinade over olives occasionally. Serve with toothpicks. Store in original jars which makes it easy to shake the mixture over the olives. Will keep for two months if under refrigeration.

Lou Deaton

Mary Knight's Scratch

YIELD: 1 gallon
CALORIES: 713
CARBOHYDRATES: 28g

FAT: 63g
PROTEIN: 12g

1   7 ounce box Cheerios
1   box thin pretzel sticks
1   11 ounce box Rice Chex
3   cups pecans
1   large can mixed nuts
3   cups cheese flavored gold
    fish crackers

2¼ cups butter or margarine
4   tablespoons Worcestershire
    Sauce
1½ teaspoons Tabasco Sauce
1½ teaspoons red pepper
1   teaspoon garlic salt

Mix dry ingredients in a large roaster pan. Melt butter or margarine and add seasonings and sauces and mix well. Bake the cereal mixture at 225 degrees for 15 minutes. Add ¼ of the butter mixture to the cereal mixture and toss well. Return to oven for 1 hour. Add ¼ of the sauce at 15 minute intervals, tossing to mix and returning to the oven after adding the sauce. Be sure to stir the sauce each time and to lift from the bottom of the pan when you are tossing it to mix well.

Lockie Sue Bissett

Soups

White-tailed deer — plentiful game and beautiful to look at.

Cream of Artichoke Soup

YIELD: 8 servings
CALORIES: 257
CARBOHYDRATES: 11g

FAT: 22g
PROTEIN: 4g

CHICKEN STOCK

8 cups chicken stock
bay leaf
celery leaves
pepper

salt
parsley
onion

Simmer ingredients for 1 hour.

SOUP

6   tablespoons butter
½   cup finely chopped onion
½   cup finely chopped celery
6   tablespoons flour
6   cups chicken stock
¼   cup lemon juice
1   bay leaf

1   teaspoon salt
¼   teaspoon pepper
¼   teaspoon thyme
1   can artichoke hearts
2   egg yolks
2   cups light cream

Saute onion and celery in butter until soft, not brown. Add flour
and cook 1 minute stirring constantly. Add stock and lemon
juice. Blend and add bay leaf, salt, pepper, thyme and artichoke
hearts. Cover and simmer 20 minutes until slightly thickened.
Remove bay leaf. May be pureed in blender if smooth, creamy
consistency is desired. If serving hot, heat to boiling point, remove from heat and add cream and egg yolks which have been
beaten together. If serving cold, add cream and eggs and chill.
Correct seasoning before serving. Garnish with thin lemon
slices and parsley.   **Kay Stewart**

Avocado Bisque

YIELD: 4 to 6 servings
CALORIES: 250
CARBOHYDRATES: 12g

FAT: 22g
PROTEIN: 6g

2½ ripe avocados, peeled
1   can cream of chicken soup
3   green onions, chopped

1   soup can of milk
salt, pepper and cayenne
½   cup chopped green onion
    tops

Reserve half of 1 avocado for garnish. Mix rest of avocados,
soup, onions, milk and seasonings in a blender or food processor until smooth. Refrigerate overnight or at least 2 hours before
serving. Garnish with chopped green onion and sliced avocado.
This soup does not freeze.   **Sandy Baggett**

Potato Cheese Soup

YIELD: 8 to 10 servings
CALORIES: 230
CARBOHYDRATES: 23g

FAT: 13g
PROTEIN: 6g

4   beef bouillon cubes
6   cups water
1   small jar Cheez-Whiz
1   package frozen
    hashbrowns

garlic salt
celery salt
1   grated carrot, optional

Dissolve bouillon cubes in boiling water. Add remaining ingredients. Bring to a boil and simmer until potatoes are tender.

Jill Seahorn

Excellent and easy.

Cheese Soup

YIELD: 4 cups
CALORIES: 400
CARBOHYDRATES: 27g

FAT: 25g
PROTEIN: 21g

1   medium onion, chopped
2   tablespoons butter
1-2 tablespoons flour
1½ cups chicken broth
½   pound American cheese,
    grated
1   bell pepper, cut into strips
15 ounce can red kidney
    beans, drained

1   teaspoon Worcestershire
    sauce
salt
white pepper
cayenne pepper
paprika

Brown onion in butter, add flour to thicken and stir until smooth, adding chicken broth until soup is of desired consistency. Add cheese, heat, stirring until it melts. Add bell peppers, kidney beans, sauce and seasonings to taste. Heat gently, stirring until flavors blend.

Sandy Baggett

Can be increased easily.

Cheese Soup

YIELD: 8 to 12 servings
CALORIES: 289
CARBOHYDRATES: 15g

FAT: 18g
PROTEIN: 17g

½ gallon milk
1 pound American or
  Velveeta cheese, grated
2 14½ ounce cans chicken
  stock
½ cup celery, finely chopped

½ cup onion, finely chopped
1 to ½ of a jalapeno pepper,
  very finely chopped
  (optional)
flour and butter to thicken
salt and pepper to taste

In one pot, melt the cheese in the milk. You might want to use a double boiler, deep well, or microwave for this step so it won't stick. In the second pot, cook celery and onion in chicken broth. Add a small amount of flour and butter to thicken. After it is smooth and well-blended, pour in milk and cheese. Cook until a nice, yellow color and really thick. Add jalapeno and stir well. DO NOT ALLOW TO BOIL or it will curdle.

Nancy Vannoy

This recipe was printed in the San Angelo paper several years ago after it was requested by a reader. This is the soup served at Zentner's Daughter Steakhouse on Fridays.

Cheese Soup

YIELD: 8 to 12 servings
CALORIES: 196
CARBOHYDRATES: 9g

FAT: 17g
PROTEIN: 9g

½ cup butter or margarine
2 carrots, grated
2 celery stalks, chopped
3 green onions, chopped
2 cans chicken broth
3 cans cream of potato soup

½ pound jalapeno cheese,
  grated
½ pound longhorn cheese,
  grated
3 heaping tablespoons sour
  cream

Saute carrots, celery and onions in butter. Add remaining ingredients, stirring frequently and heat thoroughly. Remove from heat, stir in sour cream, salt and pepper to taste.

Nancy Miller Johnson

This is great left-over and reheated in a microwave. Mild cheese can be substituted for half of the jalapeno cheese according to family taste.

Cream of Corn Soup

YIELD: 4-6 servings
CALORIES: 510
CARBOHYDRATES: 22g

FAT: 45g
PROTEIN: 8g

2   strips bacon, chopped
2   tablespoons onion,
    chopped
2   cups corn, fresh, frozen or
    canned
2   tablespoons butter

2   tablespoons flour
2   cups milk
1   teaspoon salt
½   teaspoon pepper
2   cups light or heavy cream,
    or one cup of both

Fry bacon until crisp. Add onion and saute until soft. If using fresh corn, put corn through food chopper. Add corn to onion and bacon and fry until brown. Add butter, and then flour and stir well. Cook slowly for 3 minutes, stirring frequently. Add milk, salt, and pepper and cook until thickened. Add cream and beat until smooth before serving. Serve with buttered hot rolls or toast points.

Sherry Scott

A good winter-time chowder.

Broccoli Soup

YIELD: 4 to 6 servings
CALORIES: 660
CARBOHYDRATES: 11g

FAT: 65g
PROTEIN: 15g

3   to 4 cups chopped fresh
    broccoli
2   cups water
6   tablespoons butter
½   cup chopped onion

2½ cups heavy cream
1   cup chicken broth
salt and pepper to taste
1   cup grated Gruyere or
    Parmesan cheese

Puree broccoli in food processor using metal blade, adding water to make a smooth puree. Melt butter in large sauce pan and saute onions until golden. Add broccoli puree, stirring constantly about 2 to 3 minutes or until cooked. Add cream, salt and pepper, simmer 15 minutes. Garnish with cheese and place in oven. Broil until cheese is slightly browned.

Ann Childress

Frozen broccoli may be substituted.

Bean Soup

YIELD: 8 cups
CALORIES: 293
CARBOHYDRATES: 24g

FAT: 12g
PROTEIN: 19g

2 cups dried navy beans
2 quarts water
1 pound diced ham
1 large onion, chopped
1 clove garlic, minced

½ teaspoon salt
1 16 ounce can tomatoes, chopped with juice
1 10 ounce can Rotel tomatoes with juice

Wash beans, place in dutch oven, fill with water 2 inches above beans and soak overnight. Drain, add 2 quarts of water and next 4 ingredients, cover and bring to a boil. Reduce heat, simmer 1½ hours until beans are tender. Add remaining ingredients, simmer 30 minutes, stirring constantly.

Luann Pierce

White Bean Soup

YIELD: 12 to 16 servings
CALORIES: 205
CARBOHYDRATES: 16g

FAT: 10g
PROTEIN: 14g

4 cups Great Northern beans
2½ cups cooked and diced ham
2 cups diced celery, with leaves
¾ cup green onions, with tops, chopped

1½ cups sliced carrots
1 cup tomatoes, peeled and chopped
2 teaspoons salt
¾ teaspoon pepper
1 pod hot pepper, optional

Sort and wash beans, place in a large pot and cover with water at least two inches above top of beans. Soak overnight. Drain and add 4 quarts fresh water and bring to boil. Reduce heat and simmer uncovered for 1½ hours stirring occasionally. Add ham, celery, carrots, onions and hot pepper and simmer for 1½ hours, stirring occasionally. Add tomatoes, salt and pepper and cook for 30 minutes. Serve with cornbread.

Ann Childress

A hearty winter dish that freezes well.

Zucchini Soup

YIELD: 6 servings
CALORIES: 204
CARBOHYDRATES: 17g

FAT: 14g
PROTEIN: 6g

5 small zucchini, sliced
7 chicken bouillon cubes
1 8 ounce package
  Philadelphia cream cheese

5 cups water
cayenne pepper

Combine zucchini, bouillon cubes and 5 cups of water. Boil 10 minutes or until zucchini is tender. Put mixture in the blender with cream cheese and blend until smooth. When ready to serve put a dash of cayenne pepper on each serving.

Jeannine Henderson

Can be served hot or cold.

Zucchini Soup

YIELD: 4-6 servings
CALORIES: 383
CARBOHYDRATES: 29g

FAT: 24g
PROTEIN: 16g

2 cloves garlic
¼ cup butter or margarine
1 onion, chopped
3 carrots, chopped
1 bell pepper, chopped

4 or 5 zucchini, chopped
4 cups chicken stock
½ to 1 pound Velveeta cheese
salt and pepper to taste

Vegetables can be cut in large pieces. In a large pot saute all vegetables in butter and garlic. Pour ½ of chicken stock and ½ of vegetables in a blender. Blend so that little chunks of vegetables remain. Pour this into a separate pot. Repeat procedure. Add cheese to blended mixture. This will be somewhat thick.

Susan McMullan

Zucchini Soup

YIELD: 6 to 8 servings
CALORIES: 162
CARBOHYDRATES: 27g

FAT: 3g
PROTEIN: 5g

3 pounds slender zucchini
¼ pound bacon, whole-slab
1 can consomme
3½ cups water

1 teaspoon white pepper
sour cream and chopped basil
or chives

Scrub zucchini, trim ends, cut into chunks and set aside. Cut bacon into chunks and brown in a skillet. Place squash and bacon chunks and the drippings in a saucepan with the next three ingredients. Bring to a boil and simmer for 30 minutes. Remove bacon and discard. Pour soup into a food processor and blend until smooth. Serve hot or cold. Garnish with sour cream and fresh herbs.

Camille Jones

Freezes well. Would make a nice appetizer served in demitasse cups served either cold or hot.

Crab Bisque

YIELD: 4 servings
CALORIES: 189
CARBOHYDRATES: 21g

FAT: 14g
PROTEIN: 8g

1 tablespoon flour
2 tablespoons butter
1 can cream of potato soup
1 cup half and half
2 teaspoons lemon juice

salt and pepper
dash of garlic powder
1 cup crab meat, cooked,
cubed or flaked

Make a roux with flour and butter, stirring constantly. Liquify potato soup with half and half in blender and stir into roux. Add lemon juice and seasonings. Simmer soup for 5 to 10 minutes. Add crab meat last. Always cook over low heat.

Wanda Bunger

Onion Soup

YIELD: 8 servings
CALORIES: 179
CARBOHYDRATES: 27g

FAT: 6g
PROTEIN: 6g

8 to 10 cups water
14 to 16 beef bouillon cubes
4 large yellow onions
2 to 4 tablespoons butter
1½ tablespoons flour

pepper to taste
8 slices French bread, toasted
4 slices mozzarella cheese,
cut in half

Bring water to a boil. Add bouillon cubes and simmer. Slice onions and saute in butter. Lightly stir in flour to onions and butter. Pour into hot broth. Add pepper to taste. Cover and simmer 20 minutes. Ladle soup into individual oven-proof soup dishes. Place a round of bread in each, topped with a slice of cheese. Place bowls on a cookie sheet and brown the cheese under a preheated broiler for three minutes until cheese is bubbling, or microwave until cheese is melted.

Belinda Wilkins

Very tasty and easy.

Onion Soup

YIELD: 6 to 8 servings
CALORIES: 151
CARBOHYDRATES: 14

FAT: 7
PROTEIN: 8

1½ pounds or 5 cups thinly
sliced yellow onions
3 tablespoons butter or
margarine
1 tablespoon oil
1 teaspoon salt

¼ teaspoon sugar
3 tablespoons flour
2 quarts boiling beef stock
½ cup dry white wine
salt and pepper to taste
3 tablespoons Cognac

Cook the onions over very low heat with the butter and oil in a heavy bottomed 4 quart covered sauce pan. Uncover and raise heat to moderate. Add salt and sugar. Cook for 30 minutes, stirring frequently until onions have turned an even brown. Sprinkle in the flour and stir for 3 minutes. Blend in boiling liquid off of the heat. Add the wine, and season to taste. Cover and simmer for 30 minutes. Correct seasoning. This soup can be set aside uncovered until ready to serve the same day or refrigerated covered for 1 week. Then reheat to simmer. Just before serving, stir in the Cognac, optional.

Cathy Carson

Turkey or Chicken Soup

YIELD: 16 servings
CALORIES: 101
CARBOHYDRATES: 14g

FAT: 1g
PROTEIN: 9g

8 to 10 cups water
12 to 14 chicken bouillon
   cubes
1 small chopped onion
3 carrots, peeled and sliced
3 celery stalks, sliced
1 bay leaf
1½ teaspoons thyme
1½ teaspoons sage
salt and pepper to taste

2 cups uncooked shell
   macaroni
2 cups turkey or chicken,
   bite size pieces
1 15 ounce can green beans,
   cut, drained
1 15 ounce can corn, drained
1 15 ounce can tomato
   wedges, chopped

Bring water to a boil. Add bouillon cubes, onion, carrots, celery, bay leaf, thyme, sage, salt, pepper, and macaroni. Cook until macaroni is tender. Add remaining ingredients and simmer 1 to 1½ hours. When using chicken that has not been cooked, reduce the number of bouillon cubes to 8 and use the stock from boiling the chicken.

Belinda Wilkins

Almost like chicken stew, the tester says. Sage can be decreased according to taste.

Chicken Noodle Soup

YIELD: 6 to 8 servings
CALORIES: 124
CARBOHYDRATES: 12g

FAT: 2g
PROTEIN: 14g

1 4 pound chicken
8 to 10 cups water
¼ teaspoon basil, dried whole
1 tablespoon parsley, fresh
   and chopped
¼ teaspoon celery salt
⅛ teaspoon garlic salt

1 bay leaf
2 teaspoons salt
¼ teaspoon pepper
4 medium carrots, chopped
1 onion, chopped
1 cup fine egg noodles

Combine first 9 ingredients in large dutch oven or soup kettle, making sure chicken is covered in liquid. Cook 1½ hours. Remove from heat. Remove chicken; discard bay leaf. Let chicken cool, then remove from bones, dice and set aside. Bring broth to a boil, add carrots and onions and simmer for 30 minutes. Add chicken and noodles and cook 30 minutes longer.

Cathy Carson

This is wonderful to have on hand for a sick family or friend.

Cream of Chicken Noodle Soup

YIELD: 8 servings
CALORIES: 416
CARBOHYDRATES: 25g

FAT: 28g
PROTEIN: 17g

1 chicken, cut up
1 package noodles, extra-
  wide
2 bell peppers, chopped
1 onion, chopped

1 box fresh mushrooms,
  sliced
3 cans cream of chicken soup
1 stick butter or margarine

Boil chicken, cool and remove bones and chop. Set aside. Add noodles and chopped vegetables to boiling broth and cook for 6 minutes. Remove from heat and add remaining ingredients. Salt and pepper to taste.

Carolyn Stuart Wilson

More noodles can be used than recipe calls for. Add or substitute other vegetables: 1 cup celery, chopped or 1 cup zucchini, chopped.

Sopa De Arroz Con Gallina

YIELD: 6 to 8 servings
CALORIES: 267
CARBOHYDRATES: 23g

FAT: 11g
PROTEIN: 15g

4 tablespoons oil
1 cup uncooked rice
1 medium onion, minced
½ cup tomato sauce
2 quarts chicken broth,
  heated

salt and white pepper to taste
2 cups cooked chicken, cut in
  bite-size pieces

Heat oil and brown rice lightly in it. Add onion, tomato sauce, broth, salt and pepper. Cover tightly and simmer for 30 minutes. Add chicken during the last 10 minutes of cooking.

Ann Childress

Tortillas filled with guacamole make a delicious accompaniment along with pico de gallo for picante enthusiasts.

Tortilla Soup

YIELD: 4 to 6 servings
CALORIES: 995
CARBOHYDRATES: 11g

FAT: 34g
PROTEIN: 25g

2 tablespoons oil
1 onion, chopped
2 cloves garlic, crushed
2 14½ ounce cans tomatoes,
   pureed
4 cups chicken stock
¼ teaspoon ground cumin

½ bunch cilantro, chopped
   fine
salt to taste
2 packages corn tortillas, cut
   in strips and fried (hot)
1 pound cheddar cheese,
   grated

In a large pot, saute onions, garlic and cumin. Add tomatoes and chicken stock. Stir and simmer for about 20 minutes. Add chopped cilantro and salt; stir. Place fried tortilla strips and cheese in individual bowls, pour soup over and serve immediately.

Susan McMullan

Wonderful with any Mexican dish. Cilantro is a must!

Bill's Mexican Soup

YIELD: 3 to 4 servings
CALORIES: 105
CARBOHYDRATES: 17g

FAT: 4g
PROTEIN: 3g

1 tablespoon butter
1 medium onion, finely
   chopped
1 cup canned pumpkin
2 cups chicken bouillon
¼ cup milk
1/16 teaspoon ground coriander

1/16 teaspoon ground mace
¼ teaspoon pepper
1 large tomato, peeled and
   seeded, finely chopped,
   about ¾ cup
3 scallions, finely chopped,
   with tops

In a medium saucepan, quickly brown onion in butter. Whisk in pumpkin, bouillon, coriander, mace, milk, pepper, tomato and scallions. Bring to a boil. Reduce heat to simmer. Simmer, covered, stirring occasionally, until hot and onion is very soft. Good served with corn sticks.

Lockie Sue Bissett

This has a very different flavor and is an authentic Mexican soup.

Breads

Sotol — lonely sentinels of the ranch country.

Biscuits

YIELD: 12
CALORIES: 157
CARBOHYDRATES: 16g

FAT: 9g
PROTEIN: 2g

2 cups flour
½ teaspoon salt
4 teaspoons baking powder
½ teaspoon cream of tartar

2 teaspoons sugar
½ cup shortening
⅔ cup milk

Mix all ingredients well. Roll dough on floured surface. Use biscuit cutter to shape dough. Bake on ungreased baking sheet at 450 degrees for 12 to 15 minutes or until golden brown. Tester baked these at 475 degrees.

Teri Jackson

Cooking Oil Biscuits

YIELD: 12 to 16 servings
CALORIES: 99
CARBOHYDRATES: 11g

FAT: 5g
PROTEIN: 2g

2 cups flour
2 teaspoons salt
3 teaspoons baking powder

⅓ cup vegetable oil
⅔ cup milk

Sift dry ingredients together. Mix milk and oil together and add to dry ingredients. Roll between two pieces of wax paper to ½ inch thickness. Cut with biscuit cutter. Bake on ungreased cookie sheet 8 to 10 minutes in preheated oven at 475 degrees. These are not light and fluffy but short and crusty.

Jean Read

Very easy and good.

Sour Cream Biscuits

YIELD: 1 dozen
CALORIES: 124
CARBOHYDRATES: 3g

FAT: 12g
PROTEIN: 1g

2 cups Bisquick
½ cup melted butter

1 cup sour cream

Preheat oven to 400 degrees. Line muffin tin with paper cups. Mix ingredients. Pour into muffin cups and bake for 10-15 minutes.

Sandy Baggett

Angel Biscuits

YIELD: 3 dozen
CALORIES: 107
CARBOHYDRATES: 14g

FAT: 4g
PROTEIN: 2g

1½ packages dry yeast
4   tablespoons water
5   cups flour
1   teaspoon soda
3   teaspoons baking powder

¼   cup sugar
1   teaspoon salt
¾   cup shortening
2   cups buttermilk

Dissolve yeast in lukewarm water. Sift flour into bowl with other dry ingredients. Cut in shortening. Add buttermilk, then yeast mixture. Stir until all flour is moistened. Knead on floured surface one or two minutes. Roll out to desired thickness, about ½ inch, and cut with a biscuit cutter. Bake at 400 degrees about 15 minutes. This dough will keep about a week in the refrigerator and used as needed. If desired, place a small amount of margarine in pan before baking. Can be made, frozen, and baked later. Let thaw before baking.

Sherry Scott

Louise's Angel Flake Biscuits

YIELD: 30
CALORIES: 149
CARBOHYDRATES: 19g

FAT: 7g
PROTEIN: 2.6g

1   cup shortening
½   cup sugar
1   package yeast
2   cups cold buttermilk

½   teaspoon soda
1   teaspoon baking powder
1   teaspoon salt
5   cups flour

Cream sugar and shortening. Dissolve yeast in a small amount of warm water and add to 1 cup of the buttermilk. Add soda to remaining cup of buttermilk. Add baking powder and salt to the first cup of flour. Add all ingredients to sugar and shortening. Roll or pat dough to ½ inch thickness, cut into biscuits and place on greased baking sheet. Let rise about 1 hour. Bake at 400 degrees about 15 minutes. These can be brushed with melted margarine and frozen on a baking sheet. Then transfer to plastic bags for freezer storage. Before cooking, thaw 40 minutes.

Lorelei McMullan and Jill Seahorn

Yeast Buttermilk Biscuits

YIELD: 2 dozen
CALORIES: 96
CARBOHYDRATES: 17g

FAT: 2g
PROTEIN: 2g

6-7 cups flour
¾ cup sugar
2 teaspoons salt
1 teaspoon soda
2 cups buttermilk

4 teaspoons baking powder
½ cup melted margarine
½ cup warm water
2 packages dry yeast

Combine dry ingredients. Dissolve yeast in warm water and add to buttermilk. Add melted margarine. Stir liquids into dry ingredients. Knead 10-15 times. Roll out and cut into biscuits. They are better when you let them rise at least 30 minutes. Brush with melted margarine before baking. Bake at 425 degrees for 15 minutes. Tip: May be refrigerated for up to 3 weeks. Let rise for 1½ to 2 hours after refrigeration.

Janie Chandler

Hot Rolls

YIELD: 2 dozen rolls
CALORIES: 86
CARBOHYDRATES: 14g

FAT: 2g
PROTEIN: 2g

½ cup lukewarm water
1 cup lukewarm milk
3 tablespoons shortening
2 tablespoons sugar

1 scant teaspoon salt
½ teaspoon baking powder
3½ cups sifted flour
1 package yeast

Dissolve the yeast in the lukewarm water. Add the lukewarm milk. Add the shortening, sugar and salt. Sift the dry ingredients and add to the first mixture. Beat 5 minutes. Roll out to ½ inch thick and cut or shape as desired. Let rise for 30 minutes. Bake in a 425 degree oven for 8 to 10 minutes.

Helen Bean

Icebox Rolls

YIELD: 6 dozen
CALORIES: 69
CARBOHYDRATES: 12g

FAT: 1g
PROTEIN: 2g

2	cups milk, scalded	2	packages dry yeast
½	cup sugar	2	eggs
2	teaspoons salt	7	cups flour
3	tablespoons butter		

Add sugar, salt and butter to scalded milk. Cool to lukewarm. Dissolve yeast in ¼ cup lukewarm water. Add 1 teaspoon sugar and stir into lukewarm milk mixture. Next add 2 eggs, well beaten. Stir in 4 cups sifted flour and beat well. Add 3 more cups of flour and as much more as can be stirred into dough without kneading. Put into a greased bowl, cover with oiled paper and use as needed from the refrigerator. For clover leaf rolls, make three marble sized balls for each roll and let rise in small muffin tins. To freeze rolls, partially cook first. Bake rolls at 400 degrees for 15 to 20 minutes.

Belinda Wilkins

Edna's Icebox Rolls

YIELD: 5 dozen
CALORIES: 113
CARBOHYDRATES: 16g

FAT: 4g
PROTEIN: 2g

1¼	packages dry yeast	8	cups flour
1	cup sugar	1	tablespoon salt
1	cup shortening	1	teaspoon soda
4	cups scalded milk	2	teaspoons baking powder

Dissolve yeast in 2 tablespoons warm water. Set aside. Put sugar, shortening, milk and flour in a large bowl, mix. When cooled to warm, add yeast. Stir and cover. Put in a warm place to rise undisturbed for 2 hours. After the 2 hours, stir the batter down. Sift together the salt, soda, baking powder and 2 more cups flour. Stir into dough and add 2 more cups flour. You don't want the dough to get too stiff. Place in a greased covered container and put in refrigerator. Prepare rolls about 10:30 for lunch. Pinch off desired dough, knead down, let rest 10 minutes. Roll out to ½ inch thick and let rest 10 minutes. Cut with biscuit cutter, fold over. Place on a greased pan and let rise for 45 minutes. Bake at 400 degrees for 10 minutes. Hint: Dough keeps for several days in covered container and freezes well after baked.

Jane Richardson

Refrigerator Rolls

YIELD: 2½ dozen
CALORIES: 113
CARBOHYDRATES: 21g

FAT: 1.6g
PROTEIN: 3g

¾ cup water
½ cup sugar
2 teaspoons salt
3 tablespoons margarine
2 packages dry yeast

1 cup lukewarm water
1 egg
6 cups sifted flour
⅓ cup dry milk

Mix water, sugar, salt, and margarine and heat until margarine is melted. Cool to lukewarm. Dissolve yeast in lukewarm water. Mix with first mixture. Pour into bowl. Add egg, 3 cups flour, and dry milk (in dry form). Beat until smooth. Stir in about 3 cups additional flour. Knead for 5 minutes. Brush with melted shortening. Let rise until double in size. Punch down and knead again. Shape into rolls. Let rise. Bake at 375 degrees for 10 minutes.

Teri Jackson

Whole Wheat Dinner Rolls

YIELD: 1 dozen
CALORIES: 136
CARBOHYDRATES: 20g

FAT: 5g
PROTEIN: 4g

¾ cup warm water
1 package dry yeast
¼ cup sugar
1 teaspoon salt

2¼ cups whole wheat flour
1 egg
¼ cup shortening or soft margarine

Dissolve yeast in water in mixing bowl. Add sugar, salt, and about half of the flour. Beat two minutes. Add egg and shortening, then remaining flour. Let rise 40 to 50 minutes. Stir down batter and drop into muffin tins. Let rise another 30 minutes or until doubled. Bake at 425 degrees about 10 minutes.

Barbara Malone

Beer Bread

YIELD: 24 servings
CALORIES: 98
CARBOHYDRATES: 16g

FAT: 3g
PROTEIN: 21g

4 cups Bisquick
1 tablespoon sugar

1 can beer

Mix and drop into greased muffin tins. Bake at 400 degrees for fifteen minutes.

Martha Henderson, Charter Member

Very quick and easy.

French Bread

YIELD: 20 slices
CALORIES: 94
CARBOHYDRATES: 19g

FAT: .20g
PROTEIN: 3g

4 cups flour
2 teaspoons salt
1 tablespoon sugar

1 package dry yeast
2 cups water
1 cup butter

Mix ingredients in one bowl as listed except butter. Let rise until double in size, about 3 hours. Put in 2 greased bread pans. Let bread rise again. Heat oven to 400 degrees. Put approximately ½ cup melted butter on top of each loaf. Bake for 1 hour.

Teri Jackson

Garlic Bread

YIELD: 2 loaves, 24 slices
CALORIES: 222
CARBOHYDRATES: 31g

FAT: 9g
PROTEIN: 4g

1 cup sugar
1 cup shortening
1 cup lukewarm water
1 teaspoon salt

2 packages dry yeast
2 eggs, beaten
6 cups flour
½ cup Bran Buds or All Bran

Put sugar, shortening, and salt in a large bowl. Mix water and yeast, stir well and add to bowl. Add one cup tap water and the beaten eggs. Add flour gradually. Put mixture in a greased, covered container. Let rise until double in bulk. Punch down and add bran. Knead well for about 10 minutes. Place in greased loaf pans (2) and bake for 30 minutes at 350 degrees. Let cool then slice and spread with garlic butter.

Debbie Glasscock

Monkey Bread

YIELD: 12 servings
CALORIES: 187
CARBOHYDRATES: 31g

FAT: 5g
PROTEIN: 4g

2 packages active dry yeast
1 cup milk heated to lukewarm
4 tablespoons sugar

1 teaspoon salt
½ cup melted butter
3½ cups sifted flour

Dissolve yeast in lukewarm milk. Stir in sugar, salt and butter. Add the flour and beat well. Let rise until double in bulk. Punch down and roll out on lightly floured surface to ¼ inch thickness. Cut dough into 2 inch squares. Dip each square in melted butter. Arrange in buttered tube pans ½ full. Let rise until double. Bake at 400 degrees for 30 minutes until golden brown.

Carol Hunnicutt

Pan Bread

YIELD: 3 to 4 servings
CALORIES: 238
CARBOHYDRATES: 27g

FAT: 13g
PROTEIN: 4g

1 cup flour
1 teaspoon salt
1 teaspoon baking powder

1 tablespoon sugar
⅓ to ½ cup milk
½ cup margarine or butter

Mix dry ingredients. Add enough milk to help ingredients stick together. Turn out on to a floured board and make one big biscuit. Melt butter in a heavy cast iron skillet. Put biscuit in skillet and cook on burner on low heat until brown. Turn once. It will take about 30 minutes to reach a golden brown. This recipe can be doubled and still baked in one skillet. Be prepared to get up in the middle of supper and fix another pan of this bread!

Nancy Vannoy

This recipe was given to me by Peggy Hagelstein Holden who prepared it for her family often.

Texas Onion Bread

YIELD: 6 servings
CALORIES: 227
CARBOHYDRATES: 17g

FAT: 15g
PROTEIN: 8g

¼ cup finely chopped onion
1 tablespoon butter
1½ cups biscuit mix
1 cup mild cheddar cheese, grated

1 egg, slightly beaten
½ cup milk
1 tablespoon butter, melted

Pre-heat oven to 425 degrees. Saute onions in butter. Blend biscuit mix, milk, egg, half of the cheese and the onion. Pour mixture into well greased 8 inch baking pan. Top with remaining cheese and butter. Bake for 20 minutes.

Benny Gail Hunnicutt

Squaw Bread

YIELD: 6 to 7 dozen
CALORIES: 124
CARBOHYDRATES: 5g

FAT: .28g
PROTEIN: .75g

1 package dry yeast
2 cups warm water
4 teaspoons sugar

1 teaspoon salt
5 cups flour
4 teaspoons oil

Mix all ingredients except flour and oil in a large bowl and let stand for 5 minutes. Add 4½ cups flour and beat well. Add oil and beat with a large spoon. Cover and let rise 30 minutes in a warm place. Knead in the remaining ½ cup flour, about 2-3 minutes of kneading. Pull off pieces and fry in shortening until browned on both sides. Tip: Serve with butter, jelly, chocolate sauce, strawberry sauce or powdered sugar. Can be frozen after it is fried. Place in Zip-Loc bags and reheat in microwave.

Lisa Wagoner

Banana Bread

YIELD: 12 slices
CALORIES: 198
CARBOHYDRATES: 41g

FAT: 3g
PROTEIN: 3g

3   ripe bananas, 4 if small
1   cup sugar
1   egg
1½ cups flour
¼   cup butter or margarine,
    melted

1   teaspoon baking soda
1   teaspoon salt
1   cup pecans, chopped
    (optional)

Mash bananas with a fork, stir in other ingredients, pour into Teflon or buttered loaf pan. Bake at 325 degrees for one hour. Freezes well.

Mary Jo Mason

Cranberry Bread

YIELD: 10 slices
CALORIES: 374
CARBOHYDRATES: 43g

FAT: 9g
PROTEIN: 4g

2   cups flour
1   teaspoon salt
½   teaspoon soda
1   cup plus 2 tablespoons
    sugar
1¾ teaspoons baking powder
1   egg, beaten

¼   cup water
⅓   cup orange juice
2   tablespoons margarine
¾   cups pecans, chopped
2   cups fresh cranberries,
    halved

Sift together dry ingredients. Combine beaten egg, water, orange juice and cooled melted margarine. Pour into flour mixture and mix just until moistened. Add pecans and cranberries and stir slightly. Bake in 9×5×3 inch greased and floured loaf pan at 350 degrees for 70 minutes.

Jeannine Henderson

Haley's Cranberry Orange Bread

YIELD: 9 inch loaf 12 slices
CALORIES: 238
CARBOHYDRATES: 30g

FAT: 6.5g
PROTEIN: 3g

2 cups flour, sifted
¾ cup sugar
1½ teaspoons baking powder
1 teaspoon salt
½ teaspoon soda
1 cup cranberries, coarsely cut

½ cup pecans, chopped
1 teaspoon orange peel, grated
1 egg, beaten
¾ cup orange juice
2 tablespoons salad oil

Sift the first five ingredients together. Stir in cranberries, pecans and orange peel. Combine egg, juice and salad oil. Add to dry ingredients, stirring just until moistened. Bake in a greased 9 inch loaf pan at 350 degrees for 50 minutes. Remove from pan and cool. This is excellent sliced and spread with cream cheese or butter. Freezes well.

Cathy Carson

Peanut Butter Bread

YIELD: 24 slices
CALORIES: 200
CARBOHYDRATES: 27g

FAT: 8g
PROTEIN: 6g

1½ cups sugar
1 cup peanut butter
2 cups milk

2 tablespoons baking powder
2 cups flour
2 eggs

Cream sugar and peanut butter and add eggs one at a time. Mix dry ingredients and add to creamed mixture alternately with the milk. Pour into 2 greased and floured loaf pans and bake at 350 degrees for 1 hour.

Carmen Sutton

Bran Muffins

YIELD: 6 dozen muffins
CALORIES: 135
CARBOHYDRATES: 23g

FAT: 4g
PROTEIN: 2.6g

4 beaten eggs
1 cup corn oil
2½ cups sugar
1 quart buttermilk

5 cups flour
4 teaspoons soda
2 teaspoons salt
1 15 ounce box raisin bran cereal

In a large bowl mix eggs, oil and sugar. Sift together flour, soda, and salt. Add flour mixture alternately with buttermilk. Mix well. Stir in raisin bran. Bake in greased muffin pans at 400 degrees for 12 minutes. If desired, dough may be stored in refrigerator for six weeks.

Barbara Malone

Oatmeal Muffins

YIELD: 12-24 muffins
CALORIES: 66
CARBOHYDRATES: 10g

FAT: 2.5g
PROTEIN: 1g

1 cup oatmeal
1 cup buttermilk
1 egg
½ cup brown sugar
1 cup flour

½ teaspoon salt
1½ teaspoons baking powder
½ teaspoon soda
¼ cup melted shortening

Pour buttermilk over oatmeal and let sit. Sift dry ingredients. Add eggs and sugar to buttermilk and oatmeal and mix well. Add dry ingredients and then shortening and mix well. Pour in Teflon or greased muffin tins, half full, and bake at 400 degrees for 18 minutes.

Mary Jo Mason

Good for brunch or shower.

Sweet Breakfast Muffins

YIELD: 2 dozen
CALORIES: 176
CARBOHYDRATES: 21g

FAT: 10g
PROTEIN: 21g

½ cup margarine
1½ cups brown sugar
1 cup sour cream
2 eggs
1¾ cups flour

1 teaspoon soda
½ teaspoon salt
1 teaspoon vanilla
1 cup chopped pecans

Mix together in order given. Bake in muffin tins 15 minutes at 375 degrees. Batter keeps well in refrigerator. This may be mixed up ahead of time and used as needed. May be baked and frozen, then microwaved for a quick breakfast.

Patti May

Streusel Filled Coffee Cake

YIELD: 4 servings
CALORIES: 683
CARBOHYDRATES: 102

FAT: 29g
PROTEIN: 6g

2 tablespoons flour
2 teaspoons cinnamon
½ cup brown sugar
2 tablespoons melted butter
½ cup chopped nuts
1½ cups sifted flour

3 teaspoons baking powder
¼ teaspoon salt
¾ cup sugar
¼ cup shortening
1 egg, beaten
½ cup milk

Combine first 5 ingredients and set aside. Sift flour, baking powder, salt and sugar. Cut in shortening with a pastry blender. Blend in beaten egg and milk. Spread half of batter in a greased and floured 8×8 inch pan, sprinkle half of the first mixture over the batter and top with the remaining filling mixture. Bake in preheated 375 degree oven for 25 to 30 minutes. Serve hot.

Sandy Baggett

Best Ever Homemade Pancakes

YIELD: 8
CALORIES: 177
CARBOHYDRATES: 23g

FAT: 7g
PROTEIN: 5g

1½ cups flour
1 teaspoon salt
3 tablespoons sugar
1¾ teaspoons baking powder

2 slightly beaten eggs
3 tablespoons melted butter
1 to 1¼ cups milk

Mix all dry ingredients together. Quickly mix liquid ingredients into dry mixture. Cook on hot griddle or waffle iron.

Nancy Miller Johnson

Lovie's Pancakes

YIELD: 8
CALORIES: 228
CARBOHYDRATES: 31g

FAT: 9g
PROTEIN: 5g

½ cup margarine, melted
½ cup sugar
3 eggs
1½ cups flour

1 cup milk
3 teaspoons baking powder
dash of salt

Cream margarine and sugar. Add eggs and beat well. Add baking powder and salt to flour. Add alternately with milk, mixing well. Pour about ⅓ cup on greased griddle. Lightly brown on each side.

Barbara Malone

Oat Pancakes

YIELD: 8
CALORIES: 226
CARBOHYDRATES: 29g

FAT: 9g
PROTEIN: 7g

1 cup flour
½ cup oats
1 tablespoon baking powder
½ teaspoon salt (optional)

1 cup skim milk
1 egg, beaten
2 tablespoons vegetable oil

Mix ingredients in order listed. Bake on a hot griddle.

Mary Jo Mason

Caribbean French Toast

YIELD: 4-6 servings
CALORIES: 229
CARBOHYDRATES: 24g

FAT: 8.5g
PROTEIN: 9.5g

8 slices French bread
4 eggs
1 cup evaporated milk
2 tablespoons rum

1 tablespoon sugar
¼ teaspoon salt
½ teaspoon cinnamon
¼ teaspoon nutmeg

Mix all ingredients and pour over bread or dip bread into mixture. Saute in hot butter. Serve with honey, maple syrup, or powdered sugar.

Mary Jo Mason

Magic Marshmallow Crescent Puffs

YIELD: 16
CALORIES: 218
CARBOHYDRATES: 35g

FAT: 7g
PROTEIN: 3g

¼ cup sugar
1 teaspoon cinnamon
2 8 ounce refrigerated quick crescent dinner rolls

16 large marshmallows
¼ cup margarine, melted
¼ cup chopped pecans, if desired

GLAZE:
½ cup powdered sugar
2 to 3 teaspoons milk

½ teaspoon vanilla

Heat oven to 375 degrees. Combine sugar and cinnamon. Separate crescent dough into 16 triangles. Dip a marshmallow in melted margarine. Roll in cinnamon-sugar mixture. Place marshmallow on shortest side of triangle. Fold corners over marshmallow and roll to opposite point, completely covering marshmallow and pinching edges of dough to seal. Dip in melted margarine and place margarine side down in deep muffin cup. Repeat with remaining marshmallows. Place pan on foil or cookie sheet during baking to guard against spillage. Bake at 375 degrees for 10 to 15 minutes or until golden brown. Immediately remove from pans. Combine glaze ingredients and drizzle over warm rolls. Sprinkle with nuts. To reheat, wrap in foil: heat at 375 degrees for 5 to 10 minutes.

Nancy Vannoy

Corn Bread

YIELD: 6 servings
CALORIES: 215
CARBOHYDRATES: 22g

FAT: 11g
PROTEIN: 5g

¾ cup flour
1 teaspoon salt
1 tablespoon baking powder
2 tablespoons sugar

1 cup corn meal
1 cup milk
¼ cup shortening
2 eggs

Mix dry ingredients together. Add other ingredients and stir well. Bake in greased skillet or corn bread stick pan at 400 degrees for 20 minutes.

Teri Jackson

Southern Corn Bread

YIELD: 8 servings
CALORIES: 74
CARBOHYDRATES: 6g

FAT: 4g
PROTEIN: 2g

2 tablespoons shortening
1⅓ cups white corn meal
1 teaspoon baking powder
pinch of baking soda

pinch of salt
1 egg
1⅓ cups buttermilk

Preheat oven to 450 degrees. Place shortening in cast iron skillet. Put in oven while preparing batter of remaining ingredients. When shortening is beginning to smoke, pour batter into skillet. Bake for 15 to 20 minutes or until golden brown. Serve immediately.

Elizabeth Clark

Jalapeno Corn Bread

YIELD: 9 servings
CALORIES: 200
CARBOHYDRATES: 20g

FAT: 10g
PROTEIN: 7g

1 cup yellow corn meal	3 tablespoons cooking oil
½ teaspoon soda	1 cup cream-style corn
½ teaspoon salt	¾ cup buttermilk
1 tablespoon sugar	1 cup cheddar cheese, grated
2 eggs	2 fresh jalapenos, chopped, or less according to taste

Sift the dry ingredients together. Beat the eggs, oil, corn and buttermilk together. Add the dry ingredients and blend well. Stir in the pepper. Pour into a well greased pan. Sprinkle the cheese on top. Bake at 400 degrees for 45 minutes.

Sherry Scott

Jalapeno Corn Bread

YIELD: 6 servings
CALORIES: 293
CARBOHYDRATES: 41g

FAT: 12g
PROTEIN: 8g

2 tablespoons oil	½ teaspoon salt
½ cup whole wheat flour	½ cup sour cream
½ cup white flour	¾ cup buttermilk
1 cup yellow corn meal	2 small eggs
2½ tablespoons brown sugar	1 large jalapeno, diced finely
1¼ teaspoons baking soda	

Pre-heat oven to 425 degrees. Place the oil in a heavy iron skillet and put in oven until very hot. Combine dry ingredients and mix well. In a separate bowl, combine sour cream, buttermilk, eggs and jalapeno. Stir the two mixtures together making sure the dry ingredients are mixed. Pour into the prepared skillet and bake for 25 minutes.

Camille Jones

Great with butter and honey or preserves.

Green Chili Corn Bread

YIELD: 12 to 15 servings
CALORIES: 162
CARBOHYDRATES: 24g

FAT: 5g
PROTEIN: 5g

1½ cups yellow corn meal
½ cup flour
1 teaspoon salt
3 teaspoons baking powder
2 tablespoons sugar
1½ cups milk

1 egg
2 tablespoons oil
2 4 ounce cans green chilies, chopped
1 #3 can cream style corn
¾ cup grated sharp cheese

Place oiled 9×11 inch pan in 425 degree oven while preparing recipe. Blend dry ingredients well. Add milk and stir. Add egg and stir. Add remaining ingredients and mix well. Sprinkle hot, oiled pan with cornmeal before pouring mixture into it. Bake about 50 minutes. Cut into squares.

Carmen Sutton

Mexican Corn Bread

YIELD: 12 servings
CALORIES: 229
CARBOHYDRATES: 26g

FAT: 10g
PROTEIN: 8g

1 cup flour
1 cup corn meal
1 teaspoon salt
1 tablespoon baking powder
1 egg
1 cup milk

1 16 ounce can cream style corn
2 tablespoons oil
1 small jalapeno pepper, chopped
2 cups cheese, grated

Mix dry ingredients, add egg and milk and mix well. Add corn, oil and pepper and mix well. Pour half of the batter into a greased 8×12 ovenproof glass dish. Sprinkle 1 cup grated cheese on the batter. Top with the remaining batter and rest of cheese on top. Bake at 350 degrees until browned, about an hour. Tip: good with wild game. Tester says that green chili peppers can be substituted for a milder cornbread.

Jeannine Henderson

Hush Puppies

YIELD: 8 servings of 3
CALORIES: 153
CARBOHYDRATES: 20g

FAT: 7g
PROTEIN: 3g

1½ cups yellow corn meal
½ cup flour
2 teaspoons baking powder
1 teaspoon salt

1 small onion, finely chopped
¾ cup milk
1 egg

Mix dry ingredients together, add onion, milk, and egg. Drop by teaspoons into deep, hot shortening. Fry only a few at a time until golden brown.

Wanda Bunger

Flour Tortillas

YIELD: 20 to 24 tortillas
CALORIES: 95
CARBOHYDRATES: 17g

FAT: 2g
PROTEIN: 2g

4 cups flour
⅛ teaspoon baking powder
1½ teaspoons salt

¾ cup lard or shortening
1⅛ cups warm water

Mix flour, baking powder and salt with your hands in a medium mixing bowl. Cut in lard until it is well mixed. Slowly add water while mixing. Mix until dough will form a ball. If needed add more water or if too sticky add more flour. Knead dough until it is smooth. Let rest for 15 minutes. Shape into 20 to 24 balls. On a lightly floured surface roll each ball into a thin circle. Cook on an ungreased skillet or griddle over medium heat. Cook lightly on first side, turn, completely cook second side, turn back to first side and finish cooking. As you cook, stack them and cover with a cup towel. They can be made well in advance and reheated for a few seconds in a microwave or place in a steamer for about 5 minutes to soften and heat.

Cookbook Committee

Turkey Dressing

YIELD: 8 servings
CALORIES: 387
CARBOHYDRATES: 64g

FAT: 9g
PROTEIN: 13g

1   can biscuits
2   pans corn bread
1   cup chopped onion
1   cup chopped celery
2   eggs

2   14½ ounce cans chicken
     broth
sage to taste, about 2
     teaspoons

Bake biscuits and corn bread and let cool. Simmer onion and celery in chicken broth until tender. Break biscuits and corn bread into small pieces. Add eggs and mix well. Add celery, onion, and chicken broth mixture and sage and mix well. Pour in greased oven proof glass dish. Bake at 350 degrees until brown. Another can of chicken broth may be added if too dry.

Helen Bean

Cornbread Dressing with Oysters

YIELD: 10 to 12 servings
CALORIES: 315
CARBOHYDRATES: 37g

FAT: 13g
PROTEIN: 11g

1   large pan buttermilk
     cornbread
1   package saltine crackers (36
     crackers)
8 to 10 slices stale bread, dried
     in oven
1   large onion, chopped
4   ribs celery, chopped
½   cup butter

2   small bell peppers,
     chopped
4   eggs, beaten
stock from giblets
stock from turkey
chicken broth if needed
½   cup parsley, fresh
poultry seasoning to taste
1   pint fresh oysters

The day before, crumble cornbread, crackers and bread together. Saute onions, celery, and pepper in butter until soft. Add to cornbread mixture. Refrigerate at this point. When ready to bake add enough stock and broth to 1st ingredients until it is quite moist. Add eggs and seasonings to taste. You may divide dressing and add oysters to one half. Pour into large roasting pans and bake at 350 degrees for 30 to 45 minutes.

Mary Jo Mason

Main Dishes

Pecos River — wild rugged scenery and memories of many
happy fishing trips.

Chinese Peppered Steak

YIELD: 6 servings
CALORIES: 638
CARBOHYDRATES: 52g

FAT: 22g
PROTEIN: 55g

3 tablespoons oil
1 round steak, cubed
1 small can mushrooms
1 can Chinese vegetables
1 cup chopped celery

2 bell peppers, diced
soy sauce to taste
¼ to ⅓ cup cornstarch
cooked rice
Chinese noodles

Brown meat in 2 tablespoons oil. Saute pepper and celery in 1 tablespoon oil until tender. Mix the meat, pepper and celery together and add soy sauce for flavor. Mix cornstarch with the juice from the Chinese vegetables and then mix with above ingredients. Simmer until tender and serve over hot rice with Chinese noodles on top.

Tammy Bunger

Try adding pineapple tidbits for a change.

Rolled Steak

YIELD: 4 to 6 servings
CALORIES: 593
CARBOHYDRATES: 4g

FAT: 30g
PROTEIN: 69g

1 large round steak, pounded
   slightly with mallet
1 cup finely chopped onions
2 cups grated American
   cheese
1 teaspoon salt

1 teaspoon pepper
½ teaspoon garlic salt
2 tablespoons oil
2 cups water
2 tablespoons flour
toothpicks for securing

Rub pounded steak with salt, pepper and garlic salt. Place onions and 1 cup of the grated cheese at one end of the steak. Roll steak up as you would cinnamon rolls and secure at the end and sides with toothpicks. Flour steak roll well and brown the outside by rolling to get all sides. When well browned, pour water over steak, cover and simmer for 45 minutes, turning occasionally. Sprinkle top of steak with remaining cheese. Add more water if necessary. Simmer on low heat for 20 minutes or until done.

Shawn Mitchell

Good tasting, with a great gravy for mashed potatoes.

Filet of Beef Tenderloin

YIELD: 6 servings
CALORIES: 800
CARBOHYDRATES: 3g

FAT: 46g
PROTEIN: 85g

4   pounds beef tenderloin
5   cloves garlic, slivered
½   teaspoon Tabasco Sauce
1   cup soy sauce
½   cup oil

1   cup port wine
1   teaspoon thyme
2   bay leaves, crushed and
     stem removed
bacon slices

Season meat with salt and pepper. Make small slits in beef and fill with garlic slivers. Place in shallow enamel baking dish and pour remaining ingredients, except bacon, over beef. Marinate about 2 hours, turning frequently. Preheat oven to 425 degrees. Remove beef from marinade, saving liquid and place on a rack in a shallow roasting pan. Top with the bacon slices and cover. Roast for 30 to 40 minutes depending on desired doneness. Baste beef frequently with marinade. For slower cooking, roast, covered, at 300 degrees for 2 hours. Serve on a heated platter with marinade poured on au jus. Garnish with parsley.

Sandy Baggett

Wonderful!

Chicken Fried Steak and Cream Gravy

2 pounds round steak	2 eggs, beaten
1 cup flour	¼ cup milk
1 teaspoon salt	garlic salt (optional)
1 teaspoon pepper	

Cut steak into serving size pieces. Tenderize thoroughly with a meat mallet or with the edge of a saucer. Season the steak and tenderize a little longer. Dip steak pieces in flour and then in the egg and milk mixed together and then return to flour and coat well. Let set for a few minutes before frying in deep, hot grease until golden brown. Drain on paper towels. Serve with fried potatoes and cream gravy.

CREAM GRAVY

4 tablespoons pan drippings	salt
3 to 4 tablespoons flour	pepper
2 to 3 cups milk	

Pour off all but 4 tablespoons of grease or pan drippings. Over medium heat, blend in flour, stirring constantly with a fork until bubbly. Stir in milk, salt and pepper to taste. Continue cooking and stirring, scraping cooked on goodies from bottom and sides of skillet, until gravy thickens to desired consistency.

Cookbook Committee

Swiss Steak with Mozzarella Cheese

YIELD: 8 to 10 servings	FAT: 26g
CALORIES: 566	PROTEIN: 65g
CARBOHYDRATES: 14g	

4 pounds beef round steak, ½ inch thick	2 cups water
¾ cup flour	1 cup chopped celery
4 to 6 tablespoons shortening	1 cup chopped bell pepper
1 teaspoon salt	2 1 pound cans tomatoes
¼ teaspoon savory	½ pound mozzarella cheese

Cut meat into 8 to 10 pieces. Dredge in ½ cup of the flour. Brown floured meat in hot shortening. Remove meat to a large roasting pan. Blend remaining flour in hot drippings and add seasonings. Gradually blend in water. Add vegetables. Cook and stir until slightly thickened. Pour mixture over meat and bake uncovered in a slow oven 350 degrees for 2½ to 3 hours or until meat is tender. Top meat with cheese and return to 425 degree oven just long enough to melt cheese.

Ann Childress

Texas Brisket

YIELD: 12 to 16 servings
CALORIES: 766
CARBOHYDRATES: 3g

FAT: 50g
PROTEIN: 70g

9 to 12 pound brisket
1   4 ounce bottle liquid
    smoke
3 to 4 ounces Worcestershire
    sauce
1 to 2 teaspoons lemon pepper

1   teaspoon garlic pepper
½   teaspoon salt
½   teaspoon pepper
Pam
1   bottle Cattleman's
    Barbecue Sauce

Spray brisket with Pam. Place brisket in pan and pour smoke and Worcestershire sauce over it. Generously season with remaining ingredients. Cover and refrigerate for 24 hours or overnight. Cook at 275 degrees for 5 hours; remove drippings. Pour 1 bottle Cattleman's Barbecue Sauce over brisket. Cook for one more hour.

Nancy Vannoy

Easy and excellent

Oven Barbeque Brisket

YIELD: 8 to 10 servings
CALORIES: 583
CARBOHYDRATES: 20g

FAT: 34g
PROTEIN: 47g

brisket — 4 pounds or larger
1   tablespoon salt
1   tablespoon pepper
1   tablespoon onion salt
2   tablespoons celery seed

1   tablespoon garlic salt
2   tablespoons Worcestershire
    sauce
1   tablespoon liquid smoke

SAUCE:
1   cup Woody's barbeque
    sauce
1   cup catsup

½   cup brown sugar

Place meat fat side up in a pan lined with heavy foil. Mix marinade ingredients and put on top of meat. Wrap tightly with foil, refrigerate for 24 hours. Bake brisket at 300 degrees for 1 hour per pound. Mix sauce ingredients together and bring to a boil. While cooking, baste brisket with juice. One hour before serving, put sauce over meat, rewrap and cook for 1 more hour.

Sandy Baggett

Microwave Veal Parmigian

YIELD: 6 servings
CALORIES: 592
CARBOHYDRATES: 46g

FAT: 25g
PROTEIN: 41g

6   veal loin chops
1   egg, beaten
1   cup buttery cracker crumbs
¼   teaspoon pepper
½   cup grated Parmesan
    cheese

1   cup shredded mozzarella
    cheese
2   8 ounce cans tomato sauce
1   teaspoon crushed oregano
¼   cup grated Parmesan
    cheese

Coat chops with beaten egg, then with mixture of crumbs, salt, pepper and ½ cup Parmesan cheese. In a 12×8×2 inch dish, arrange chops so thickest areas are close to edges. Cover with waxed paper. Microwave at medium for 10 minutes. Turn chops over, sprinkle with mozzarella cheese. Mix tomato sauce and oregano and spread over chops. Top with ¼ cup Parmesan cheese. Microwave at medium for 10 to 14 minutes or until tender. Let stand covered for 10 minutes before serving.

Cathy Carson

This recipe is for an 800 watt microwave oven, adjust time for individual oven.

Beef Stroganoff

YIELD: 6 servings
CALORIES: 939
CARBOHYDRATES: 108g

FAT: 27g
PROTEIN: 59g

2   pounds beef filet
    (tenderloin), cubed
2   tablespoons butter
1   cup chopped onion
1   clove of garlic, crushed
½   pound mushrooms, sliced
3   tablespoons flour
2   teaspoons meat extract
    paste
1   tablespoon catsup

½   teaspoon salt
¼   teaspoon pepper
10½ ounce can beef bouillon
¼   cup dry white wine
1   tablespoon dill or ¼
    teaspoon dill weed
1½ cups sour cream
1½ cups wild rice
    fresh dill or parsley, snipped

Sear beef in butter, remove and reserve. Saute onion, mushrooms and garlic. Reduce heat and add flour, meat extract paste, catsup, salt and pepper and simmer. Stir in wine, sour cream and dill. Add reserved beef and simmer. Serve over rice.

Lee Allen

Better if prepared 1 day early.

Jack's Favorite Beef Stroganoff

YIELD: 6 servings
CALORIES: 1296
CARBOHYDRATES: 46g

FAT: 78g
PROTEIN: 90g

⅓ cup butter
½ cup finely chopped onions
⅓ cup butter
1½ pounds fresh mushrooms, sliced, or 1 large can sliced mushrooms
⅓ cup butter
3½ pounds sirloin steak, cut in ½ × ½ × 2 inch strips
6 tablespoons flour
3 bouillon cubes

3 cups salted water
6 tablespoons tomato paste (1-6 ounce can)
2 tablespoons Worcestershire sauce
¾ cup sour cream
½ cup heavy cream
½ cup burgundy
1 teaspoon instant coffee
Noodles or rice, cooked

Saute onion in butter until tender; remove and set aside. Saute mushrooms in butter until brown; remove and set aside. Roll the beef strips in flour; salt and pepper to taste. Brown all sides in butter. Dissolve bouillon in boiling salted water; add to beef. Add onions. Cover and simmer gently until the beef is tender, approximately 1½-2 hours. Add mushrooms, tomato paste, Worcestershire sauce and sour cream. Heat thoroughly. Add heavy cream, burgundy and instant coffee. Heat thoroughly. Adjust seasonings. Serve over buttered noodles or fluffy rice.

Sandy Baggett

If made ahead and frozen, do not add the sour cream, cream, and wine until stroganoff has thawed and been heated slightly.

Beef Stroganoff

YIELD: 4 servings
CALORIES: 822
CARBOHYDRATES: 28g

FAT: 43g
PROTEIN: 76g

2 pounds lean sirloin
4 tablespoons butter
1 8 ounce jar mushrooms, sliced
1 cup tomato juice

1 teaspoon garlic salt
1 can cream of mushroom soup
1 cup sour cream
cooked rice or noodles

Trim fat from meat and cut into cubes. Melt butter in electric skillet at 400 degrees. Saute meat and mushrooms. Add tomato juice and seasonings. More juice can be added if needed. Cover and simmer for 40 minutes. Add sour cream and soup. Heat and serve over rice or noodles.

Wanda Bunger

Juicy Meat Loaf

YIELD: 6 servings
CALORIES: 557
CARBOHYDRATES: 6g

FAT: 46g
PROTEIN: 26g

1½ pounds ground beef
¾ cup oatmeal
2 eggs, beaten
onion salt, or small amount
   onion, chopped

1 teaspoon salt
black pepper to taste
1 10 ounce can tomatoes or
   tomato sauce

Combine all ingredients thoroughly and pack firmly into a loaf pan. Bake at 325 degrees for one hour. DO NOT OVERCOOK. You may need to reduce oven time. Drain accumulated grease once or twice during cooking time. Let stand 5 minutes before serving.

Nancy Miller Johnson

Meat Loaf Hero

YIELD: 10 to 12 servings
CALORIES: 308
CARBOHYDRATES: 23g

FAT: 11g
PROTEIN: 26g

1½ pounds lean ground beef
   or ground round
⅓ cup evaporated milk
¼ cup bread crumbs
1 egg
1 medium onion, minced
1 teaspoon salt

¼ teaspoon pepper
½ tablespoon mustard
¼ teaspoon garlic powder
¼ teaspoon Tabasco Sauce
1 loaf Italian bread, split
   lengthwise
8 strips American cheese

Mix first 10 ingredients. Place bottom half of bread on a large sheet of foil. Spread meat on bread. Close foil. Place on grill or in 350 degree oven for 45 minutes. Open and top with cheese. Re-wrap loosely and return to oven for 5 minutes. Toast top half of bread with the cut side down and put on top of meat. Cut into serving pieces.

Elizabeth Clark

Cheesy Meat Loaf

YIELD: 10 servings
CALORIES: 591
CARBOHYDRATES: 7g

FAT: 49g
PROTEIN: 29g

2   pounds ground meat
salt and pepper to taste
1   egg

1   16 ounce can tomato sauce
1   pound American cheese or
    8 slices

Mix meat, egg, salt and pepper. Bake at 350 degrees for one hour or until done, draining grease as meat cooks. Pour tomato sauce on top of meat; cook for 5 more minutes. Top with grated cheese or cheese slices.

Helen Bean

Can also pat the meat out and put the cheese in the middle and roll it up.

Meat Loaf

YIELD: 6 servings
CALORIES: 603
CARBOHYDRATES: 24g

FAT: 36g
PROTEIN: 44g

1½ to 2 pounds ground meat
1   can cream of mushroom
    soup
1   small onion, chopped
½   package saltine crackers,
    about 22
2   eggs
½   bell pepper, chopped

salt and pepper to taste
garlic powder
1   8 ounce can tomato sauce
3-4 strips bacon

Crumble crackers and mix with meat, onion, bell pepper and seasonings. Add the soup and bake at 350 degrees for 1 hour. Pour tomato sauce over meatloaf and top with strips of bacon. Cook 30 minutes longer. Let stand for 10 minutes before serving.

Tammy Bunger

Very moist!

Tallerine

YIELD: 8
CALORIES: 423
CARBOHYDRATES: 33g

FAT: 20g
PROTEIN: 26g

1   pound ground beef
1   onion, chopped
1   small bell pepper, chopped
⅔   cup cooked noodles
1   can tomato soup
1   small can whole kernel
    corn
1   small can chopped ripe
    olives

1   small can tomato sauce
1   small can water
chili powder
garlic
salt and pepper to taste
1   cup grated cheddar cheese
    (more if you like)

Cook meat with onion and green pepper until done. Cook noodles separately, then add meat mixture and remaining ingredients, except cheese. Top with cheese and refrigerate overnight. Bake at 350 degrees for 1 hour.

Jean Rippetoe

Stuffed Pepper Cups

YIELD: 6 servings
CALORIES: 536
CARBOHYDRATES: 21g

FAT: 39g
PROTEIN: 24g

6   medium bell peppers
1   pound ground beef
⅓   cup chopped onion
1   16 ounce can tomatoes, cut
    up
½   cup uncooked long grain
    rice

½   cup water
1   teaspoon Worcestershire
    sauce
4   ounces sharp processed
    American cheese, shredded

Cut tops off the bell peppers and remove the seeds. Scallop the edges. Boil in salted water for 5 minutes; drain. (For crisp peppers, omit boiling). Salt the inside of the peppers generously. Brown the ground beef and onion. Salt and pepper to taste. Stir in the tomatoes, rice, water, and Worcestershire sauce. Stuff the peppers with the meat mixture. Place in 10×6×1½ inch baking dish. Bake at 350 degrees for 20 minutes. Top peppers with shredded cheese and bake 5 minutes more.

Tammy Bunger

Excellent! Great for family suppers.

Chinese Beef

YIELD: 6 to 8 servings
CALORIES: 281
CARBOHYDRATES: 10g

FAT: 13g
PROTEIN: 30g

1½ pounds round steak
1 onion, sliced
1 cup fresh mushrooms, sliced
1 to 2 cups celery, sliced
1 8 ounce can water chestnuts, sliced and drained
4 cups cabbage, thinly sliced

2 6 ounce cans beef-mushroom steak sauce
salt and pepper
2 to 4 tablespoons cooking oil
garlic salt
2 tablespoons or more soy sauce

Cut round steak in thin strips, 1 inch × 3 inches. Sprinkle with salt, pepper and garlic salt. Brown meat strips in hot oil in wok or large skillet. Remove and keep warm. Saute onion, mushrooms, celery and cabbage until tender-crisp. Add water chestnuts and meat strips. Cover and heat for 2 minutes. Add gravy, warm until bubbly and add soy sauce. Serve over rice or chinese rice noodles.

Sherry Scott

Tester says it is fast and kids like it too.

Julie's Connecticut Beef Supper

YIELD: 6-8 servings
CALORIES: 627
CARBOHYDRATES: 18g

FAT: 42g
PROTEIN: 42g

2 pounds beef for stew cut into 1 inch cubes
salt and pepper to taste
2 large onions, sliced
2 tablespoons olive oil
1 4½ ounce jar whole mushrooms
4 medium potatoes, peeled and thinly sliced

1 10½ ounce can cream of mushroom soup
¾ cup sour cream
1 teaspoon salt
¼ teaspoon pepper
2 cups grated cheddar cheese
¾ cup milk

Season meat with salt and pepper to taste. Cook and stir meat and onions in oil in large skillet in medium heat until meat is brown and onions are tender. Pour off oil. Drain mushrooms, reserving liquid to make 1 cup. Stir mushrooms and liquid into meat and onions. Heat to boiling; reduce heat and cover. Simmer one hour. Heat oven to 350 degrees. Pour meat mixture into a 9 × 13 inch baking dish. Arrange potatoes over meat. Mix soup, milk, sour cream, salt and pepper; pour over potatoes. Bake uncovered for one hour. Sprinkle with cheese and cook for five more minutes or until cheese melts.   **Cathy Carson**

Beef and Green Beans

YIELD: 6 servings
CALORIES: 371
CARBOHYDRATES: 11g

FAT: 11g
PROTEIN: 52g

1½ to 2 pounds round steak, cut into ½ × 2-inch strips
3 teaspoons dry mustard
1½ teaspoons salt
¼ teaspoon pepper
2 beef bouillon cubes
1 cup hot water

1½ cups buttermilk
3 tablespoons cornstarch
1 4 ounce jar pimientos, cut in strips
1 8 ounce can mushrooms
1 16 ounce package frozen green beans, thawed

Brown beef in a small amount of vegetable oil in a heavy dutch oven. Combine mustard, salt and pepper and sprinkle over browned meat. Dissolve bouillon in hot water and pour over beef. Cover tightly and simmer for 40 minutes. Stir cornstarch into buttermilk until smooth and add slowly to beef mixture stirring well. Simmer 20 minutes, stirring occasionally. Add pimientos, mushrooms and green beans and continue simmering an additional 10 minutes. Serve over hot cooked rice.
Martha Gries

Huntington Stew

YIELD: 6 to 8 servings
CALORIES: 550
CARBOHYDRATES: 34g

FAT: 25g
PROTEIN: 42g

STEW

2   tablespoons oil
2   pounds round steak, cubed
2   onions, chopped
½   pound mushrooms, sliced
2   cups beef broth
1   teaspoon salt

½   teaspoon pepper
⅛   teaspoon cloves
½   teaspoon paprika
1   small clove garlic, minced
½   cup dry red wine

Brown meat in hot oil and drain off excess fat. Add remainder of ingredients except wine and bring to a boil. Cover, reduce heat to a simmer and cook for 1 hour. Stir in wine and pour into oven-proof serving dish. Top with drop or shaped biscuits. Bake at 400 degrees for 10 to 15 minutes or until biscuits are browned.

DROP BISCUITS

2   cups sifted flour
4   teaspoons baking powder
½   teaspoon salt
½   teaspoon cream of tarter

2   teaspoons sugar
½   cup shortening
1   cup milk

Sift dry ingredients together. Cut in shortening until mixture resembles coarse crumbs. Add milk all at once. Stir only until dough is moistened. Drop by heaping tablespoonsfull on top of stew. Makes approximately 16 biscuits. Decrease amount of milk to ⅔ cup for rolled and shaped biscuits.

Cathy Carson

The biscuit recipe is also good when rolled out and shaped into regular biscuits, baked at 450 degrees for 10 minutes and served with butter and jelly.

Mexican Hamburger Stew

YIELD: 4 to 6 servings
CALORIES: 408
CARBOHYDRATES: 46g

FAT: 14g
PROTEIN: 26g

1 pound ground beef
2 onions, diced
2 large potatoes, diced
1 16 ounce can whole kernel
  corn

1 13 ounce can Spanish rice
1 can Rotel tomatoes

Brown ground meat and onion. Add remaining ingredients and cook for 45 minutes or until the potatoes are tender.

Nancy Vannoy

Baked Stew

YIELD: 6 servings
CALORIES: 416
CARBOHYDRATES: 15g

FAT: 15g
PROTEIN: 50g

2 pounds stew meat, bite-
  size pieces
1 large onion, quartered
2 carrots, sliced
1 can golden cream of
  mushroom soup

1 small can whole
  mushrooms, drained
1 package dry onion soup
  mix
½ cup red wine, Burgundy
  type

Brown meat and onions. Stir in remaining ingredients and place in a casserole. Do not add salt. Cover with foil and bake at 300 degrees for 3 hours.

Martha Henderson

Can be prepared ahead of time. Especially good with noodles or rice.

Herb Beef Stew with Almond Noodles

YIELD: 6 to 8 servings
CALORIES: 903
CARBOHYDRATES: 29g

FAT: 66g
PROTEIN: 46g

¼ cup butter
1 large round steak, cubed
1½ cups fresh mushrooms, sliced
1 onion, chopped fine
2 cloves garlic, chopped
1 teaspoon salt
1 teaspoon dill weed
4 to 5 bay leaves
¾ teaspoon basil
½ teaspoon thyme

1 16 ounce can tomatoes, blended
2 to 3 cups beef bouillon
3 carrots, chopped
1 to 2 tablespoons flour
¼ cup water
1 package noodles
¼ cup butter
3 ounces almonds, slivered
poppy seeds

In a large pot, brown the meat in butter, a few pieces at a time. Add mushrooms, onions, garlic and spices. Saute slowly until vegetables are tender. Add bouillon and tomatoes and simmer covered about 30 minutes. Add carrots and cook until tender. Combine flour and water, stir until smooth and add to meat mixture stirring until thickened. Boil noodles and drain. Add butter, almonds and poppy seeds to taste. To serve, place approximately ½ cup noodles on each plate, top with serving of stew and garnish with parsley. Serve with salad or green vegetable.

Susan McMullan

Family Style Beef Stew

YIELD: 8 servings
CALORIES: 680
CARBOHYDRATES: 49g

FAT: 28g
PROTEIN: 57g

3 pounds stew meat, cubed
2 tablespoons shortening
2 large onions, sliced
2 cloves garlic
1 cup chopped celery
¼ cup chopped parsley
2¼ cups canned tomatoes
1 bay leaf, crumbled
½ teaspoon thyme

1 tablespoon salt
black pepper
2½ cups water
1 cup green peas
12 small carrots
12 small onions
6 potatoes, quartered
½ cup flour,if thickening is
desired

Melt shortening in a dutch oven and brown meat. Add onions, garlic, celery, parsley, tomatoes, bay leaf, thyme, salt and pepper and the 2½ cups of water. Bring to a boil, reduce heat; cover and simmer for 2 hours. Add remaining vegetables and simmer for 1 hour. Just before serving, thicken with flour if desired.

Nancy Vannoy

No Peep Stew

YIELD: 8 to 10 servings
CALORIES: 458
CARBOHYDRATES: 10g

FAT: 36g
PROTEIN: 20g

2 pounds ground beef
2 cups sliced potatoes
1 cup chopped celery
1 cup chopped onion
1 cup sliced carrots

2 cans Snap-E-Tom Tomato
Juice Cocktail
2 tablespoons tapioca
1 to 2 tablespoons Season All
salt and pepper, optional

Dissolve tapioca in tomato juice. Mix remaining ingredients in a large dutch oven. Pour tapioca mixture over all. Bake at 250 degrees for 5 hours. Do not peep.

Carol Hunnicutt

This is good with cornbread and a green salad.

Cabbage Patch Stew

YIELD: 8 to 10 servings
CALORIES: 350
CARBOHYDRATES: 25g

FAT: 21g
PROTEIN: 16g

1	pound lean ground beef	1	small head cabbage,
1	medium onion, chopped		chopped
1	bell pepper, chopped	1	teaspoon chili powder
2	ribs celery, chopped		garlic powder, salt and pepper
1	15 ounce can corn		to taste
1	15 ounce can ranch style	1	cup water
	beans	1	jalapeno pepper, chopped,
1	15 ounce can tomatoes		optional

Saute the first 4 ingredients. Add the remaining ingredients and cook until cabbage is tender.

Katharine Russell

A meal in itself.

Hamburger Goulash

YIELD: 8 servings
CALORIES: 512
CARBOHYDRATES: 44g

FAT: 21g
PROTEIN: 36g

2	pounds ground beef		chili powder
1	onion, chopped		salt
1	bell pepper, chopped		pepper
1	14½ ounce can tomatoes	1	can water chestnuts,
1	8 ounce can tomato sauce		drained and sliced
1	package ready cut		
	spaghetti, cooked and		
	drained		

Brown the ground meat, onion, and bell pepper. Drain excess grease. Add the tomatoes, tomato sauce, spaghetti and spices. Add enough water to make the mixture soupy. Simmer for 10 to 15 minutes to cook the liquid down. Add the water chestnuts five minutes before serving.

Sherry Scott

Clifford's Pizza

YIELD: 8 servings
CALORIES: 287
CARBOHYDRATES: 35g

FAT: 9g
PROTEIN: 17g

SAUCE

1 8 ounce can tomato sauce
1 tablespoon fresh oregano
   or 1 teaspoon dried
1 teaspoon brown sugar
1 teaspoon Accent
½ onion, chopped
1 clove garlic, chopped
6 to 8 ounces mozzarella
   cheese, grated

fennel seeds, to taste
toppings of your choice:
   hamburger, cooked
green onions
mushrooms
pepperoni
peppers, etc.

Mix all ingredients except toppings and fennel seeds in small saucepan and simmer 5 minutes. If making pepperoni pizza, add a few chopped slices to the sauce for flavor. Set sauce aside.

DOUGH

2 cups flour
½ cup water, lukewarm
1 package yeast

½ teaspoon salt
1 teaspoon sugar
1 teaspoon cooking oil

Mix sugar, salt and yeast in water. Gradually add to flour. Mixture should be sticky, not too wet or too dry. Knead for about 5 minutes until smooth. Add cooking oil and knead into dough until dough is satiny. Set aside, cover, and let rise at least an hour. After dough has risen, roll out on 15 inch pizza tin. Turn edges up to contain sauce. Rub about 2 teaspoons oil over surface of dough. This will give the crust much better texture. Spread sauce over dough. Sprinkle cheese over sauce and sprinkle lightly with fennel seeds. Add toppings of your choice. Bake at 450 degrees for about 15 minutes or until cheese bubbles and crust shows light brown edges.

Mary Jo Mason

This recipe came from Clifford Kite, a dear friend in Austin, and has been a favorite in our family for years.

Pizza

YIELD: 12 servings, 2 pizzas
CALORIES: 237
CARBOHYDRATES: 26g

FAT: 9g
PROTEIN: 14g

DOUGH
1   package dry yeast
1   cup lukewarm water
1   teaspoon sugar

2   teaspoons salad oil
2½ cups flour

SAUCE:
½   cup onion, chopped
1   8 ounce can tomato sauce
¼   teaspoon salt

½   teaspoon garlic salt
⅛   teaspoon pepper
½   teaspoon basil

TOPPING:
sprinkle of oregano
Parmesan cheese
3   to 4 ounces cheddar cheese
1   package sliced pepperoni
    or 1 cup cooked ground
    meat

8   ounces mozzarella cheese,
    shredded

Dissolve yeast in water. Stir in remaining ingredients and beat dough vigorously, about 20 strokes. Allow dough to rest while preparing sauce. Let it rise until double in bulk, about 1 hour. Mix sauce ingredients and set aside. Preheat oven to 425 degrees. Divide dough in half. On lightly greased baking pizza pan, pat each half into 10 inch circles. Flour fingers while patting down. Spread sauce on each circle. Sprinkle with Parmesan and oregano. Arrange cheese and then meat on top. Add extras if desired. Bake 20-25 minutes.

Debbie Glasscock

Orphie's Beans

YIELD: 8 servings
CALORIES: 371
CARBOHYDRATES: 25g

FAT: 21g
PROTEIN: 19g

1   pound ground meat
1   to 2 onions, chopped
½   tablespoon cumin
½   tablespoon chili powder
1   small can chopped green
    chilies

1   small can taco sauce
1   15 ounce can whole
    tomatoes
1   pound cooked pinto beans

Brown the ground meat and onions. Drain excess grease. Add the remaining ingredients. Simmer 1 hour.

Cynthia Berry

Great quick meal served with cornbread. Freezes well.

Baked Country Ham

YIELD: 8 to 12 servings
CALORIES: 714
CARBOHYDRATES: 24g

FAT: 48g
PROTEIN: 45g

4   to 6 pound cooked ham
15 to 20 cloves
1   cup brown sugar

½   cup dry sherry
¼   cup honey
¼   cup Dijon mustard

Score the top of the ham into diamonds and place a clove in the middle of each diamond. Put the ham, scored side up, in a foil lined metal baking pan. Cover with foil and bake at 300 degrees for 1½ hours. Pour the excess fat from the pan. Line the pan with fresh foil and place the ham in the pan. Combine the remaining ingredients to make the glaze. Spoon the glaze over the ham and bake 20 minutes. Glaze once more and bake 15 minutes. Cool and carve.

Sandy Baggett

A versatile glaze that can be served on the side or over baked pork chops.

Leota's Ham

YIELD: 8 servings
CALORIES: 1183
CARBOHYDRATES: 81g

FAT: 67g
PROTEIN: 63g

ham, your choice
1   box brown sugar
1   can beer

cloves, pineapple slices,
    cherries (optional)

Place ham in roaster, fat side down. Pour beer over ham then pat brown sugar firmly onto ham. Cover and bake at 350 degrees for 20 minutes per pound of ham. Halfway through baking, remove cover, turn ham over. Score and stud ham with cloves. Decorate with pineapple and cherries if desired. Return to oven and continue baking uncovered until done, basting occasionally. If ham is very large use 2 boxes of brown sugar and 2 cans of beer.

Lockie Sue Bissett

Strawberry Sauce

CALORIES: 93

CARBOHYDRATES: 22g

10 ounce package frozen,
    sweetened strawberries

2   tablespoons cornstarch
1   teaspoon cinnamon

Combine all ingredients in a small saucepan and mix well. Cook over low heat until thickened and bubbly. Serve with hot baked ham, pork chops or lamb.

Cathy Carson

Individual Ham Loaves

YIELD: 14 servings
CALORIES: 202
CARBOHYDRATES: 18g

FAT: 11g
PROTEIN: 9g

½ pound ground ham
½ pound ground pork
¼ cup cracker crumbs
1 small onion, chopped

1 egg, beaten
¾ cup milk
¼ teaspoon salt
dash of pepper

Mix all ingredients, pack tightly into muffin tins. Pour sauce over and bake at 350 degrees for 20 minutes. Serve with a side sauce of mayonnaise with horseradish to taste.

SAUCE
3 tablespoons vinegar
1 cup brown sugar

1 teaspoon dry mustard

Combine and boil for 1 minute. Spoon over meat mixture before baking.

Lee Allen

Quick Sausage n' Potatoes

YIELD: 4 servings
CALORIES: 615
CARBOHYDRATES: 38g

FAT: 45g
PROTEIN: 15g

1 pound Polish sausage (or beef), sliced ¼ inch thick
2 tablespoons vegetable oil
24 ounce package frozen potatoes O'Brien

1 cup fresh or frozen onions, chopped
salt and pepper to taste

In a large non-stick skillet cook sausage over medium heat, about 3 minutes until browned. Remove with a slotted spoon. Add oil to skillet and heat over medium high heat. Add potatoes, onions, salt and pepper. Cover and cook 10 minutes or until potatoes are golden brown and tender, stirring once. Stir in sausage and heat through.

Marilyn Chalmers

Easy to prepare.

Barbequed Pork Chops

YIELD: 4 servings
CALORIES: 758
CARBOHYDRATES: 12g

FAT: 58g
PROTEIN: 45g

2   tablespoons butter or
    margarine
4   thick center cut pork chops
¼   teaspoon salt
¼   teaspoon pepper
¼   teaspoon paprika
1   large onion, peeled

½   bottle chili sauce
2   tablespoons Worcestershire
    sauce
¼   teaspoon Tabasco
¼   cup water
1   large green pepper, thinly
    sliced

Saute pork chops in butter. Season with salt, pepper and paprika. Brown well on both sides. Slice onion into four large slices. Place one slice on top of each chop. Mix together the chili sauce, Worcestershire, Tabasco and water. Pour this sauce over the chops and onions. Cover skillet and simmer slowly for about 1½ hours or until very tender. Serve on warmed platter garnished with green pepper.

Sandy Baggett

Sweet and Sour Pork

YIELD: 4 to 6 servings
CALORIES: 489
CARBOHYDRATES: 56g

FAT: 17g
PROTEIN: 27g

1   pound lean pork, cut into
    ¾ inch cubes
1   egg, slightly beaten
1   cup flour
½   teaspoon monosodium
    glutamate

⅛   teaspoon salt
¼   teaspoon pepper
peanut oil for deep frying

SAUCE

1   14 ounce can pineapple
    chunks, drained(reserve
    liquid)
½   cup sugar
½   cup white vinegar
¼   cup tomato catsup

1   teaspoon soy sauce
2   tablespoons cornstarch
2   tablespoons water
1   medium bell pepper, cut
    into ½ inch squares

Dip pork cubes in the beaten egg until well coated. In a medium sized bowl, mix the flour, MSG and salt. Add pork and stir gently until well coated. Fry pork in 375 degree oil for 6 to 8 minutes or until brown. Drain well and keep warm. In a wok or deep skillet, mix soy sauce, sugar, catsup, vinegar, ⅓ cup pineapple liquid and bring to a boil. Taste for seasoning. Mix corn starch and water and add to sauce. Simmer, stirring until thick. Add pork, pineapple chunks and green pepper. Continue to heat until heated throughout. Serve over rice.

Paula Bailey

Fran's Egg Rolls

YIELD: 4 to 6 servings
CALORIES: 620
CARBOHYDRATES: 19g

FAT: 45g
PROTEIN: 34g

1   pound ground pork
½   pound shrimp, cleaned,
    deveined and chopped
2   cups bean sprouts, chopped
2   cups Nappa cabbage,
    chopped

1   cup celery, chopped
1   tablespoon cornstarch
2   tablespoons soy sauce
egg roll skins
cooking oil
1   egg, beaten

Chop all vegetables, cook pork in a small amount of oil for 2 minutes, add shrimp and cook 1 minute. Add all vegetables, cook 2 minutes. Mix cornstarch and soy sauce and add, cooking until thickened. Let cool. Place 2 tablespoons of the mixture on egg roll skins. Place bottom point of skin over and under mixture. Fold sides over this and roll up neatly. Seal with beaten egg. Fry in deep oil. Serve with mustard sauce or sweet sour sauce. Egg rolls may be frozen before frying.

Mary Jo Mason

Leg of Lamb

YIELD: 2 or 3 servings per pound
CALORIES: 260

FAT: 10g
PROTEIN: 40g

1   leg of lamb, trimmed of
    excess fat and de-boned if
    desired

2   pods garlic
salt
pepper

Peel the garlic and slice thinly. Make tiny slits in the lamb flesh and bury the garlic pieces. Season the meat. Place in a roasting pan and cover with foil. Bake at 325 degrees for 30 minutes per pound.

Paula Bailey

Broiled Lamb Chops

YIELD: 6 to 8 servings
CALORIES: 360

FAT: 32g
PROTEIN: 18g

6 to 8 lamb chops
2   teaspoons lemon pepper

1   teaspoon garlic salt

Sprinkle both sides of chops with lemon pepper and garlic salt. Broil 2 inches from heat source for 10 minutes per side for medium.

Helen Bean

Baked Leg of Lamb

YIELD: 4 to 8 servings   FAT: 38g
CALORIES: 564   PROTEIN: 53g

1   leg of lamb   lemon-pepper seasoning

Let lamb thaw completely. Season heavily both sides of leg with lemon-pepper seasoning. Place on a rack in roaster and cover. Bake at 350 degrees for 3 to 4 hours. It is important to place the leg of lamb on a rack so the fat can drip away and you won't have a strong taste.

Helen Bean

Roast Leg of Lamb

YIELD: 4 servings   FAT: 38g
CALORIES: 564   PROTEIN: 53g

7   to 8 pound leg of lamb   1   tablespoon corn oil
2   large cloves garlic, peeled 1   small onion, peeled
Freshly ground black pepper   1   cup unsalted chicken broth
1   tablespoon dried crumbled
    rosemary or 2 sprigs fresh

Bone or have butcher bone it, saving the bone, and trim away much of the top fat, leaving a light layer. Cut each garlic clove into 4 slivers. Make gashes in the fat and insert garlic slivers. If using fresh rosemary, insert a small piece along with garlic. Place roast in shallow roasting pan fat side up. Sprinkle with a generous grinding of pepper. If using dried rosemary, rub the meat all over with it. Now rub with oil. Place bone around the lamb. Add the onion. Bake, basting occasionally at 400 degrees for about 1½ hours for rare. Cook 30 minutes more if you like it well done. Remove lamb, add both and stir to dissolve the bits left in bottom of pan. Strain gravy and serve with the lamb.

Camille Jones

Lamb Chops with Tarragon

YIELD: 4 servings
CALORIES: 281

FAT: 28g
PROTEIN: 9g

4 double lamb chops, about 2 pounds, each about 1¾ inches thick.
Freshly ground black pepper to taste.
2 to 4 tablespoons unsalted butter or margarine

2 tablespoons finely chopped shallots or green onions
1 tablespoon finely chopped fresh tarragon, or half the amount dried.

Heat large iron skillet. When skillet is very hot, rub with a piece of lamb fat. Sprinkle the chops with pepper. Place chops in hot skillet and sear until crusty on each side, about five minutes per side. Lower the heat and cook about five to ten minutes more. This method of cooking is a little smokey, but delicious. In the microwave, melt the butter or margarine and add the shallots and tarragon. Remove from the heat and swirl the butter around. Pour over the chops.

Camille Jones

The ranch provides us with meat the year round and in fall and summer, the garden supplies fresh herbs and vegetables. One of my favorite herbs is tarragon, especially combined with lamb.

Lamb Chops Two Ways

CALORIES: 360

FAT: 32g
PROTEIN: 18g

lamb chops
Pick A Peppa Sauce

soy sauce

Rub lamb chops on both sides with "Pick A Peppa Sauce" then pan broil. No other seasonings are needed.

Marinate lamb chops in soy sauce at least 2 hours then cook in pan with soy sauce.

Paula Bailey

Allow 1 chop ½ inch thick per serving.

Bill's Goat Meat

YIELD: 6 servings
CALORIES: 368
CARBOHYDRATES: 8g

FAT: 18g
PROTEIN: 38g

2 tablespoons salad oil
2 pounds cubed goat meat
1 teaspoon salt
½ teaspoon garlic powder
¼ teaspoon oregano
⅛ teaspoon ground cumin

1 large onion, chopped
1 tablespoon flour
1 10 ounce can Rotel
  tomatoes and green chiles
1 10 ounce can water

Brown meat in hot oil. Add salt, garlic powder, oregano, cumin and onion. Cook until onion is soft. Sprinkle flour over all and allow to brown, stirring constantly. Add tomatoes and water. Simmer uncovered for 40 minutes, stirring occasionally. Most of the liquid will be absorbed.

Cathy Carson

Serve with homemade flour tortillas

Fried Goat Ribs

YIELD: 4 to 6 servings
CALORIES: 547
CARBOHYDRATES: 15g

FAT: 34g
PROTEIN: 38g

1 set of goat ribs
salt
coarse gound pepper

flour
lard or shortening

Cut ribs into segments of 2 ribs each. Salt and pepper liberally. Dredge in flour. Have shortening 1½ inches deep in skillet. Place only 2 or 3 into hot grease at a time. Fry until light brown. Drain on paper towel.

Lou Deaton and Helen Bean

Lamb or Goat Fries

YIELD: 24 fries

24 prepared fries, thinly sliced crosswise	¼ cup water or milk
2 cups flour	1 tablespoon oil
cayenne pepper	3 cups breadcrumbs
4 eggs	3 tablespoons extra-spicy Mrs. Dash

To prepare fries, carefully cut into the loose outer skin for the entire length of the swelled surface. Remove this skin and again cut into the two inner skins in the same manner, disturbing the flesh as little as possible. An oval flesh form will remain. Soak the peeled fries in the refrigerator in enough cold water to cover. The fries should soak about three hours, changing the water several times. Drain, then cover the fries with fresh cold water in a saucepan. Bring to a boil, then reduce heat at once and simmer about 6 minutes. Drain the fries and then plunge them into cold water until cool. To prepare batter, season the flour with cayenne. In another bowl, beat the eggs slightly and mix with water and oil. Place the breadcrumbs and Mrs. Dash in a third bowl. Coat a handful of the fries in the flour, shaking off the excess. Dip them in the egg/milk mixture, and then coat with the seasoned breadcrumbs. Place on a rack to dry for at least 20 minutes, but no longer than 1 hour. Do not chill the fries because they will absorb more fat and become soggy. When all the fries are ready to cook, fry in deep fat, very hot until they float to the top.

Camille Jones

In the spring time, all the young male goats and lambs must be castrated (these are called fries). At this time the lamb's tails are cut off, they are vaccinated and they are ear marked. The whole proce-dure has come to be called "marking" In the old days the cowboys threw the fries on the fire and cooked them as a great delicacy. Some still consider them so.

Baked Goat Meat

YIELD: 6 servings
CALORIES: 330

FAT: 18g
PROTEIN: 36g

goat meat
garlic salt

pepper

Season meat on both sides. Place in a roasting pan with a small amount of water to cover the bottom of the pan. Cover and bake at 300 degrees to 350 degrees for 3 or 4 hours. Meat should fall off of the bone.

Helen Bean and Lou Deaton

Dean's Baked Goat

YIELD: 6 servings
CALORIES: 330

FAT: 18g
PROTEIN: 36g

goat meat, any parts
salt and pepper

garlic salt
Worcestershire sauce

Place goat meat in bottom of large roaster. Season liberally with salt and pepper and garlic. Sprinkle liberally with Worcestershire. Seal pan with foil. Bake at 250 degrees for 4 hours or more.

Lockie Sue Bissett

Your kitchen will smell heavenly while this is cooking.

Son-of-a-Gun Stew

YIELD: 8 servings
CALORIES: 583
CARBOHYDRATES: 16g

FAT: 37g
PROTEIN: 44g

shoulder meat, goat or mutton
heart
liver
sweetbreads
marrow-gut

salt, pepper, flour
1   clove garlic, minced
1   medium onion, chopped
¼   cup lard or suet
water

Cut equal parts of all meat and marrow-gut into ½ inch cubes. Dredge in salt, pepper and flour. Heat suet or lard, brown the onion and garlic in hot fat. Add meat and brown. Cover with water and cook very slowly until tender and thick.

Lou Deaton

An old time West Texas Bar–B–Que favorite.

Texas Barbeque Sauce

YIELD: 2 cups
CALORIES: 164
CARBOHYDRATES: 17g

FAT: 12g
PROTEIN: 1g

¼ pound butter or margarine
1 cup vinegar
1 cup water
½ cup tomato catsup
2 tablespoons Worcestershire
  sauce
juice of one lemon
1 tablespoon dry mustard
2 tablespoons Texas chili
  powder

¼ teaspoon cayenne
1 teaspoon black pepper
1 teaspoon salt
¼ cup sugar
2 bay leaves, crushed
2 garlic cloves,minced
1 large onion,minced

Melt butter or margarine. Add vinegar, water, tomato catsup, Worcestershire sauce and lemon juice. Mix mustard, chili powder, cayenne, pepper, salt, sugar, bay leaves and add to butter mixture. Add garlic and onion. Simmer for about 10 to 15 minutes.

Nancy Vannoy

This is enough sauce to swab 4 to 5 pounds of meat.

Sandy's Barbeque Sauce

YIELD: 2½ quarts
CALORIES: 150
CARBOHYDRATES: 13g

FAT: 11g
PROTEIN: 1g

½ cup cooking oil
½ cup butter
2 onions,chopped
4 cloves garlic,crushed
2 dried hot red peppers,
  chopped or bellpeppers
  with seeds
3 8 ounce cans tomato sauce
2 cups water
1 pound can tomatoes
¾ cup chili sauce

3 tablespoons Liquid Smoke
3 tablespoons Worcestershire
  sauce
2 tablespoons wine vinegar
2 tablespoons prepared
  mustard
½ cup sugar
2 tablespoons salt
2 tablespoons pepper
3 bay leaves, crushed
4 slices lemon

Combine all the ingredients. Simmer for 4 hours. Baste meat often with sauce while cooking.

Sandy Baggett

Use on chicken, pork, ribs or venison. Freezes well.

Bar-B-Que Sauce

YIELD: 1½ cups
CALORIES: 176
CARBOHYDRATES: 9g

FAT: 15g

½ cup margarine
3 tablespoons mustard
3 tablespoons catsup
3 tablespoons brown sugar
3 tablespoons vinegar

3 tablespoons Worcestershire sauce
salt and pepper
Louisiana Hotsauce
celery and garlic salt

Melt margarine, add next 5 ingredients. Then add next 4 ingredients to taste.

Sammye Pierce

Very good on chicken.

Venison Stew

YIELD: 6 servings
CALORIES: 799
CARBOHYDRATES: 14g

FAT: 30g
PROTEIN: 105g

½ pound salt pork, diced
3 pounds venison shoulder, cut into cubes
2 ribs celery, chopped
3 onions, chopped
2 carrots, sliced
3 tablespoons flour

salt and pepper to taste
3 cups beef broth
1 bay leaf
juice of half a lemon
2 cloves
½ cup dry red wine

Saute salt pork until lightly browned. Add venison and brown quickly. Add celery, onions, and carrots, cook until wilted. Sprinkle with flour and cook, stirring, 2 minutes. Add remaining ingredients except wine, and bring to a boil. Cover and simmer gently about one hour. Remove bay leaf, stir in wine and cook 15 minutes longer.

Cathy Carson

If you're tired of fried deermeat, try this. It's a great change.

Fried Venison Backstrap and Gravy

YIELD: 4 servings

2 pounds venison backstrap	3 eggs plus 1 tablespoon
1 teaspoon salt	water, beaten together
1 teaspoon pepper	bacon grease or cooking oil
2 cups flour	garlic salt, optional

Slice backstrap crosswise in ¾ inch slices. Salt and pepper on both sides and place on a cutting board. Pound the meat to ¼ inch thickness with a meat mallet. Dredge the meat slices in flour, dip into a bowl of egg and water, then back into the flour. In skillet, place 1 to 1½ inches of cooking oil or bacon grease and heat until hot. Add the backstrap and fry about 3 minutes on each side or until light brown. Do not overcook. Drain on paper towel.

GRAVY

1 to 2 tablespoons grease or oil	2 to 3 cups milk
1 to 2 tablespoons flour	salt and pepper to taste

To make gravy, drain oil from skillet leaving the dregs in the skillet. Return 1 to 2 tablespoons grease to skillet. Place skillet on heat and add 1 to 2 tablespoons flour to make a paste or roux. Stirring constantly with a fork or whisk, add 2 to 3 cups milk and bring to a boil. Season to taste. Simmer until gravy is at desired thickness.

Lou Deaton

Lemon Chicken

YIELD: 4 servings
CALORIES: 212
CARBOHYDRATES: 1g

FAT: 9g
PROTEIN: 31g

1 chicken, about 2½ pounds, cut into serving pieces
2 teaspoons finely minced garlic
1 tablespoon corn oil
1 tablespoon finely grated lemon rind
3 tablespoons lemon juice

3 tablespoons chicken broth or water
1 teaspoon dried oregano, or 2 tablespoons fresh
½ teaspoon dried thyme or 1 tablespoon fresh
parsley, fresh and chopped, for garnish

Preheat oven to 400 degrees. Rub chicken pieces with garlic. Rub the oil over the inside of a baking dish that is large enough to hold chicken pieces in one layer. Add chicken, skin side down. Sprinkle with lemon rind and pour lemon juice and broth over all. Sprinkle with the herbs, place in oven and bake for 30 minutes. Turn the pieces and continue baking for about 30 minutes. Sprinkle with parsley and serve.

Camille Jones

Chicken with Chinese Vegetables

YIELD: 6 servings
CALORIES: 489
CARBOHYDRATES: 12g

FAT: 29g
PROTEIN: 39g

2 pounds raw chicken, cut into 1 inch cubes
2 tablespoons cornstarch
1 teaspoon salt
½ cup chopped onion
¼ cup peanut oil
1 tablespoon ginger, optional
½ pound mushrooms, sliced

1 cup bamboo shoots or 2 cups bean sprouts
¼ cup soy sauce
2 tablespoons sweet sherry or sake
1 8½ ounce can sliced water chestnuts
1 package frozen pod peas

Dredge chicken in cornstarch and salt. Saute with onions in oil until chicken is almost tender stirring frequently. Add ginger, mushrooms, bamboo shoots or bean sprouts, soy sauce and sherry or sake. Cook for 5 minutes, add peas and chestnuts. When this comes to a boil, serve at once over rice. This can be prepared ahead of time, adding the last ingredients when you heat to serve.

Paula D. Bailey

Chicken Breast with Green Peppercorn Sauce

YIELD: 4 servings
CALORIES: 584
CARBOHYDRATES: 24g

FAT: 35g
PROTEIN: 40g

4   chicken breasts, split, skinned and boned
3   tablespoons butter or margarine
2   tablespoons flour
1   cup chicken broth

½   cup light cream
2   teaspoons Dijon mustard
2   teaspoons green peppercorns
rice

Brown chicken in butter until done, about 20 minutes. Remove and keep warm. Stir flour into skillet drippings. Add broth, cream and mustard. Add peppercorns and mash a few while stirring sauce. Cook and stir sauce about 10 minutes. Pour over chicken and rice.

Mary Jo Mason

Sauce is also excellent on veal.

Hawaiian Chicken

YIELD: 4 servings
CALORIES: 250
CARBOHYDRATES: 12g

FAT: 7g
PROTEIN: 21g

2   chicken breasts, split, skinned and boned
1½ cups rose wine
1   tablespoon cornstarch
1   tablespoon brown sugar

¼   teaspoon oregano
⅛   teaspoon garlic powder
1   tablespoon cooking oil
½   cup pineapple juice
2   tablespoons soy sauce

Marinate chicken in half of the rose wine. Drain and pierce with cooking fork. Arrange in casserole. Combine remaining ingredients including the other half of the wine. Mix well and pour over chicken. Cover and microwave on high for 13 minutes, rotating dish ½ turns after 6 minutes. Serve over rice if desired. Remember when cooking with wine or liquor use the best that you can afford because of the taste. The alcohol content is gone after 5 minutes of cooking time.

Cathy Carson

Chicken L'Aiglon

YIELD: 4 servings
CALORIES: 1173
CARBOHYDRATES: 47g

FAT: 79g
PROTEIN: 60g

Chicken
4 small chicken breasts, skinned and deboned
4 very thin smoked ham slices
4 strips Swiss cheese
1 egg

1½ cups very fine cracker crumbs
salt and pepper
¾ cup butter
1 cup white rice
1 box long grain and wild rice mix

WHITE WINE SAUCE
1 can cream of chicken soup
⅓ cup milk
1 tablespoon pimientos, chopped

2 tablespoons dry white wine or sherry
1 3 ounce can button mushrooms, drained

Place chicken between sheets of wax paper and flatten with a cleaver. Place a slice of ham and a strip of cheese in the center of each breast. Fold edges of chicken over the ham and cheese and secure with toothpicks or string. Dip the rolled chicken in the egg which has been beaten with 1 teaspoon water, roll in the cracker crumbs. Season with salt and pepper. Heat butter in skillet until foamy. Brown chicken until golden on both sides, reduce heat and cook until done. In the meantime, cook rice according to directions on package and prepare the White Wine Sauce by mixing all of the listed ingredients and heat, but do not boil. Serve chicken breasts on a mound of rice with sauce spooned over. Serve extra sauce as gravy.

Belinda Wilkins

Iri-Dori

YIELD: 4 servings
CALORIES: 761
CARBOHYDRATES: 68g

FAT: 31g
PROTEIN: 46g

4   boned chicken breasts, cut into bite sized pieces
4 or 5 carrots, cut into bite sized pieces
1   cup bamboo shoots, drained
fresh broccoli, cauliflower, bean sprouts, scallions, spinach, as desired

3   tablespoons cooking oil
⅓ to ½ cup soy sauce
1   teaspoon chicken bouillon granules in 1 cup water
1   teaspoon sugar, optional
½   cup or less mirin-sweet cooking rice wine
rice

Heat the wok on high and add oil. Cook chicken until done. Add desired vegetables except spinach. Add soy sauce, chicken bouillon, sugar and wine. Cook for 5 minutes. Add the spinach last and cook for 1 minute more, covered. Serve over rice.

Mary Jo Mason

This is a recipe from Linda Whitten, Richardson, Texas, a very good friend and fellow artist.

Cornish Hens

YIELD: 1 hen per person
CALORIES: 547
CARBOHYDRATES: 23g

FAT: 31g
PROTEIN: 46g

1   cornish hen per person
1   new potato, quartered
1   large carrot, sliced
1   beef bouillon cube

2   tablespoons butter or margarine
salt and pepper to taste

Place the hen on a sheet of heavy duty foil. Place all other ingredients on top of hen, including giblets. Fold foil and seal around the hen. Bake at 350 degrees for 1 hour.

Benny Gail Hunnicutt

Try this for your next tailgate picnic.

Apricot Glazed Cornish Hens

YIELD: 4 to 6 servings
CALORIES: 226
CARBOHYDRATES: 12g

FAT: 13g
PROTEIN: 16g

4 cornish hens
salt
pepper
thyme
¼ cup melted butter
4 slices of bacon
1 onion, chopped

1 tablespoon flour
1 tablespoon sugar
1 to 2 teaspoons curry powder
2 teaspoons instant chicken bouillon
8 to 12 ounces apricot nectar

Season hens with salt, pepper and thyme on outside and rubbing the cavity. Brush with butter and place in a long ovenproof glass dish. Roast at 325 degrees. Make glaze by sauteing onion with bacon. Do not drain. Add the flour, sugar, curry powder and bouillon. Cook into a paste. Slowly add the apricot nectar. After the hens have cooked for 1 hour remove from the oven and baste with glaze. Return to oven and cook for 30 minutes more.

Belinda Wilkins

Perfect Turkey

YIELD: 4 to 6 ounce servings per person
CALORIES: 337

FAT: 25g
PROTEIN: 27g

Turkey
salt
pepper
poultry seasoning

ground sage
peanut oil
melted butter

Wash the turkey by scrubbing with salt. Rinse the salt off. Season heavily inside and out with salt, pepper, poultry seasoning and sage. Seal seasonings by rubbing turkey with peanut oil, inside and out. Baste turkey frequently with melted butter while cooking. Bake in a 325 degree oven for 30 minutes per pound or follow directions on an electric roaster.

Sandy Baggett

Do not stuff this turkey with dressing.

Grilled Dove or Quail

YIELD:
CALORIES: 553

FAT: 40g
PROTEIN: 48g

dove or quail
bacon slices

margarine

Make slits in each side of the breast of the bird and stuff each slit with butter. Wrap each bird with a slice of bacon and secure with a toothpick. Charcoal birds until done (about 20 to 30 minutes), turning often. Bacon should be crisp.

Jeannine Henderson

Can baste the birds in BBQ sauce. Great change from frying.

Wild Duck

YIELD: 1 to 2 servings
CALORIES: 825
CARBOHYDRATES: 2g

FAT: 72g
PROTEIN: 40g

1   or more wild ducks
¼   medium white onion per
    duck
2   slices bacon per duck,
    chopped finely

2   tablespoons butter
salt
pepper
flour

Make a putty of bacon, butter, and onion. Stuff putty into the cavity of the duck. Rub the bird with butter, salt, pepper, and wrap in heavy foil. Bake in oven for 1½ hours at 300 degrees. Cut slit in foil (over breast of bird) and pour off liquid into a container. Baste the breast of the bird with liquid. With the remaining liquid make a thick paste of the broth and flour. Spread the breast of the bird with paste. Return the bird to the oven with the foil open to brown the crust on the bird.

Steve Sessom

Can use domestic duck.

Buddy's Flounder Elegante

YIELD: 2 servings
CALORIES: 621
CARBOHYDRATES: 22g

FAT: 12g
PROTEIN: 92g

1   flounder fillet (½-1 pound)
½   teaspoon salt
flour
½   cup butter (1 stick)
½   medium white onion,
      chopped fine

3   ribs celery, sliced thin
½   pound fresh, medium
      shrimp, peeled and
      deveined
1   can chicken broth
½   cup dry white wine

Salt and flour flounder fillet. Saute in butter until light brown and remove fillet to shallow casserole dish. Add just enough flour, about ¼ cup, to the butter left in the skillet to make a smooth blend. Add chopped onion and celery to mixture and saute for 10 minutes. Add shrimp and saute 5 minutes. Add chicken broth and wine then cook until smooth. Pour sauce over fillet and place in an oven preheated to 350 degrees for 20 minutes.

Jodie Sessom

Fried Fish Batter

YIELD: 6 servings
CALORIES: 312
CARBOHYDRATES: 20g

FAT: 20g
PROTEIN: 3g

sour cream
prepared mustard

cornmeal or cracker crumbs
fish fillets

Mix equal parts of sour cream and mustard. Dip fillets in mixture and roll in cornmeal or crumbs before frying.

Lockie Sue Bissett

Fillets are also good cold when you use this batter.

Fried Fish Fillets

YIELD: 6 servings
CALORIES: 603
CARBOHYDRATES: 12g

FAT: 37g
PROTEIN: 57g

3   pounds fish fillets
2   teaspoons salt
¼   teaspoon black pepper

2   cups buttermilk
flour
1   teaspoon Accent (optional)

Dry fish with paper towels. Season on both sides. Dip into buttermilk and then into flour, coating on both sides evenly. Shake off excess. In skillet, place 1 inch of cooking oil and heat until very hot, then add the fish, a few pieces at a time. Fry for about 3 minutes on both sides or until light brown. Serve at once.

Lou Deaton

This recipe came from a restaurant in Oxaca, Mexico.

Ben's Shrimp Artichoke

YIELD: 4 main course servings
CALORIES: 436
CARBOHYDRATES: 10g

FAT: 29g
PROTEIN: 65g

2-6 ounce jars marinated
    artichoke hearts
1   pound fresh mushrooms,
    sliced
1   pound medium sized
    shrimp, shelled and
    deveined

1   cup chopped parsley
¼   cup fresh lemon juice
salt and pepper to taste

Drain artichokes marinade into skillet, reserving the hearts. Cook mushrooms in marinade until tender, about three minutes. Add the shrimp, ½ cup parsley, and the lemon juice. Cook, turning often, until shrimp are pink and firm, about two minutes. Stir in artichoke hearts, cook until heated through. Garnish with remaining ½ cup parsley. Serve with rice as main dish or at room temperature in lettuce cups as appetizers. Season with salt and pepper.

Lou Deaton

Shrimp Victoria

YIELD: 4 to 6 servings
CALORIES: 318
CARBOHYDRATES: 18g

FAT: 17g
PROTEIN: 24g

1 pound raw shrimp, peeled and deveined
1 small onion, finely chopped
¼ cup butter or margarine
1 6 ounce can mushrooms

¼ teaspoon salt
1 tablespoon flour
dash of cayenne pepper
1 cup sour cream
1½ cups rice, cooked

Saute the shrimp and onion in the butter or margarine for 10 minutes or until shrimp are tender. Add the mushrooms and cook for 5 minutes more. Sprinkle with flour, salt and cayenne pepper. Stir in the sour cream and cook gently for 10 minutes. Do not allow to boil. Serve over rice.

Lou Deaton

Shrimp and Okra Gumbo

YIELD: 8 servings
CALORIES: 278
CARBOHYDRATES: 11g

FAT: 9g
PROTEIN: 39g

2 pounds okra, sliced
2 medium onions, chopped
1 medium bell pepper, chopped
½ cup chopped celery
4 tablespoons cooking oil

1 can tomato sauce
1 cup water
2 pounds shrimp
salt and pepper
red pepper

Cook okra, onions, bell pepper and celery in oil. Smother for 45 minutes until okra is done. Add tomato sauce and water. Add shrimp and season to taste. Cook another 15 minutes. Serve over rice.

Kay Stewart

Shrimp Scampi

YIELD: 2 to 4 servings
CALORIES: 399
CARBOHYDRATES: 5g

FAT: 14g
PROTEIN: 32g

1   pound small shrimp
3   cloves garlic, mashed
½   cup butter, melted
½   cup dry white wine

juice of one lemon
¼   cup chopped fresh parsley
½   teaspoon oregano
rice

Peel and devein shrimp. Mix other ingredients except rice, pour over shrimp and marinate 30 minutes in refrigerator. Broil shrimp about 5 minutes on each side. Serve over rice.

Debbie Glasscock

Shrimp Creole

YIELD: 6 servings
CALORIES: 106
CARBOHYDRATES: 6g

FAT: 3g
PROTEIN: 15g

½   cup chopped onion
½   cup chopped celery
1   clove garlic, minced
2   teaspoons salad oil
16 ounce can tomatoes
1   8 ounce can tomato sauce
1½ teaspoons salt
1   teaspoon sugar

2   teaspoons chili powder
1   tablespoon Worcestershire
    sauce
dash Tabasco sauce
1   teaspoon cornstarch
12 ounces raw shrimp,
    cleaned
½   cup chopped bell peppers

Cook onion, celery and garlic in hot oil until tender. Do not brown. Add tomatoes, tomato sauce, seasonings, Worcestershire and Tabasco sauce. Simmer 45 minutes. Mix cornstarch with 2 teaspoons water, stir into sauce. Cook and stir until mixture thickens slightly. Add shrimp and bell pepper. Cover and simmer 5 minutes. Serve with rice.

Cathy Carson

Tuna Roll

YIELD: 4 to 6 servings
CALORIES: 345
CARBOHYDRATES: 19g

FAT: 24g
PROTEIN: 14g

1   cup flour
⅓   cup shortening
½   teaspoon salt
3 to 4 tablespoons water
½   cup onion
¼   cup margarine
1½ tablespoons flour
¼   cup milk

¼   teaspoon salt
¼   teaspoon pepper
6½ ounce can tuna, water
    packed
1   egg, beaten
¼   cup grated Parmesan
    cheese

Blend first 4 ingredients and roll out into a ½ inch thick rectangular shape. Saute onion in margarine. Add flour and stir. Blend in milk, salt and pepper. Cook until thickened. Add tuna and egg. Place filling on pastry and roll jelly-roll fashion. Brush with butter. Sprinkle with Parmesan cheese. Bake at 350 degrees for 30 minutes. Allow to sit at least 5 minutes before slicing.

Kay Stewart

Lobster Thermidor

YIELD: 4 servings
CALORIES: 300
CARBOHYDRATES: 11g

FAT: 20g
PROTEIN: 16g

2	tablespoons butter	⅛	teaspoon paprika
⅓	cup mushrooms, sliced	¼	cup chicken broth
2	tablespoons onion, chopped	½	cup Half and Half
		1	egg yolk, beaten
¼	teaspoon salt	2	tablespoons sherry
2	tablespoons flour	2	cups cooked lobster, chopped
⅛	teaspoon pepper		

In a 1½ quart casserole, place butter, mushrooms and onions. Microwave on high 3 minutes, stirring after 2 minutes. Stir in flour, salt, pepper and paprika until smooth. Microwave on high 1 minute. Slowly stir in broth and cream. Microwave on high 3 to 4 minutes, stirring after 2 minutes, until thickened. Stir a portion of the hot mixture into the egg yolk, then add egg to the rest of the hot mixture. Stir in the sherry. Microwave on low 3 to 4 minutes, stirring after 2 minutes. Stir in lobster. Fill 4 individual au gratin dishes or large scallop shells with mixture. Cover with crumb mixture. Cover with waxed paper. Microwave on high for approximately 6 minutes, rearranging dishes after 3 minutes. Adjust the time for individual microwave ovens. The higher the wattage, the less time needed for cooking.

CRUMB COATING

2	tablespoons butter	2	tablespoons Parmesan cheese
¼	cup fine dry bread crumbs		

Place butter in a small bowl. Microwave on high 30 seconds or until melted. Stir in bread crumbs and cheese.

Cathy Carson

A microwave is required for this recipe.

Steve's Crawfish Etouffe

YIELD: 8 servings
CALORIES: 228
CARBOHYDRATES: 9g

FAT: 8g
PROTEIN: 30g

4 tablespoons bacon drippings
2 tablespoons flour
½ white onion, chopped fine
4 green onions, chopped fine
½ teaspoon garlic powder
4 ribs celery, chopped fine
1 cup finely chopped bell pepper

2 pounds crawfish tail(meat)
3 sprigs parsley
2 boiled egg yolks
1 cup hot tap water
½ cup tomato sauce(optional)
cayenne pepper to taste

Place flour and drippings in a microwave dish and cook on high for 3 minutes. Stir, cook 2 minutes, stir and at 1 minute intervals, until chocolate colored. Transfer to skillet and add next 5 ingredients and cook until tender. Add water, tomato sauce, pepper and meat and cook 15 minutes. Mash egg yolks with chopped parsley in 2 tablespoons water and add to the first mixture. Cook 5 minutes more, then serve over rice.

Jodie Sessom

Langostinos or shrimp may be substituted for the crawfish meat.

Bob's Oyster Stew

YIELD: 6 servings
CALORIES: 332
CARBOHYDRATES: 10g

FAT: 28g
PROTEIN: 11g

1 pint or 2-10 ounce containers raw oysters with liquid
¼ cup butter
¾ teaspoon celery salt
¾ teaspoon salt
⅛ teaspoon white pepper

⅛ teaspoon paprika
⅛ teaspoon red pepper, optional
1 quart half and half
2 green onions with tops, finely chopped

Check oysters for bits of shell. Save liquid. Heat butter, celery salt, salt, pepper and onion in large skillet. Cook about 1 minute on medium heat. Add oysters and heat until edges of oysters curl slightly. Reduce heat to simmer. Heat half and half in top of double boiler. When hot, add oyster mixture, stir and heat 15 minutes longer. Top each serving with lump of butter and a dash of paprika.

Lockie Sue Bissett

Steve's Seafood Gumbo

YIELD: 10 Servings
CALORIES: 489
CARBOHYDRATES: 12g

FAT: 24g
PROTEIN: 52g

1   cup oil
3   cups okra, sliced thin
1   large white onion, chopped fine
½   cup flour
1   stalk celery, plus leaves, cut finely
1   bunch parsley, chopped
4   cups green onions, minced
1   bell pepper, minced
1½ teaspoons garlic powder
3   tablespoons salt
1   teaspoon black pepper
1   teaspoon red pepper

2   quarts boiling water
2   cans chicken broth
1   8 ounce can tomato sauce special
1   tablespoon Worcestershire Sauce
5   14 ounce packages of frozen cooked shrimp
3   3½ ounce cans fancy white lump crab meat
1   teaspoon liquid crab boil
gumbo file to taste
Tabasco sauce to taste

Place ½ cup oil in a big, heavy skillet and saute onion and okra until soft. While this is cooking, place the other half cup of oil and flour in a microwave proof dish and blend well. Place in microwave for three minutes on high and then stir. Cook two more minutes, stir, and then stir at one minute intervals until the roux is the desired color (chocolate). Add celery, parsley, green onions, bell pepper, garlic powder, salt and pepper to the onion and okra mixture. Continue to saute until soft. When roux is ready, add to the vegetables and mix well. Transfer to a large soup pot. Add boiling water and chicken broth to mixture. Add tomato sauce and Worcestershire sauce and let mixture heat up to a slow bubble. Add shrimp, liquid crab boil and simmer for 30 minutes. Add crab meat and simmer for one hour. Serve over rice and add file and Tabasco to taste if desired.

Jodie Sessom

Great to prepare ahead of time. Freezes well.

Eggplant Parmigiana

YIELD: 6 servings
CALORIES: 706
CARBOHYDRATES: 33g

FAT: 53g
PROTEIN: 28g

2 small eggplants,
approximately 2 pounds
salt
2 cups ricotta cheese
2 eggs
¼ cup Parmesan cheese,
grated

1 cup parsley, chopped
fresh ground pepper to taste
½ cup olive oil
2 cups Quick Tomato Sauce
(recipe included)
½ pound mozzarella cheese,
grated

Slice the eggplant into ½ inch thick pieces and layer in a colander, salting the slices heavily as you go. Set aside for 30 minutes. Combine the ricotta, eggs, Parmesan, and chopped parsley. Season to taste with salt and pepper. Rinse eggplant slices well, pat dry and heat 2 tablespoon olive oil in large skillet until it smokes. Add a single layer of eggplant slices and turn quickly to coat both sides. (Do not add more oil) Brown the slices and drain on paper towel. Pour 2 tablespoon more oil into skillet, cook another layer and repeat until all slices are browned. Spread ½ cup tomato sauce in the casserole. Add a layer of eggplant. Top each slice with ricotta mixture. Sprinkle with ⅓ of the mozzarella cheese. Repeat layers. Add a final layer of eggplant. Cover with the tomato sauce. Spoon remaining ricotta mixture down the center of the dish. Sprinkle with remaining mozzarella cheese over tomato sauce only. Place dish on the middle rack of preheated oven. Bake at 400 degrees for 25 to 30 minutes or until well browned. Let stand for 10 minutes before serving.

QUICK TOMATO SAUCE
½ cup olive oil
3 cups yellow onions, finely
chopped
2 medium size carrots,
peeled and chopped
2 28 ounce cans peeled plum
tomatoes in tomato puree
1 tablespoon dried basil
1 teaspoon dried thyme

1 teaspoon salt
⅛ teaspoon cayenne pepper
1 bay leaf
1 cup finely chopped parsley
4 garlic cloves, peeled and
chopped
1 tablespoon balsamic or
mild vinegar, optional

Heat oil and add onions and carrots. Cook until tender or for 25 minutes. Add the tomatoes and seasonings and cook for 30 minutes on medium heat, stirring occasionally. Remove the bay leaf and puree sauce in food processor. Return sauce to pan over

Continued on next page

medium heat and add parsley and garlic. Cook for another 5 minutes. Taste and correct seasonings. Add vinegar if the sauce lacks intensity. Serve immediately or cool to room temperature and cover. Refrigerate or freeze. Makes 2 quarts.

Sandy Baggett

Basic Egg Pasta

YIELD: 8 servings
CALORIES: 227
CARBOHYDRATES: 3g

FAT: 7g
PROTEIN: 7g

3   cups all purpose flour
1   teaspoon salt
4   large eggs (may need 5 depending on size.)

2   tablespoons oil (olive oil is best.)

With the metal blade in place on a food processor, measure flour and salt into the workbowl. Process briefly to blend. Drop the eggs and oil through the feed tube. Process until the dough "chases" itself around the workbowl. If is doesn't do this in about 15 seconds, add a little flour if it is too sticky or a little water or an egg if it is too dry. Process again. Turn out onto floured board and knead for 3 to 5 minutes until it is smooth and elastic. Leave it to rest under a dish towel for at least 15 minutes. It can wait hours if necessary.

To roll and cut: Cut the dough into the same number of pieces as eggs in dough. Repeat the following steps with each piece of dough. Flatten, sprinkle with flour and pass through widest space on smooth roller. Fold in thirds, sprinkle with flour and roll again through smooth roller and continue this for 6 to 8 times. This kneads the dough. Move the wheel to the next notch. Pass the flour dusted dough through rollers once. Do not fold. Move the wheel to next higher number, each time dusting with a little flour. Stop at desired thickness. To cut Taglierini, pass through the narrow teeth. To cut Tagliatelle, pass through the wide teeth. To cut spaghetti, use Taglierini teeth #5. To cook, place in boiling, salted water for about 15 seconds. It will float to the top. To freeze, dry for ten minutes and coil on paper plates and cover with foil.

Camille Jones

Red Beans and Rice

YIELD: 10 servings
CALORIES: 312
CARBOHYDRATES: 55g

FAT: 5g
PROTEIN: 15g

2 onions, chopped
4 green onions, chopped
2 cloves garlic, minced
3 tablespoons bacon grease
1 tablespoon butter
1 bell pepper, finely chopped
2 8 ounce cans tomato sauce

1 8 ounce can water
2 fresh tomatoes, chopped
4 cans #300 red kidney
   beans, drained and rinsed
1 teaspoon salt
½ teaspoon red pepper flakes
1 tablespoon chili powder

Saute all onions and garlic in the grease and butter until lightly browned. Add tomato sauce, water and bell pepper. Simmer for 30 minutes. Add beans and remaining ingredients and cook for 45 minutes. Serve with steamed white rice.

Cathy Carson

Can be prepared ahead of time and reheated. Great for working moms.

Fresh Tomato Sauce

YIELD: 6 servings
CALORIES: 143
CARBOHYDRATES: 15g

FAT: 9g
PROTEIN: 3g

3 pounds ripe tomatoes,
   chopped
1 meduim onion, chopped
2 teaspoons salt
1 carrot, chopped

1 rib of celery, chopped
½ pound mushrooms (1 box),
   thinly sliced
4 tablespoons butter
½ cup sliced black olives

Cook chopped tomatoes in large skillet until slightly soft, add onion and cook until transparent. Then add salt, carrot and celery and cook about 20 minutes. Saute mushrooms in 4 table-spoons butter until they loose their liquid. Add olives and mushrooms to sauce and cook 4 to 5 minutes. Pour over freshly cooked pasta. Sprinkle with cheese and freshly ground pepper.

Camille Jones

Great summer recipe, light and fresh for hot weather.

Fresh Tomato Pasta Sauce

YIELD: 10 servings
CALORIES: 137
CARBOHYDRATES: 24g

FAT: 4g
PROTEIN: 4g

15 to 20 very ripe fresh
   tomatoes, peeled and
   seeded.
1 to 2 large onions, chopped
3 or 4 cloves garlic, minced

3 tablespoons or more fresh
   basil, minced
4 tablespoons olive oil
½ cup fresh parsley, minced
salt and pepper, if desired

Put peeled and seeded tomatoes in processor or blender. Process until smooth. Put tomato sauce and rest of ingredients in large saucepan and simmer until thick. Put in pint freezer cartons and freeze. Heat and serve over pasta.

Mary Jo Mason

A great way to use a surplus of fresh, ripe tomatoes. The processor makes a chunkier sauce than the blender.

Pesto Sauce with Spaghetti

YIELD: 8 servings
CALORIES: 389
CARBOHYDRATES: 33g

FAT: 25g
PROTEIN: 9g

2 rounded tablespoons dried basil or 2 cups fresh basil
¾ cup grated Parmesan cheese
¾ cup oil (can use ½ olive oil and ½ vegetable oil)

2 tablespoons pinenuts or walnuts
4 cloves garlic
16 ounces spaghetti or other pasta

Place first 5 ingredients in blender or food processor. Cover and blend until smooth, stopping occasionally to scrape sides. Cook pasta according to directions on package. Drain, pour sauce over, toss well and serve immediately.

Lockie Sue Bissett

Pesto Sauce

YIELD: 2 cups
CALORIES: 78 per tablespoon
CARBOHYDRATES: .41g

FAT: 8g
PROTEIN: 1g

4 cups fresh basil leaves
3 cloves garlic
½ cup pignoli nuts or almonds

1 teaspoon salt
½ to 1 cup oil (olive oil is best)
½ cup Parmesan cheese

Place the basil, garlic, nuts and salt into a food processor or blender with ½ cup oil. Process, adding enough oil to make a smooth paste. Add the cheese and process a few seconds longer. If freezing, pour into egg carton and freeze. Pop out when frozen and transfer to a freezer bag. Use it to season soups as well as a quick topping for pasta.

Camille Jones

Lasagna

YIELD: 8 servings
CALORIES: 851
CARBOHYDRATES: 54g

FAT: 41g
PROTEIN: 65g

2 pounds ground meat
1 onion, chopped
1 bay leaf
½ to ¾ teaspoon oregano, to taste
2 cans tomato sauce, special
garlic salt, to taste

salt and pepper
lasagna noodles, at least 6
16 ounces ricotta cheese or cottage cheese
12 to 16 ounces mozzarella cheese

Brown meat, season with garlic salt, salt, pepper, bay leaf and oregano. Add onion and tomato sauce special. Simmer. While simmering, boil lasagna noodles. Drain, then layer in a large baking pan, the meat sauce, noodles and cheese. Repeat until all is gone, ending with the ricotta cheese. Cover and cook at 350 degrees for about 45 minutes. Remove the cover and brown a few minutes before serving. Can use more cheese if you like.

Jane Richardson

Old-Fashioned Lasagne

YIELD: 10 to 12 servings
CALORIES: 1494
CARBOHYDRATES: 44g

FAT: 111g
PROTEIN: 78g

2	16 ounce cans tomatoes	2	pounds ground chuck
4	8 ounce cans tomato sauce	2	teaspoons monosodium
2	tablespoons sugar		glutamate
2	teaspoons salt	6	ounce can tomato paste
1	tablespoon oregano	¾	cup water
¼	teaspoon pepper	1	pound lasagne noodles
2	teaspoons onion salt	2	egg whites, slightly beaten
4	ounce can mushrooms,	1½	pounds ricotta cheese
	drained	1½	pounds Parmesan cheese,
½	cup olive oil		grated
2	cups minced onion	1	pound mozzarella cheese,
3	cloves garlic, crushed		thinly sliced

Combine tomatoes, tomato sauce, 1 tablespoon sugar, salt, oregano, pepper, onion salt and mushrooms; simmer uncovered for 10 minutes. Pour the olive oil in a heavy skillet and saute onions, garlic and meat. Add monosodium glutamate, tomato paste and water. Combine the tomato mixture and meat mixture in a large heavy pan. Simmer 2 to 3 hours or until thick. Cook lasagna noodles in salted water, drain. Dry on wax paper to prevent sticking. Combine egg whites, 1 tablespoon sugar and ricotta cheese. In a large, deep, rectangular baking dish, layer noodles, ricotta cheese mixture, meat sauce, Parmesan cheese and mozzarella cheese. Repeat layers. Cover and bake 45 minutes at 350 degrees. Uncover and bake 15 minutes more. Let stand for 15 minutes before serving.

Sandy Baggett

May be prepared ahead and baked just before serving.

Lazy Lasagne

YIELD: 6 to 8 servings
CALORIES: 470
CARBOHYDRATES: 40g

FAT: 19g
PROTEIN: 33g

1 pound ground beef
14½ ounce can tomatoes, sliced
8 ounce can tomato sauce
1 envelope spaghetti sauce mix

2 cloves garlic, minced
8 ounces lasagne noodles
1 6 ounce package mozzarella cheese
1 cup cream style cottage cheese

Brown meat slowly and drain. Add tomatoes, tomato sauce, sauce mix and garlic. Cover and simmer 40 minutes, stirring occasionally. Salt to taste. Cook noodles until tender. Place half of the noodles in an oblong baking dish and cover with half of the sauce, half of the mozzarella cheese and cottage cheese. Repeat layers ending with the sauce. Top with thin slices of mozzarella cheese. Bake in a moderate oven, about 350 degrees for 30 minutes.

Carmen Sutton

This recipe freezes well.

Fettuccine Alfredo

YIELD: 6 servings
CALORIES: 314
CARBOHYDRATES: 1g

FAT: 32g
PROTEIN: 11g

¾ cup unsalted butter
½ pint whipping cream
1½ cups freshly grated Parmesan cheese

white pepper
nutmeg, freshly grated
fettuccine

Put a pot of salted water on to boil and place oven-proof platter in oven set on low. Place large skillet with the butter in it on very low heat. Do not allow butter to boil. When water boils add freshly made pasta, cook 15 seconds, if frozen it will take about 8 minutes. Add the cooked, drained pasta to the butter in the skillet and toss gently with 2 forks. Add the cream and Parmesan cheese, toss until sauce is creamy and the cheese is melted. Pour onto the heated platter, add white pepper and nutmeg. Serve immediately. For family dinners I put the skillet on the table, as it stays hot longer.

Camille Jones

Fettuccine Carbonara

YIELD: 4 servings
CALORIES: 443
CARBOHYDRATES: 48g

FAT: 22g
PROTEIN: 17g

1 cup bacon, crumbled
½ cup onion
½ cup bellpepper
3 ounces cream cheese
1½ cups milk

1 teaspoon basil
½ teaspoon oregano
salt and pepper to taste
fettuccine
2 eggs, slightly boiled

Fry bacon, drain and crumble. Saute onion and pepper in three tablespoons of bacon grease. Add other ingredients and cook over low heat until cheese melts. Adjust seasonings. Cook one package of fettucine until done. Drain in colander. Slightly boil 2 eggs and toss with fettucine. Put back in pan fettucine was cooked in and add first mixture and bacon, toss together. Ready to serve.

Paula Bailey

Looks pretty on a plate or in a bowl. Served with salad and bread, it makes a wonderful meal.

Basil Tagliatelle

YIELD: 4 servings
CALORIES: 899
CARBOHYDRATES: 82g

FAT: 42g
PROTEIN: 46g

½ pound fresh pasta, or dried lasagne noodles
½ cup pesto sauce
1 cup ricotta cheese or cottage cheese

1 egg
½ cup grated parmesan cheese
½ pound mozzarella cheese, grated

Using the metal blade, process the pesto sauce, ricotta cheese, egg and parmesan cheese. Cook pasta al dente(firm to the teeth). Fresh pasta, 20 seconds; fresh frozen, 8 minutes; dried pasta, 10 minutes. Drain pasta and make a layer of it in a buttered casserole dish. Cover with the ricotta, pesto mixture and then with a second layer of pasta. Spread the mozzarella on top and sprinkle with more parmesan. Bake at 350 degrees for 25 minutes.

Camille Jones

Chicken Spaghetti

YIELD: 8 to 10 servings
CALORIES: 160
CARBOHYDRATES: 4g

FAT: 9g
PROTEIN: 15g

1   quart or more chicken
    broth
12 ounce package spaghetti
2   cups cooked chicken,
    chopped
14 ounce can tomatoes

10 ounce can Rotel tomatoes
4   ounce jar diced pimientos
salt
2   cups grated Old English
    cheese

Cook spaghetti in broth until tender. Add all ingredients, except cheese. Simmer until thick. Place in serving bowl and sprinkle with grated cheese. You can add cheese while cooking or wait until served.

Lisa Wagoner

This recipe freezes well and reheats in the microwave.

Italian Meat Sauce and Spaghetti

YIELD: 6 to 8 servings
CALORIES: 483
CARBOHYDRATES: 44g

FAT: 26g
PROTEIN: 18g

1   pound ground chuck
4   tablespoons Schilling
    Italian spices
15 ounce can tomato sauce
15 ounce can water

2   6 ounce cans tomato paste
2   6 ounce cans water
garlic powder to taste
½   pound thin spaghetti,
    cooked

Brown ground chuck. Drain excess fat. Add remaining ingredients except noodles. Bring sauce to a boil, cover and simmer for 2 hours. On heated platter mix 1 cup sauce with spaghetti. Then pour rest of sauce over spaghetti. Can be served on individual plates.

Cathy Carson

This recipe freezes well and can be doubled for a crowd.

Marge McMullan's 'Johnny Knows It'

YIELD: 8 servings
CALORIES: 1010
CARBOHYDRATES: 40g

FAT: 73g
PROTEIN: 46g

2 pounds lean ground beef	1 10 ounce package noodles
1 large onion	1 10 ounce can tomato juice
1 clove garlic	1 can cream of tomato soup
1 large bell pepper	1 can mushroom soup
1 stalk celery	1 small can mushrooms,
1 10-12 ounce jar salad olives	drained
1 pound cheddar cheese, grated	

Brown meat and drain. Cook noodles and drain. Dice ingredients 2 through 6. Grate cheese. Mix all ingredients together except cheese. Place in 9×13 inch casserole. Top with cheese and brown in 350 degrees oven for 15 to 20 minutes. This dish freezes well. Do not add cheese until dish is thawed and ready to be baked.

Jean Read

Miss Marge said the name originated from people asking what was in it and the cook saying, 'Only Johnny knows it'.

'Tater Top Casserole

YIELD: 6 servings
CALORIES: 536
CARBOHYDRATES: 40g

FAT: 27g
PROTEIN: 33g

1 pound ground beef	6 potatoes
1 medium onion, chopped	milk
1 16 ounce can green beans, drained	2 tablespoons butter
1 8 ounce can tomato sauce	8 ounces Colby cheese, grated

Boil potatoes, drain, add milk and butter and mash to desired consistency. Season to taste and set aside. Brown meat and onions, season to taste. Using a 1½ quart casserole, layer meat, green beans and tomato sauce. Top with mashed potatoes and sprinkle with cheese. Bake at 400 degrees for 1 hour or microwave until cheese melts and it is heated thoroughly.

Lisa Wagoner

Spaghetti Casserole

YIELD: 12 servings
CALORIES: 509
CARBOHYDRATES: 10g

FAT: 41g
PROTEIN: 24g

2   pounds hamburger meat
½   cup chopped bell pepper
½   cup chopped onion
garlic salt and pepper to taste

15½ ounce jar spaghetti sauce
12 ounce package spaghetti
6-8 slices Velveeta cheese
longhorn cheese, grated

Brown meat and add bell pepper, onion, garlic salt and pepper. cook until done and add jar of sauce. Meanwhile, cook the spaghetti and mix with meat mixture. Pour ½ of the mixture in a Pyrex dish. Layer the 6-8 slices of Velveeta on top. Pour on the remaining mixture and top with the longhorn cheese. Place in a microwave or conventional oven (about 350 degrees) until cheese melts.

Patti May

This recipe freezes well.

Steak and Onion Casserole

YIELD: 4-6
CALORIES: 461
CARBOHYDRATES: 18g

FAT: 18g
PROTEIN: 51g

2   pounds of sliced round
     steak
salt
pepper

flour
3   tablespoons cooking oil
3   large onions, sliced
½   cup dry red wine

Season sliced steak with salt and pepper, cover with flour. Heat oil in a skillet and brown onions slightly. Push onions aside. Place the steak in the skillet and brown well on both sides. Transfer to shallow casserole with onions. Pour wine in skillet and scrape up glaze, pour over the steak. Cover tightly. Bake at 300 degrees for about 2 hours or until steak is very tender. Add more liquid if necessary.

Mary Jo Mason

Heavenly Hash

YIELD: 8 servings
CALORIES: 540
CARBOHYDRATES: 49g

FAT: 25g
PROTEIN: 28g

1	pound ground beef	1	cup small curd cottage cheese
½	cup chopped onion		
1	16 ounce can tomato sauce	1	8 ounce package cream cheese
1	teaspoon sugar		
¾	teaspoon salt	⅓	cup sliced green onions
¼	teaspoon pepper	¼	cup sour cream
¼	teaspoon garlic salt	¼	cup chopped green pepper
4	cups uncooked medium noodles	¼	cup grated Parmesan cheese

Brown meat and onion, stir in tomato sauce and seasonings. Remove from heat. Cook noodles according to directions and drain. Combine cottage cheese, cream cheese, sour cream, onion, green peppers. Spread half of cooked noodles in bottom of 11×7 inch baking dish. Top with half of meat sauce mixture. Follow with all of the cheese mixture. Add remaining noodles, then meat sauce, sprinkle with Parmesan cheese if desired. Bake at 350 degrees for 30 minutes.

Marilyn Chalmers

Hamburger Casserole

YIELD: 10 to 12 servings
CALORIES: 508
CARBOHYDRATES: 25g

FAT: 31g
PROTEIN: 31g

2	pounds ground beef	1	8 ounce can sliced mushrooms
1	onion, chopped		
1	15 ounce can tomatoes	1	cup chopped celery
1	15 ounce can tomato sauce	1	8 ounce package egg noodles, cooked according to package directions
1	8 ounce jar chopped green olives		
1	8 ounce can sliced water chestnuts	1	pound Velveeta cheese, grated
½	10 ounce can black olives, chopped	1	tablespoon soy sauce

In a medium skillet, brown meat, saute onion until limp and set aside. Mix together in a large bowl, the tomatoes, tomato sauce, water chestnuts, green olives, black olives, celery, mushrooms, noodles and soy sauce. Combine with meat. Place in casserole. Bake at 350 degrees in oven about 30 minutes or until bubbly.

Teri Jackson

Make in 2 pans and freeze one for later use.

Pork Chop Casserole

YIELD: 4 servings
CALORIES: 613
CARBOHYDRATES: 29g

FAT: 31g
PROTEIN: 56g

4 medium pork chops, center cut
2 large potatoes, peeled and sliced
5 carrots, peeled and sliced

1 onion, thinly sliced
1 can cream of mushroom soup
salt and pepper to taste

Brown pork chops in frying pan. Layer vegetables in a greased casserole dish. Season to taste and lay pork chops on top. Add soup to drippings in frying pan with ½ cup water. Stir to make gravy. Pour over meat. Cover and bake in a 350 degree oven for 1 hour.

Cathy Carson

A meal in one dish.

Ham n Broccoli Bake

YIELD: 6 to 8 servings
CALORIES: 562
CARBOHYDRATES: 43g

FAT: 34g
PROTEIN: 23g

2 11 ounce packages Green Giant Frozen Rice Original Rice Pilaf
2 11 ounce packages Green Giant Cut Broccoli in Cheese Sauce
1½ cups cubed cooked ham
½ cup shredded cheddar cheese

10¾ ounce can cream of mushroom soup
½ cup dairy sour cream
2 teaspoons lemon juice
¾ of 1½ ounces canned french fried onions

Heat oven to 350 degrees. Prepare rice according to directions. Defrost broccoli. Layer rice, broccoli, ham and cheese in a 7 × 11 inch pan. Combine soup, sour cream and lemon juice, spoon over ingredients in pan. Bake at 350 degrees for 30 minutes. Sprinkle onions over top. Bake an additional 5 minutes.

Nancy Vannoy

Smothered Chicken

YIELD: 6 servings
CALORIES: 163
CARBOHYDRATES: 5g

FAT: 9g
PROTEIN: 17g

1 chicken, cut in serving pieces
2 eggs, hard boiled

2 cans cream of mushroom soup

Brown chicken in frying pan and season to taste. Place in baking dish. Pour cream of mushroom soup and eggs over chicken. Bake at 350 degrees until bubbly, about 30 minutes.

Tammy Bunger

Pork chops are also good prepared like this.

Donna's Chicken Divan

YIELD: 4 to 6 servings
CALORIES: 660
CARBOHYDRATES: 5g

FAT: 55g
PROTEIN: 36g

3 broccoli stalks
1 chicken, cooked and diced
1 cup mayonnaise
2 cans cream of mushroom soup

½ teaspoon curry powder
1 cup shredded Swiss cheese

Cook broccoli in microwave on high for 8 minutes. Arrange stalks in greased 9×13 inch baking dish. Place chicken over broccoli. Combine mayonnaise, soup and curry powder and pour over chicken. Sprinkle with cheese. Bake at 350 degrees for 30 minutes.

Barbara Malone

Great for Sunday lunch.

Chicken in Wine Sauce

YIELD: 6 servings
CALORIES: 403
CARBOHYDRATES: 9g

FAT: 22g
PROTEIN: 23g

6 large chicken breasts, boned
salt and pepper to taste
½ cup butter or margarine

2 cans cream of chicken soup
1¼ cups Sauterne (white wine)
1 5 ounce can of sliced water chestnuts

Season chicken with salt and pepper. Brown the chicken in the butter in a skillet. Once browned, arrange chicken pieces in a Pyrex baking dish. Add remaining ingredients to drippings from browning the chicken and cook these ingredients until bubbly and slightly thickened. Pour over chicken, cover with foil and bake at 350 degrees for 25 minutes. Uncover and continue baking for 25 to 30 minutes longer. Serve over white or wild rice.

Ann Childress

Wine may be added just before pouring sauce over chicken.

Chicken Rice Casserole

YIELD: 6 to 8 servings
CALORIES: 179
CARBOHYDRATES: 22g

FAT: 4g
PROTEIN: 13g

1 chicken, cut in serving pieces
¼ cup chopped celery
¼ cup chopped onion
1 cup regular rice

1 can cream of mushroom soup
1 can chicken with rice soup
salt and pepper

Mix rice, onion, celery, and soups in a 9×13 baking dish. Salt and pepper the chicken pieces. Lay chicken pieces on top of the rice mixture. Bake at 350 degrees for 45 minutes to 1 hour or until chicken is done.

Sherry Scott

This recipe was a wedding gift 20 years ago and is still a family favorite!

Chicken with Wine Sauce

YIELD: 6 to 8 servings
CALORIES: 209
CARBOHYDRATES: 3g

FAT: 9g
PROTEIN: 26g

1 chicken, cut up or 6 to 8
   chicken breasts or pieces of
   your choice
½ cup chopped onion
⅛ cup margarine
garlic salt or minced garlic
salt

pepper
tarragon
1 can cream of mushroom
   soup
½ cup white wine or cooking
   wine

Place chicken in a baking dish. Sprinkle with garlic, salt, pepper and tarragon. Place chopped onion and margarine on chicken. Cover with foil and bake at 350 degrees for one hour. One half hour before you are ready to serve, mix the wine and soup together and pour over the chicken. Bake uncovered at 375 degrees for 30 minutes. Good to serve with rice. The soup and wine may be heated separately and used as a gravy over the chicken and rice.

Sandra Childress

May want to use skinned and boned chicken pieces.

Sour Cream Chicken

YIELD: 6 to 8 servings
CALORIES: 1171
CARBOHYDRATES: 12g

FAT: 8g
PROTEIN: 13g

4 whole boned chicken
   breasts, greased with
   butter
1 cup sour cream
1 teaspoon Worcestershire
   sauce

1 teaspoon celery salt
2 tablespoons lemon juice
1 teaspoon salt

Marinate chicken for several hours in sauce made from the above ingredients. Top with butter and bread crumbs. Cover and bake at 350 degrees for one hour. Remove covering and bake for 10 more minutes.

Cynthia Berry

Easy and elegant.

Easy Chicken Casserole

YIELD: 4 to 6 servings
CALORIES: 288
CARBOHYDRATES: 34g

FAT: 8g
PROTEIN: 19g

1   cup uncooked rice
1   can mushroom soup
1   package dry onion soup
    mix

1½ soup cans of milk
1   fryer, cut up
    salt
    pepper

Mix rice, soup and milk. Pour into 9 × 13 inch greased casserole. Place chicken on top, skin side down. Season with salt and pepper. Cover and bake at 250 degrees for 3 hours. Turn chicken once during cooking time.

Carol Hunnicutt

Chicken Tetrazzini

YIELD: 8 servings
CALORIES: 322
CARBOHYDRATES: 22g

FAT: 15g
PROTEIN: 24g

½   cup mushrooms, sliced and drained
½   cup thinly sliced onions
¼   cup margarine
¼   cup flour
2   cups chicken broth
1   cup light cream or half and half
1   teaspoon salt

¼   teaspoon pepper
1   teaspoon poultry seasoning
1   8 ounce package spaghetti, cooked and drained
3   cups chicken, cooked and diced
½   cup cheddar or mozzarella cheese, shredded

Lightly brown mushrooms and onions in margarine. Stir in the flour and cook until bubbly. Stir in the broth and cream. Add salt, pepper and poultry seasoning. Cook, stirring often until mixture begins to boil and thickens. Place a layer of cooked spaghetti in a buttered 2 quart casserole dish, cover with a layer of diced chicken and a layer of sauce. Repeat layers finishing with a layer of spaghetti and top with grated cheese. Bake at 400 degrees for 20 minutes or until bubbly.

Ann Childress

Black olives add color to this dish as does a garnish of fresh parsley.

Turkey or Chicken Tetrazzini

YIELD: 6 servings
CALORIES: 405
CARBOHYDRATES: 40g

FAT: 12g
PROTEIN: 33g

12 ounces spaghetti
5 quarts boiling water
¾ cup fat-free white sauce mix
3 cups chicken broth
1½ cups fresh mushrooms, sliced

1 tablespoon Worcestershire sauce or low-salt soy sauce
3 cups chicken or turkey, cooked and diced
3 tablespoons grated parmesan

Gradually add spaghetti to rapidly boiling water so that the water continues to boil. Cook uncovered, stirring occasionally for 8 to 10 minutes. Drain in a colander and rinse with cold water to prevent sticking. While pasta is cooking, combine the white-sauce mix with the broth in a sauce pan. Add the mushrooms and Worcestershire or soy sauce. Cover and cook for 3 minutes. Add the sliced turkey and cooked spaghetti. Pour mixture into a greased 9×13 inch casserole dish. Top with grated cheese and bake in a 350 degree oven for 25 minutes.

Fat Free White Sauce Mix

YIELD: 3 cups mix makes 12 cups sauce
CALORIES: 50 calories per ½ cup reconstituted sauce

2 cups nonfat dry powdered milk
¾ cup cornstarch
¼ cup chicken bouillon powder

4 teaspoons onion powder
1 teaspoon dried thyme
1 teaspoon dried basil
½ teaspoon freshly ground white pepper

Stir all ingredients together or process until well mixed. Store at room temperature in a tightly covered jar. Reconstitute as follows.

1 cup milk or water
¼ cup mix

1 tablespoon butter

Add mix to liquid and stir until well mixed. Add butter, heat and stir until thickened.

Continued on next page

Low Calorie Cheese Sauce

YIELD: 2 servings
CALORIES: 155 calories per ½ cup serving

¼ cup fat-free white sauce
    mix
1 cup water
¼ teaspoon dry mustard

¼ teaspoon paprika
2 ounces sharp cheddar
    cheese, grated

Heat mix and water, stirring until blended. Add seasonings and grated cheese. Stir until cheese is melted.

Camille Jones

This is a great way to begin a diet!

Chicken and Dressing Casserole

YIELD: 8 servings
CALORIES: 650
CARBOHYDRATES: 31g

FAT: 43g
PROTEIN: 33g

1 package Pepperidge Farm
    Cornbread Stuffing Mix, (8
    ounces)
½ cup margarine, melted
1 cup water
2½ cups diced cooked chicken,
    4 whole chicken breasts
¾ cup diced onion
½ cup diced celery

¾ teaspoon salt
½ cup mayonnaise (no
    subsitute)
2 eggs
1½ cups milk
1 can cream of mushroom
    soup
8 ounces grated cheddar
    cheese (2 cups)

Mix melted margarine and water with dressing mix and toss lightly to mix well. Place half of dressing in bottom of greased 8×12×2 inch dish. Mix together chicken, onion, celery, salt, and mayonnaise. Spread this mixture over bottom layer of dressing. Put other half of dressing over top. Beat eggs and milk together and pour over top of casserole. Cover and refrigerate overnight or for several hours. Remove one hour before baking and spread soup over top. Bake uncovered at 325 degrees for 40 minutes. Remove and sprinkle grated cheese on top.

Nancy Vannoy

Submitted by Whitney Vannoy, 10 year old daughter of Nancy Vannoy. This was a first place prize in county and district food shows in December, 1985.

Sour Cream Chicken Casserole

YIELD: 6 to 8 servings
CALORIES: 318
CARBOHYDRATES: 8g

FAT: 21g
PROTEIN: 24g

4 cups cubed, cooked chicken
8 ounces sour cream
1 can cream of chicken soup

6 tablespoons melted margarine
1 roll Ritz crackers, crumbled

Mix the soup and sour cream. Place a layer of chicken in the bottom of a 2½ quart casserole dish. Place soup mixture on top of chicken. Make another layer of chicken. Top with cracker crumbs and melted butter. Bake at 350 degrees for 30 to 45 minutes, uncovered.

Ann Childress

Try this with left over turkey, too.

Chicken Macaroni

YIELD: 10-12 servings
CALORIES: 289
CARBOHYDRATES: 20g

FAT: 15g
PROTEIN: 19g

1 fryer
1 package macaroni
1 can chicken broth
1 can tomato soup
1 can cream of mushroom soup

1 medium onion, diced
1 teaspoon garlic salt
1 pound American cheese, grated

Boil fryer until tender. Bone the chicken and reserve the stock. Add broth to the stock and cook the macaroni, onion and garlic salt. Add the chopped chicken, tomato soup, cream of mushroom soup and cheese. Pour into 13×9×2 inch pan or two 8×8×2 pans and bake at 325 degrees until cheese bubbles, approximately 30 minutes.

Janie Chandler

Tuna Casserole

YIELD: 4 servings
CALORIES: 352
CARBOHYDRATES: 24g

FAT: 21g
PROTEIN: 19g

1   can cream of mushroom
    soup
¼   cup water
1   3 ounce can chow mein
    noodles

dash of pepper
1   can tuna, drained
1   cup chopped celery
¼   cup chopped onion
½   cup cashew nuts

Combine water and soup. Add 1 cup of noodles. Toss with other ingredients. Place in ungreased baking dish. Sprinkle with remaining noodles. Bake at 350 degrees for 15 minutes or until thoroughly heated. Garnish with drained, canned mandarin orange sections.

Jo Nel Stokes

Tuna Casserole

YIELD: 5
CALORIES: 350
CARBOHYDRATES: 22g

FAT: 17g
PROTEIN: 27g

½   6 ounce package elbow
    macaroni
1   teaspoon salt
1   9¼ ounce can tuna
2   eggs, hard boiled
½   cup grated American
    cheese

2   tablespoons margarine
2   tablespoons flour
1½ cups milk
½   teaspoon salt

Bring 1½ quarts of water and 1 teaspoon salt to boil. Add ½ package macaroni and boil, stirring occasionally, for 8 minutes or until tender. Drain and set aside. Boil 2 eggs for 15 minutes. Shell and slice and set aside. Grate ½ cup cheese. Make a white sauce by melting margarine in a pan. Add 2 tablespoons flour and stir. Stir in ½ teaspoon salt and 1½ cups milk. Cook slowly until smooth and thick. Set aside. Alternate ingredients in a casserole dish by placing a layer of macaroni, tuna, egg and white sauce. Make two layers of each. Top with grated cheese and cook at 400 degrees for 20 minutes.

Jeannine Henderson

Good when you're in a hurry!

Tuna Macaroni Casserole

YIELD: 6
CALORIES: 445
CARBOHYDRATES: 32g

FAT: 27g
PROTEIN: 19g

6 ounces elbow macaroni	1 teaspoon salt
1 6 ounce can tuna, drained	1 can cream of mushroom soup
½ cup mayonnaise	½ cup milk
1 cup celery, diced	1 cup sharp cheese, shredded
⅓ cup onion, chopped	
3 tablespoons butter	
¼ cup green bell pepper, diced	

Saute vegetables in butter. Cook macaroni according to package directions and drain. Combine macaroni, tuna, mayonnaise, vegetables and salt. Blend together soup and milk in a saucepan, add cheese and heat until cheese melts, stirring constantly. Add to tuna mixture, fold together. Pour into 1½ quart casserole. Bake at 425 degrees for 20 minutes.

Ann Childress

Katy's 5 Can Casserole

YIELD: 6 servings
CALORIES: 280
CARBOHYDRATES: 17g

FAT: 17g
PROTEIN: 14g

1 small can turkey, chicken or tuna	1 can cream of mushroom soup
1 small can evaporated milk	1 5 ounce can Chinese noodles
1 can cream of chicken soup	½ cup chopped almonds or water chestnuts

Mix all together. Bake in buttered 1 quart casserole at 350 degrees for 25 minutes.

Shelly Conner

Stuffed Jalapeno Cornbread

YIELD: 6 to 8
CALORIES: 587
CARBOHYDRATES: 47g

FAT: 33g
PROTEIN: 27g

1 pound ground beef
1 onion, chopped
1 cup grated cheese
1 7½ ounce can hot jalapeno relish
1 4 ounce can chopped green chilies

1 cup yellow corn meal
1 cup buttermilk
2 eggs
1 tablespoon salt
¾ teaspoon soda
½ cup bacon drippings
1 cup cream style corn

Brown gound beef and onion and drain excess grease. Add cheese, jalapeno relish, and green chilies. Set aside. Combine corn meal, buttermilk, eggs, salt, soda, bacon drippings, and corn. Pour one-half of mixture into greased baking dish. Cover with meat mixture. Top with remaining cornbread mixture. Bake for 50 minutes at 400 degrees.

Teri Jackson

Green Enchiladas

YIELD: 6
CALORIES: 734
CARBOHYDRATES: 23g

FAT: 49g
PROTEIN: 48g

1 can cream of chicken soup
1 can evaporated milk
1 can chopped green chilies

1 pound Velveeta cheese, grated
1 pound ground beef
1 dozen corn tortillas

Blend first four ingredients together and set aside. Brown ground beef and spoon into tortillas, roll up and place in casserole dish. Pour sauce over enchiladas and bake at 350 degrees for 15 minutes or until tortillas are soft and heated through.

Teri Jackson

For chicken enchiladas: substitute chicken and flour tortillas. Follow same instructions.

Chicken Enchiladas

YIELD: 12 to 15 servings
CALORIES: 287
CARBOHYDRATES: 16g

FAT: 18g
PROTEIN: 14g

RED CHILI SAUCE

2 tablespoons bacon drippings	2 tablespoons flour
3 to 4 tablespoons chili powder	¾ teaspoon salt
	½ teaspoon garlic salt
	dash ground cumin

Heat drippings in skillet, add remaining ingredients and stir until blended. Gradually stir in 2 cups water. Bring to a boil, stirring constantly. Reduce heat and simmer for 10 minutes.

FILLING

2 tablespoons salad oil	dash of pepper
1 4 ounce can green chilies	4 ounces sour cream
1 clove garlic, crushed	½ pound cheddar cheese, grated
1 pound can tomato puree	tortillas
12 cups chopped chicken	1 can chopped olives
½ teaspoon salt	

Saute onions in oil in large skillet. Add remaining ingredients except cheese, tortillas, sour cream and olives. Simmer uncovered for 10 minutes. Preheat oven to 350 degrees. Spread about 1-2 tablespoons chili sauce on each softened tortilla, top with filling and 1 tablespoon sour cream, roll up, place on shallow, greased baking dish. Pour red sauce over tortillas, sprinkle with cheese and olives. Bake uncovered for 15 minutes.

Sharon Forehand

If you like more cheese you can add some when you put the filling in tortillas.

Janet and Gana's Enchilada Suise

YIELD: 6 servings
CALORIES: 350
CARBOHYDRATES: 19g

FAT: 22g
PROTEIN: 19g

ENCHILADAS
½ cup chopped onion
1 clove garlic, minced
¼ cup oil
¼ cup chopped green chilies
2 cups diced cooked chicken
1 can green chile salsa
2 tablespoons chopped
   parsley

2 teaspoons flour
2 chicken boullion cubes,
   crumbled
dash of paprika
1 cup milk
½ cup whipping cream
1½ cups shredded Jack cheese
corn tortillas

SALSA
⅔ cup chopped tomato
½ cup sliced green onion

⅓ cup diced green chiles

Saute onion and garlic in one tablespoon of the oil until onion is tender. Combine onion mixture, green chilies, chicken, chile salsa, and parsley. Set aside. Make sauce by combining flour, boullion and paprika. Stir in milk and cook, stirring constantly until mixture just begins to boil. It should be the consistency of thin white sauce. Remove from heat and stir in ½ cup of the cheese. Dip tortilla in remaining heated oil, then dip in cream sauce. Place 2 tablespoons of the chicken mixture in center of each tortilla and roll. Place seam down in casserole. Pour remaining sauce over all enchiladas after rolling. Sprinkle with remaining 1 cup of cheese. Cover with foil and bake at 350 degrees for 15 minutes. Uncover and bake 15 minutes longer. Combine salsa ingredients and spoon down center of casserole.

Cathy Carson

This recipe is from 2 friends in Midland. I have served it at many dinner parties and the men have always loved it.

Chicken Taco Casserole

YIELD: 8 servings
CALORIES: 448
CARBOHYDRATES: 22g

FAT: 28g
PROTEIN: 25g

12 corn tortillas or 1 medium package corn chips
1 12 ounce can evaporated milk
1 can cream of mushroom soup
1 can cream of chicken soup

1 6 ounce can boned chicken
1 4 ounce can chopped green chilies
1 small onion, chopped
1 pound longhorn or cheddar cheese, grated

Lay torn tortillas or broken corn chips in the bottom of a large flat baking dish. Heat rest of ingredients (except cheese) in a sauce pan until bubbly. Pour over tortillas. Top with grated cheese. Bake at 350 degrees for 15-20 minutes. Serve with tossed salad and dessert for an easy meal.

Sherry Scott

Freezes well.

King Ranch Chicken

YIELD: 6 to 8 servings
CALORIES: 557
CARBOHYDRATES: 20g

FAT: 33g
PROTEIN: 41g

1 2 to 3 pound fryer, cooked and diced (reserve broth)
1 dozen tortillas
1 can cream of mushroom soup
1 can cream of chicken soup
1 cup diced onions
1 cup diced green bell pepper

1 tablespoon chili powder
¾ pound grated cheddar cheese
1 can Rotel tomatoes and green chilies or 1 can tomato soup
1 tablespoon chili powder

Line large dish with layer of tortillas and sprinkle with chicken broth. Saute onions, green pepper, and chili powder. Add soups. Pour layer of soup mixture over tortillas, then layer of chicken, then layer of cheese. Repeat layers. Pour over all the Rotel tomatoes or the tomato soup with chili powder. Bake 1 hour in 350 degree oven.

Brenda Comer

Make ahead of time and cook an hour before serving time.

Lasagna Ole

YIELD: 9 to 10 servings
CALORIES: 392
CARBOHYDRATES: 26g

FAT: 24g
PROTEIN: 17g

¾ cup Monterey Jack cheese, grated
1⅔ cups Parmesan cheese, grated
2   pounds hamburger
1   onion, chopped
1   10 ounce can tomatoes

1   8 ounce can tomato sauce
1   10 ounce can Rotel tomatoes
2   cups sour cream
1   package taco seasoning
flour tortillas

Saute onions and meat. Drain and add taco seasoning, tomatoes and tomato sauce. Layer tortillas, meat, sour cream and cheeses twice in a 9 × 13 × 2 inch baking dish. Bake at 325 degrees for 45 minutes.

Patti May

You may want to freeze ½ of this recipe.

White Enchiladas

YIELD: 6 to 8 servings
CALORIES: 475
CARBOHYDRATES: 24g

FAT: 29g
PROTEIN: 29g

1   pound ground meat
1   onion, chopped
1   8 ounce package American cheese
2   cans cream of mushroom soup

1   5⅓ ounce can evaporated milk
1   4 ounce can green chilies, chopped
12 corn tortillas

Brown the meat and onions and season to taste. Add just enough cheese to hold the meat together. In a sauce pan, combine the soup, remaining cheese, milk and green chilies. Heat until cheese is melted. Soften corn tortillas by dipping in hot oil or in conventional oven or microwave. Spoon meat mixture into tortillas and roll. Place seam side down in a baking dish. Pour heated sauce over all. Bake at 350 degrees for 30 minutes.

Karen Childress

Enchilada Casserole

YIELD: 8 to 10 servings
CALORIES: 598
CARBOHYDRATES: 19g

FAT: 36g
PROTEIN: 42g

2 pounds ground beef
1 onion, chopped
salt and pepper to taste
2 to 3 jalapeno peppers,
   chopped (optional)
1 to 6 ounce can enchilada
   sauce

1 6 ounce can taco sauce
1 can cream of chicken soup
1 can cream of mushroom
   soup
10 to 12 corn tortillas
1 pound longhorn cheese,
   grated

Brown ground beef, onion, salt and pepper together. Blend in pepper sauces and soups. Dip tortillas in hot oil and line bottom of casserole with half of them. Add meat mixture and cover with cheese. Repeat layers. At this point, refrigerate until the next day or freeze for later use. Bring to room temperature and bake in a 325 degree oven for 20 to 30 minutes or until center is bubbly.   **Lorelei McMullan**

VARIATION: *Omit jalapenos and add one 4 ounce can chopped green chiles and 1 small can evaporated milk, also omit enchilada sauce and use 1 small can taco sauce. Quarter the corn tortillas and do not dip in hot oil. Continue as above.*   **Jill Seahorn**

VARIATION: *Add ground comino with other seasonings. Omit jalapenos, taco sauce, enchilada sauce and add a 4 ounce can chopped green chiles and a small can evaporated milk. Continue as above with tortillas quartered and not dipped in hot oil.*
                                             Sandra Childress

VARIATION: *Substitute ½ cup sliced green onions for 1 chopped onion. Omit jalapeno, taco sauce, enchilada sauce and substitute a 4 ounce can green chiles, an 8 ounce can chile salsa, a 2¼ ounce can sliced ripe olives drained, and ¾ teaspoon ground cumin. Cut the corn tortillas into ½ inch strips. Use 2 cups shredded Monterey Jack cheese and 2 cups of cheddar cheese. Continue as above.*   **Sharon Forehand**

VARIATION: *Use 1 pound ground turkey instead of beef. Omit jalapeno, taco sauce and enchilada sauce. Use tostados or doritos instead of tortillas dipped in oil. Use sliced Velveeta cheese. Continue layers as above.*
                                              Shelley Conner

Mexican Spaghetti

YIELD: 5 to 6 servings
CALORIES: 406
CARBOHYDRATES: 30g

FAT: 19g
PROTEIN: 29g

1 pound ground chuck	1 medium onion, chopped
oregano	2 10 ounce cans Rotel
garlic powder	Tomatoes and Green
1 tablespoon salad oil	Chiles
5 ounce box vermicelli	1 to 2 10 ounce cans water

Brown ground beef. Season with garlic powder and oregano while browning. Drain meat and set aside. Brown vermicelli in salad oil. Add onions, tomatoes and beef. Add water. Bring to a boil and reduce heat to simmer. Allow to cook down, stirring occasionally, until most of liquid is absorbed. Do not allow vermicelli to become sticky.

Cathy Carson

The testing committee says this is great.

Mexican Cornbread Casserole

YIELD: 12 servings
CALORIES: 282
CARBOHYDRATES: 20g

FAT: 14g
PROTEIN: 17g

1 pound ground meat	1 teaspoon salt
1 onion, chopped	1 egg
salt and pepper to taste	1 can cream style corn
1 cup cornmeal	2 jalapeno peppers, chopped
1 cup milk	½ pound grated cheddar
1 teaspoon baking soda	cheese

Saute ground meat, onions, salt and pepper. Drain. Make cornbread batter. Pour half of the batter into 9×13×2-inch pan. Layer with meat, then sprinkle cheese over meat. Cover with remaining batter. Bake at 350° for 50 to 55 minutes. If serving to your family, the jalapeno peppers can be omitted.

Barbara Malone

Bill's Cheese Burritos

YIELD: 1
CALORIES: 348
CARBOHYDRATES: 24g

FAT: 21g
PROTEIN: 17g

flour tortillas
Colby cheese (cheddar will
   give a different taste)
tomatoes (diced)

green onions, chopped
fresh or canned jalapeno
   peppers, chopped
lettuce, if desired, chopped

Grate or slice a small amount of cheese and place on flour tortilla. Put tortilla and cheese in microwave and cook for about 30 to 60 seconds, until cheese melts. Remove and place onions, tomatoes, peppers on top of cheese. This must be done in haste or tortilla will cool and be hard to roll. Roll tortilla into burrito and eat.

Mary Jo Mason

Additional seasoning can be placed on cheese prior to microwave cooking, such as cayenne or herbs of your choice, such as cilantro.

Fajitas

YIELD: 4
CALORIES: 837
CARBOHYDRATES: 37g

FAT: 42g
PROTEIN: 74g

1 8 ounce bottle Catalina
    salad dressing
½ package fajita seasoning
1 package fajita meat

onions, sliced and separated
    into rings
bell peppers, sliced into rings
1   package flour tortillas

Trim fat off of fajita meat and marinate it in the Catalina dressing and fajita seasoning at least 1 hour; overnight is better. Cook on sheet of foil on a grill for about 30 minutes or until done, turning occasionally. Cut the meat across the grain in thin strips after it is cooked. Cook onion and pepper rings which have been marinated along with the fajita meat. Roll fajita meat in a warmed tortilla. Serve with vegetables and guacamole.

Jeannine Henderson

Italian dressing may be substituted.

Susie Black's Party Egg Casserole

YIELD: 16 to 20 servings
CALORIES: 444
CARBOHYDRATES: 7g

FAT: 35g
PROTEIN: 27g

2   dozen eggs
2   cans stewed tomatoes, well
    drained
2½ to 3 pounds chopped and
    cooked ham
1   stick margarine, melted

1   4 ounce can drained diced
    chilies
1   cup sour cream
2   pounds Velveeta cheese,
    diced

Mix all ingredients except ham with mixer. Stir in ham. Divide
into 2 9×13×2 inch buttered casserole dishes. Bake at 350 degrees for 1 hour or until eggs are set. To freeze, reduce cooking
time to 45 minutes and place in freezer. Defrost and bake at 350
degrees for 15 to 20 minutes.

Jean Read

*VARIATION: Follow instructions above and substitute 3 chopped
green peppers, mild or hot, for the canned chilies.*
Teri Jackson

This recipe halves nicely and you can freeze it.

Poached Eggs Supreme

YIELD: 2 large or 4 small
CALORIES: 226
CARBOHYDRATES: 15g

FAT: 15g
PROTEIN: 10g

1   tablespoon minced onion
1   tablespoon margarine
10½ ounce can cream of
    chicken soup
⅔ cup milk

4   eggs
2   English muffins, split,
    toasted and buttered
paprika
parsley

Cook onion in margarine, stir in soup and milk, and heat to
boiling. Slip eggs into mixture. Cover and cook over medium
heat to desired doneness. Place egg on each half muffin. Top
with sauce and sprinkle with paprika and parsley.

Darla Jones

These are great after a dance.

Sausage Breakfast Casserole

YIELD: 8 to 10 servings
CALORIES: 264
CARBOHYDRATES: 11g

FAT: 20g
PROTEIN: 11g

1   pound bulk sausage
6   slices of white bread
butter or margarine
1½ cups grated cheddar cheese

5   eggs
2   cups half and half
1   teaspoon salt
1   teaspoon dry mustard

Cook sausage, stir to a crumble, drain. Remove crusts from bread. Butter the bread and cut into cubes. Place in $13 \times 9 \times 2$ inch baking pan. Sprinkle with sausage and top with cheese. Combine remaining ingredients in mixing bowl, beat well and pour into pan. Chill 8 hours. Bake at 350 degrees for 40 to 50 minutes.

Becky Childress

Can be made the night before, great time-saver when you have over-night guests.

Angel Egg Cups

YIELD: 4 servings
CALORIES: 210
CARBOHYDRATES: 11g

FAT: 16g
PROTEIN: 8g

4   bread slices
butter

4   eggs

Remove crusts from the bread and butter one side. Place buttered side down in a muffin tin and press into a nest shape. Drop a raw egg into each nest and bake at 350 degrees for 25 minutes.

Martha Henderson

Wonderful breakfast for company.

Omelette with Potato

YIELD: 6 servings
CALORIES: 148
CARBOHYDRATES: 7g

FAT: 10g
PROTEIN: 9g

6   slices of bacon
2   tablespoons chopped onion
1   raw potato, grated
6   eggs
Tabasco, dash

2   tablespoons fresh parsley, minced
salt and pepper to taste
dash paprika

Fry bacon until crisp. Drain and crumble. Leave two tablespoons bacon drippings in pan and saute onion over low heat until soft. Add potatoes and cook until light brown. Beat eggs slightly and pour into pan. Add Tabasco, salt and pepper and a dash of paprika. Cook omelette until firm. Sprinkle with bacon and parsley and serve immediately.

Mary Jo Mason

Good dinner dish or for brunch.

Mexican Eggs

YIELD: 4 servings
CALORIES: 335
CARBOHYDRATES: 22g

FAT: 23g
PROTEIN: 14g

1   teaspoon chili powder
1   teaspoon dried oregano
1   clove garlic, mashed
2   cans Buffalo tomato puree

1   8-ounce can tomato sauce
3   tablespoons oil
8   eggs

Mix first 3 ingredients in frying pan and heat well. Add tomato puree, tomato sauce and oil. Salt and pepper to taste. After sauce is boiling, reduce heat and break eggs into pan. Cover and cook slowly until desired doneness.

Mary Jo Mason

Good supper dish.

Egg Casserole

YIELD: 20 to 24 servings
CALORIES: 483
CARBOHYDRATES: 7g

FAT: 38g
PROTEIN: 29g

2   dozen eggs, slightly beaten
2   cans stewed tomatoes, well
     drained
2½ to 3 pounds ham, chopped
1   stick margarine, melted

3   green peppers, chopped
1   8 ounce carton sour cream
2   pounds Velveeta cheese

Mix all ingredients together. Pour into 2 13×9×2 inch casserole dishes. Bake at 350 degrees for 1 hour. This may be prepared ahead of time by baking for 45 minutes and then freezing. Defrost before baking the second time. Bake at 350 degrees for about 20 minutes, or until hot.

Teri Jackson

Brunch Eggs

YIELD: 8 servings
CALORIES: 368
CARBOHYDRATES: 18g

FAT: 24g
PROTEIN: 19g

6   slices French bread,
     crumbled
1   pound hot sausage, fried
8   ounces sharp cheddar
     cheese

2   cups milk
1   teaspoon prepared mustard,
     thinned with a little milk
8   eggs

Mix all ingredients together. Let stand in refrigerator overnight. Bake in a greased 9×13 inch dish at 350 degrees for 1 hour.

Darla Jones

Great to prepare ahead of time.

Breakfast Pizza

YIELD: 6
CALORIES: 646
CARBOHYDRATES: 62g

FAT: 35g
PROTEIN: 23g

2   cans crescent rolls
1   pound cooked sausage
1   cup uncooked hash browns
1   cup grated cheese, cheddar
    or colby

5   eggs
¼   cup milk
⅛   teaspoon pepper
½   teaspoon salt

Press crescent rolls into bottom of greased pizza pan making a raised rim around edge. Spread with the cooked sausage and sprinkle with hash browns. Mix eggs, milk, salt and pour over hash browns. Sprinkle with cheese and bake at 375 degrees for 25 to 30 minutes. The eggs tend to run over, so put a cookie sheet under the pizza pan.

Cynthia Berry

Montezuma's Quiche

YIELD: 6 servings
CALORIES: 454
CARBOHYDRATES: 24g

FAT: 33g
PROTEIN: 18g

6   tablespoons butter, chilled
1¼ cups flour
½   teaspoon salt
1   egg, slightly beaten
½   cup Monterey Jack cheese,
    grated

1   cup mild cheddar cheese,
    grated
1   4 ounce can green chilies
1   cup half and half cream
3   eggs, slightly beaten

Cut the butter into the flour and ¼ teaspoon of the salt. Add 1 slightly beaten egg and stir until dough holds together. Shape into a ball. Roll out to fit a 9 inch quiche or pie pan. Prick the dough and bake at 450 degrees for 6 minutes. Sprinkle all of the Jack and half of the cheddar cheeses on the partially baked crust. Distribute the green chilies over the cheeses. Beat the eggs with the half and half and salt, until blended. Pour into crust and top with remaining cheese. Bake at 325 degrees for 40 minutes or until well set. Let stand for 15 minutes before cutting.

Cathy Carson

Double this recipe, using a 13-inch casserole for a large brunch. Also does well served as an appetizer when cut into 2 inch squares.

John Wayne Quiche

YIELD: 6 to 8 servings
CALORIES: 493
CARBOHYDRATES: 7g

FAT: 37g
PROTEIN: 31g

1 pound Monterey Jack cheese
1 pound cheddar cheese
2-4 ounce cans chopped green chilies

4 eggs, separated
1 tablespoon flour
1 5 ounce can evaporated milk

Grate cheeses and mix. Put in a 9×13×2 inch baking dish. Smooth cheese down with hands. Sprinkle with green chilies. Beat egg whites until stiff. Set aside. Beat egg yolks with flour. Combine the egg whites, egg yolks and milk. Pour over the cheese and chilies. Bake at 325 degrees for 45 to 50 minutes, don't let it get too brown. Let set before serving.

Debbie Glasscock

Great for parties.

Golden Turkey Quiche

YIELD: 4 to 6 servings
CALORIES: 429
CARBOHYDRATES: 17g

FAT: 31g
PROTEIN: 19g

1 9 inch frozen deep dish pie shell
1 cup chopped celery
1 tablespoon butter or margarine
1 cup diced turkey or chicken
2 tablespoons chopped pimiento

3 eggs
1 cup milk
¼ cup mayonnaise
2 tablespoons prepared mustard
½ teaspoon salt
1 cup shredded cheddar cheese
paprika

Bake pie shell at 375 degrees for 10 minutes. Cook celery in margarine until tender. Stir in turkey and pimiento. Beat together eggs, milk, mayonnaise, mustard and salt. Stir into turkey mixture. Pour into pie shell. Sprinkle with cheese and paprika. Bake at 375 degrees for 25 to 35 minutes, until knife inserted near center comes out clean.

Katharine Russell

Very easy to prepare and pretty, too!

Side Dishes

Angora goats — producers of mohair, a luxury fabric. 99% of the mohair in the United States is produced in this area.

Marinated Asparagus

YIELD: 4 to 6 servings
CALORIES: 247
CARBOHYDRATES: 7g

FAT: 24g
PROTEIN: 3g

1   pound asparagus, fresh or
    frozen
¼   cup water

1   cup Italian salad dressing
    nutmeg

Cut asparagus into 2 inch pieces and place in a 2 quart casserole dish with the water. Sprinkle with nutmeg to preserve color, and cover. Microwave at high for 11 minutes, stirring after 3 minutes. Allow to cool to room temperature, gently stir in dressing, refrigerate overnight. Serve cold.

Cathy Carson

La Vaun's Beans

YIELD: 8 servings
CALORIES: 307
CARBOHYDRATES: 50g

FAT: 7g
PROTEIN: 11g

2   21 ounce cans pork and
    beans
1   small onion
½   teaspoon Worcestershire
    Sauce

1   teaspoon mustard
1   cup catsup
¼   cup packed brown sugar

Coarsely chop onion. Mix all ingredients together in a 2 quart casserole. Bake at 350 degrees for 1 hour. Serve hot.

Cathy Carson

This is my Mother's recipe and tastes as good as beans baked for hours.

Ranch Pinto Beans

YIELD: 12 servings
CALORIES: 132
CARBOHYDRATES: 16g

FAT: 4g
PROTEIN: 8g

2   pounds dried pinto beans
1½ inch by 4 inch slice salt
    pork
2   slices uncooked bacon
2   bay leaves
1   4 ounce can green chilies
1   10 ounce can Rotel
    tomatoes

1   large yellow onion,
    chopped
4   cloves garlic, chopped
¼   teaspoon cumin
salt and pepper

Rinse pinto beans, cover with water and soak for approximately 4 hours. Add more water and remaining ingredients except cumin, salt and pepper. Bring to boil, reduce to simmer and cook for about 5 hours until tender, stirring occasionally. A few minutes before serving, add cumin, salt and pepper.

Sandy Baggett

Many cowboys and ranch hands have enjoyed these beans during sheep shearing, drenching and marking lambs.

Boiled Red Pinto Beans

YIELD: 12 or more servings
CALORIES: 235
CARBOHYDRATES: 10g

FAT: 17g
PROTEIN: 9g

3 cups dried red beans
water
2 inch slab of salt pork
water

1 teaspoon salt
2 teaspoons sugar

Fill a large pot to within 2 inches from the top with water and bring to a boil. Meanwhile, pick over beans for rocks and dirt clods. Rinse and add to boiling water. Reduce heat and boil slowly for 2 hours. Add salt and sugar. Slice to the rind every ¼ inch on the slab of salt pork. Add to beans. Continue to cook until beans are done, adding water when needed. May be reheated several times or may be used to make Mexican beans or refried beans.

Lou Deaton

VARIATION: Add one small square of smoked bacon, 1 tablespoon of chili powder per cup of dried beans, comino to taste, 4 cloves minced fresh garlic. Omit onion. Soak beans in water overnight before cooking.

Mary Jo Mason

Buster adds an onion and two cloves of garlic, scored.

Green Beans with Almonds and Basil

YIELD: 4 servings
CALORIES: 130
CARBOHYDRATES: 6g

FAT: 11g
PROTEIN: 3g

1 pound fresh green beans
3 tablespoons butter
3 tablespoons almonds,
   slivered

¼ teaspoon dried basil or 1
   teaspoon fresh
1½ tablespoons fresh parsley,
   minced

Cook green beans in a small amount of water until crisp-tender. Drain if necessary. Brown almonds in butter in a small saucepan. Add basil and parsley to the almonds, then mix with the green beans.

Mary Jo Mason

Quick N' Easy Green Bean Casserole

YIELD: 6 servings
CALORIES: 96
CARBOHYDRATES: 7g

FAT: 7g
PROTEIN: 3g

1 16 ounce can green beans, drained
1 can cream of mushroom soup

1 small jar pimientos
bread crumbs or onion rings
bacon bits
almonds

Drain beans and mix with undiluted soup in a saucepan. Heat to boil and stir in the pimientos, bacon bits and almonds. Do not add salt. Put in serving dish and sprinkle with bread crumbs or broken onion rings.

Benny Gail Hunnicutt

Great color for a Christmas dish.

Broccoli with Rice

YIELD: 6 servings
CALORIES: 322 variation:363
CARBOHYDRATES: 21g 22g

FAT: 23g 27g
PROTEIN: 9g 11g

1 stick butter
1 onion, chopped
1 rib celery, chopped
1 package frozen, chopped broccoli
1 can cream of chicken soup

1 cup grated cheese or small jar Cheez-Whiz
1½ cups rice, cooked
Tabasco
salt and pepper to taste
bread crumbs

In a large skillet, saute the onions and celery in the butter until clear. Cook broccoli according to the directions on the package, drain well. Mix broccoli with soup and cheese, add to celery and onions. Stir in rice, season and mix well. Put into a greased casserole dish and top with bread crumbs. Bake at 350 degrees for 45 minutes. This can be prepared ahead of time and frozen.

Jane Richardson

VARIATION: *Follow recipe above except for the following: Bring frozen broccoli to room temperature and do not cook. Combine Cheez Whiz with rice while still hot and decrease rice to 1 cup. Use 1 cup chopped celery and 1 can cream of mushroom soup with the cream of chicken soup. Omit Tabasco.*

Teri Jackson

Cabbage Au Gratin

YIELD: 6 servings
CALORIES: 357
CARBOHYDRATES: 14g

FAT: 26g
PROTEIN: 16g

1 large head of cabbage	2 cups milk
4 tablespoons butter	2½ cups grated cheddar cheese
3 tablespoons flour	2 cups bread crumbs,
1 teaspoon salt	buttered

Cook the cabbage until tender. Drain well. Combine the butter, flour and salt in a saucepan. Blend in the milk. Cook over low heat, stirring constantly until smooth and thickened. Alternate layers of cabbage, cheese and sauce in a greased 1½ quart casserole dish. Sprinkle with bread crumbs. Bake at 350 degrees for 25 to 30 minutes.

Carol Hunnicutt

Carrots with Brandy Sauce

YIELD: 6 servings
CALORIES: 124
CARBOHYDRATES: 11g

FAT: 4g
PROTEIN: 2g

3 cups sliced carrots	2 tablespoons brandy
2 tablespoons butter or margarine	¼ cup green pepper, diced
2 tablespoons flour	1 teaspoon onion, diced
1 cup chicken broth	½ teaspoon fresh parsley, chopped

Cook the carrots, covered, in a small amount of salted boiling water for 20 minutes or until tender. Drain. Melt the butter in a heavy saucepan over low heat, add the flour and cook one minute, stirring constantly. Gradually add the chicken broth while cooking over medium heat and stirring constantly until thickened and bubbly. Gently stir in the brandy and add the cooked carrots and remaining ingredients. Cook slowly until thoroughly heated.

Ann Childress

Mom's Glazed Carrots

YIELD: 6 to 8 servings
CALORIES: 81
CARBOHYDRATES: 10g

FAT: 4g
PROTEIN: 2g

2   tablespoons margarine or
    butter
2   tablespoons chopped onion
1   tablespoon parsley,
    chopped
8   medium carrots, sliced

1   can condensed beef
    consomme
¼   teaspoon sugar
½   teaspoon monosodium
    glutamate
dash of nutmeg

Cook carrots in mixture of other ingredients until tender. Drain and serve hot. The liquid can be re-used later if refrigerated.

Sherry Scott

This is Lane's favorite recipe.

Orange Glazed Carrots

YIELD: 4 servings
CALORIES: 180
CARBOHYDRATES: 20g

FAT: 11g
PROTEIN: 3g

1   pound carrots, washed, cut
    into ½ inch slices
2   tablespoons butter
¼   cup orange juice

1   tablespoon brown sugar
1½ teaspoons cornstarch
¼   cup pecans (optional)

Place carrots in a 1 quart casserole dish with the butter, 2 tablespoons of the juice and the sugar. Cover and microwave on high for 11 minutes, stirring after 5 minutes. Mix the remaining juice with the cornstarch until smooth. Stir into the carrots and add pecans. Cover and microwave on high for 3 to 4 minutes or until thickened, stirring at end of each minute. Stir before serving.

Cathy Carson

Be sure to double the microwave time when doubling this recipe.

Baked Corn Casserole

YIELD: 8 to 10 servings
CALORIES: 224
CARBOHYDRATES: 30g

FAT: 11g
PROTEIN: 4g

2 17 ounce cans cream style corn
⅓ cup Wesson oil
2 eggs
¼ cup corn meal

1 4 ounce can chopped green chilies
½ teaspoon baking powder
1 teaspoon garlic salt

Combine all ingredients and mix well. Pour mixture into a 13 inch baking dish. Bake at 350 degrees for 50 minutes.

Sandra Childress

Great for covered dish dinners, men love it!

Cream Cheese Corn

YIELD: 8 Servings
CALORIES: 270
CARBOHYDRATES: 17g

FAT: 221g
PROTEIN: 5g

2 16 ounce packages whole kernel corn (frozen)
1 8 ounce package cream cheese

1 4 ounce can chopped green chilies
½ cup margarine

Cook and drain corn according to package directions. Add cream cheese, chilies and margarine to corn and simmer over low heat until melted. Mix well.

Nancy Vannoy

You can adjust the amount of chilies. This dish is also good cold.

Corn Fritters

YIELD: 10-12 servings
CALORIES: 103
CARBOHYDRATES: 6g

FAT: 8g
PROTEIN: 1g

1 8-ounce can cream style corn
1 egg
3 tablespoons flour

3 tablespoons vegetable oil
salt and pepper to taste

Mix all ingredients. Beat by hand until smooth. Drop by spoon into hot oil. Brown both sides and serve.

Carmen Sutton

Southwestern Corn Bake

YIELD: 6-8 servings
CALORIES: 340
CARBOHYDRATES: 35g

FAT: 18g
PROTEIN: 12g

1   16 ounce can cream corn
1   16 ounce can whole kernel
    corn
2   eggs, beaten
¾   cup yellow corn meal

1   teaspoon garlic salt
4   tablespoons vegetable oil
2   cups grated cheese
1-4 ounce can chopped green
    chilies, drained

Preheat oven to 350 degrees. Mix ingredients in large mixing bowl, and spread in 8 × 8 inch greased baking dish. Bake at 350 degrees for 30 to 35 minutes.

Karen Huffman

Easy Corn Pudding

YIELD: 6 servings
CALORIES: 300
CARBOHYDRATES: 25g

FAT: 20g
PROTEIN: 8g

24 ounces Niblet corn
3   eggs, lightly beaten
1   pint half and half
¼   cup butter, cut in small
    pieces

dash cayenne pepper
dash paprika
salt and pepper

Combine all ingredients, except butter, and season to taste with salt and pepper. Pour into buttered 2 quart casserole and dot top with butter. Bake at 350 degrees for 45 minutes. Test with a knife inserted in the center. Pudding is done when the knife comes out clean.

Sandy Baggett

This recipe is a favorite of the designer, Bill Blass.

Virginia Corn Pudding

YIELD: 4 servings
CALORIES: 213
CARBOHYDRATES: 22g

FAT: 13g
PROTEIN: 3g

1   can cream style corn
2   heaping tablespoons flour
2   heaping tablespoons sugar
½   stick margarine or butter

1   cup milk
1   egg
salt and pepper to taste

Mix all ingredients and pour into baking dish. Bake at 350 degrees for 1½ hours. Check after 1 hour. Recipe can be doubled.

Carolyn Pennington

Eggplant Almandine

YIELD: 6 servings
CALORIES: 285
CARBOHYDRATES: 9g

FAT: 24g
PROTEIN: 11g

1   medium eggplant, sliced, pared and cut in small cubes
¾   cup slivered, blanched almonds
¼   cup butter or margarine
1   small onion, finely chopped

¼   cup finely snipped parsley
¾   cup cracker crumbs
2   eggs, slightly beaten
2   tablespoons milk
1   cup thinly sliced or grated cheddar cheese

Cook the eggplant in ½ cup boiling salted water just until tender. Drain thoroughly. Mash with a fork and beat until fluffy. Lightly brown the almonds in 1 tablespoon butter. Remove from heat and keep warm. Saute the onions lightly in butter and mix with parsley and combine both with the eggplant. Heat the remaining butter and toss with the cracker crumbs to coat. Blend the crumbs and ½ cup of almonds with the vegetables. Blend in mixture of the eggs and milk. Turn into a greased 1 quart baking dish. Top with cheese and almonds. Bake at 350 degrees for 30 minutes. Remove from the oven and sprinkle with paprika. Garnish with snipped parsley. Return to the oven and heat for an additional 10 minutes.

Martha Gries

The almonds add texture and flavor.

Eggplant Creole

YIELD: 4-6 servings
CALORIES: 45
CARBOHYDRATES: 10g

FAT:
PROTEIN: 2g

1 small chopped onion
1 small chopped green
  pepper
1 8 ounce can tomato sauce
1 clove garlic, minced
½ teaspoon salt

¼ teaspoon dried whole
  oregano
¼ teaspoon pepper
¼ teaspoon hot sauce
1 small eggplant, peeled and
  coarsely chopped

Combine first eight ingredients in a heavy skillet. Cover and cook over low heat 10 minutes. Stir in eggplant. Cover and cook an additional 20 minutes stirring occasionally until eggplant is tender and completely heated.

Ann Childress

Eggplant Delicious

YIELD: 4 servings
CALORIES: 181
CARBOHYDRATES: 16g

FAT: 12g
PROTEIN: 6g

1 large firm eggplant
1 bell pepper, chopped
1 medium onion, chopped
3 stalks celery, chopped
3 tablespoons butter
1 hard cooked egg, mashed

1 raw egg
3 tablespoons cracker crumbs
cayenne pepper
salt
black pepper

Slice the top off of the eggplant. Scoop out the pulp, leaving enough wall so eggplant will retain its shape when boiled in salt water for 10 minutes. Cook pulp in salt water until tender. Drain pulp and mash well. Saute pepper, onion and celery in the butter until tender. Add the mashed pulp and cook for 5 minutes. Add the cooked egg, raw egg, 2 tablespoons of the cracker crumbs, a pinch of cayenne, and salt and pepper to taste. Fill the eggplant shell with the mixture and sprinkle with 1 tablespoon cracker crumbs and the seasonings. Dot with 1 tablespoon of butter. Bake at 375 degrees until brown.

Susan McMullan

Serve on a heated platter and garnish with parsley.

Katy's Eggplant Casserole

YIELD: 6-8 servings
CALORIES: 194
CARBOHYDRATES: 13g

FAT: 11g
PROTEIN: 10g

1   eggplant
½   teaspoon salt
¼   teaspoon pepper
½   teaspoon onion salt
1   tablespoon butter or
    margarine

2   eggs
1   cup grated cheese
2   cups corn flakes
1¼ cups milk

Peel and slice the eggplant; boil until tender, drain and mash. Add salt, pepper, onion salt and margarine. Beat the eggs. Add eggs and cheese to eggplant mixture. Stir in corn flakes and milk and pour into greased baking dish. Bake at 350 degrees until a knife inserted in the center comes out clean.

Shelley Conner

Italian Eggplant Parmigiana

YIELD: 6 servings
CALORIES: 362
CARBOHYDRATES: 10g

FAT: 31g
PROTEIN: 13g

1   large eggplant
salt and pepper
2   eggs, slightly beaten
1   cup fine, dry breadcrumbs
olive oil
1½ cups tomato sauce, heated

½   pound mozzarella cheese,
    sliced
1   teaspoon crumbled dry
    basil
¼   cup grated Parmesan
    cheese

Wash the eggplant and cut crosswise into rounds ¼ inch thick Do not peel. Season with salt and pepper. Dip into the breadcrumbs and then into the egg and then again into the breadcrumbs. More eggs and breadcrumbs may be needed, depending on the size of the eggplant. Place in the refrigerator for 30 minutes. Heat about ¼ inch of oil in a skillet. Fry eggplant slices until golden brown on both sides and drain. Line a shallow, greased baking dish with some of the sauce. Add a layer of eggplant, a layer of cheese, more sauce and a sprinkling of basil and Parmesan. Repeat layers until dish is full. Bake at 350 degrees for 25 to 30 minutes.

Shelley Conner

Val Verde County 4-H Club Hominy

YIELD: 150 servings
CALORIES: 118
CARBOHYDRATES: 5g

FAT: 62g
PROTEIN: 15g

3   pounds salt pork
7   large onions
garlic to taste, preferably fresh
3   hot peppers

9   large cans tomatoes
coarse ground black pepper
3   gallons hominy

Cut salt pork in small pieces, place in roaster and fry until brown and crisp. Chop onions, garlic, bell peppers and hot peppers and add to pork. Add tomatoes with juice. Drain the hominy and add to mixture. Season with pepper. Simmer 2-3 hours.

Jane Richardson

VARIATION: For the family, use 1 medium onion, chopped and 1 clove garlic, minced, sauteed in 1 to 2 tablespoons hot bacon grease. Use 1 can Rotel tomatoes and omit hot pepper. Use ½ cup bell peppers, chopped and 2 to 3 cups hominy. Follow above instructions adding water if needed.

Cathy Carson

A great side dish for a crowd.

Slightly Hot Cheese Grits

YIELD: 10 to 12 servings
CALORIES: 293
CARBOHYDRATES: 8g

FAT: 25g
PROTEIN: 10g

1½ cups instant grits
¾ cup margarine
1   pound Velveeta cheese, grated
½ to 1 teaspoon Tabasco

2   teaspoons paprika
3   eggs, beaten
3   teaspoons seasoning salt

Bring 6 cups water to a boil, add grits and cook until thick. Add remaining ingredients and mix well. Pour into a greased casserole and bake at 250 degrees for 1½ hours.

Benny Gail Hunnicutt

Freezes well before baking.

Okra Patties

YIELD: 8 to 10 servings
CALORIES: 159
CARBOHYDRATES: 12g

FAT: 11g
PROTEIN: 2g

12-15 fresh okra pods
½ onion
½ teaspoon salt
dash pepper
½ cup water

1 large egg
½ cup flour
1 tablespoon baking powder
½ cup corn meal
cooking oil

Chop okra and onion into very small pieces. Mix with salt, pepper, water and egg. Mix dry ingredients and add to okra mixture. Drop by tablespoon in hot oil in large skillet. Brown well over medium heat.

Mary Jo Mason

Cheese Potatoes

YIELD: 6 servings
CALORIES: 262
CARBOHYDRATES: 23g

FAT: 12g
PROTEIN: 12g

5 medium potatoes, boiled, peeled and cut
1 cup shredded cheddar or jack cheese

½ cup butter, softened
¼ to ½ cup milk
salt and pepper to taste

Cook potatoes until tender, drain. Add remaining ingredients and mix well.

Sharon Forehand

Oven Potatoes and Onions

YIELD: 4 to 6 servings
CALORIES: 243
CARBOHYDRATES: 24g

FAT: 15g
PROTEIN: 3g

4 potatoes
1 large onion

½ cup margarine
salt and pepper to taste

Peel and cube potatoes and cut up onion. Place in baking dish with margarine, salt and pepper. Cover and bake at 400 degrees for 45 minutes, stirring occasionally. Uncover early for a little browning.

Jane Richardson

From Mrs. Glen Richardson, Sonora, Texas.

Ranch Stewed Potatoes

YIELD: 4 to 5 servings
CALORIES: 198
CARBOHYDRATES: 29g

FAT: 8g
PROTEIN: 4g

4 medium potatoes
1 medium onion
3 tablespoons bacon grease

1 teaspoon salt
1 teaspoon pepper

Peel and slice potatoes ¼ inch thick. Peel and dice onion. Place bacon grease in heavy skillet that has a lid. Heat, add potatoes and onion and stir until most of the potatoes are grease coated. Add water just to the edge of the potatoes. Add salt and pepper, bring to a boil, reduce heat, cover and simmer about 5 minutes or until potatoes are tender and juice has thickened.

Lou Deaton

Hash Brown Casserole

YIELD: 10 to 12 servings
CALORIES: 178
CARBOHYDRATES: 4g

FAT: 15g
PROTEIN: 6g

1 pint sour cream
1 can cream of mushroom
  soup
1 large onion, chopped

2 cups cheddar cheese
1 package frozen hash
  browns

Mix all ingredients together and bake in a buttered casserole dish for 1½ hours at 350 degrees. Save some of the cheese for the top of the casserole, if desired.

Carol Hunnicutt

Cheese Potatoes

YIELD: 8 servings
CALORIES: 240
CARBOHYDRATES: 13g

FAT: 18g
PROTEIN: 7g

4   potatoes
1   large onion
1   small jar pimientos, diced

2   bell peppers
salt and pepper
¼   cup water

SAUCE
⅓ cup flour
½ cup butter or margarine

½   cup milk
1   8 ounce jar Cheez Whiz

Peel potatoes and onion and cut in round slices approximately ⅛ inch thick. Slice the bell peppers the same way removing seeds and membranes. Into a buttered baking dish, place a layer of potato slices topped with 2-3 slices of onion and 2 to 3 slices of bell pepper. Sprinkle diced pimientos over the layer and salt and pepper lightly. Continue to layer in this manner until the baking dish is full. Add ¼ cup of water and cover. Bake for 1 hour at 350 degrees. Prepare cheese sauce by combining flour and butter or margarine in a saucepan. Cook over low heat and stir until the butter is melted then add the milk and Cheez Whiz, stirring until smooth. Remove the cover from the potato mixture and pour the cheese sauce over the top. Bake uncovered at 350 degrees until the cheese sauce is bubbly.

Becky Childress

New Potato Casserole

YIELD: 12 to 14 servings
CALORIES: 341
CARBOHYDRATES: 14g

FAT: 27g
PROTEIN: 10g

9   medium to large new
    potatoes
6   tablespoons butter
3   cups grated cheddar cheese

salt and pepper
3   cups sour cream
½   cup chopped green onions

Boil the potatoes and chill until cool. Grate into a large bowl. Melt cheese and butter together. Blend in sour cream, onions and seasonings. Pour mixture over the potatoes and mix well. Pour into a buttered 3 quart casserole dish, dot with butter and bake at 350 degrees for 45 minutes.

Carol Hunnicutt

This freezes well.

Southwest Scalloped Potatoes

YIELD: 12 servings
CALORIES: 372
CARBOHYDRATES: 47g

FAT: 8g
PROTEIN: 9g

8   medium potatoes, peeled
    and thinly sliced
⅓   cup butter
⅓   cup flour
¾   teaspoon garlic salt
3   cups milk
2   cans condensed cheddar
    cheese soup

1   4 ounce can green chilies
1   small onion, finely
    chopped
buttered bread crumbs
dash of paprika

Cook potatoes until tender. Melt butter in a saucepan and stir in flour and garlic. Cook until bubbly. Stir in milk and cook until it thickens and bubbles, about 3 minutes. Stir soup in with a whisk. Add chilies and onion. Drain potatoes and layer with sauce in a 13×9×2 inch pan. Top with bread crumbs, cheese, reserved chilies and paprika. Cover with foil and bake at 350 degrees for 1 hour, uncover and bake 30 minutes longer.

Ann Childress

Potato Patties

YIELD: 4 servings
CALORIES: 235
CARBOHYDRATES: 19g

FAT: 16g
PROTEIN: 4g

2   cups leftover mashed
    potatoes
1   large egg, beaten
2   tablespoons flour

salt and pepper to taste
1   tablespoon grated onion
cooking oil

Mix all ingredients together making mixture stiff enough to handle. Shape into 2 inch patties, dip in flour and brown in hot oil.

Mary Jo Mason

VARIATION: Add a small can of salmon, well drained and flaked. This is Mother's recipe for leftover potatoes and it is delicious.

Easy Potato Casserole

YIELD: 8 servings
CALORIES: 341
CARBOHYDRATES: 25g

FAT: 23g
PROTEIN: 10g

6 medium potatoes
½ cup margarine
salt and pepper to taste

1 cup sour cream
6 to 8 slices American cheese

Peel and slice the potatoes. Boil in water until tender. Mash potatoes and add margarine and seasoning. Add milk if needed. Stir in sour cream and mix well. Put in a casserole dish, top with cheese slices and bake at 350 degrees until cheese melts. Baked potatoes can also be used. To use baked potatoes, cut in half, scoop out pulp, combine with margarine and sour cream and seasonings, refill potato shells, top with a cheese slice and bake until cheese melts.

Helen Bean

Wonderful with steak or chicken.

Potato Casserole

YIELD: 8 servings
CALORIES: 483
CARBOHYDRATES: 19g

FAT: 37g
PROTEIN: 18g

9 medium potatoes
½ cup butter or margarine
2 cups half and half
1 tablespoon salt

½ pound cheddar cheese, diced
1 cup cheddar cheese, grated

Boil potatoes in skins until tender. Chill for at least 24 hours. Remove skins and grate potatoes. Heat butter, half and half and salt until butter is melted. Mix in the potatoes and diced cheese. Pour into greased 2 quart casserole dish and bake for 1 hour at 350 degrees. Sprinkle with grated cheese and bake for 15 minutes longer.

Ann Childress

Cheese Soup Potatoes

YIELD: 5-6 servings
CALORIES: 243
CARBOHYDRATES: 38g

FAT: 7g
PROTEIN: 6g

5-6 medium potatoes, sliced
   thin
1 onion, sliced thin
butter

1 can cheddar cheese soup
salt and pepper to taste

Alternate potatoes and onion, layered in baking dish. Dot with butter and cover with soup. Add ½ can water. Cover and bake at 350 degrees for 1 hour.

Teri Jackson

Sweet Potato Casserole

YIELD: 10 to 12 servings
CALORIES: 317
CARBOHYDRATES: 65g

FAT: 6g
PROTEIN: 4g

8 sweet potatoes
1 cup milk
1 teaspoon vanilla
3 tablespoons sugar
¼ cup butter

¼ teaspoon cinnamon
dash of nutmeg
1 tablespoon orange juice
12 marshmallows

Bake sweet potatoes at 350 degrees until soft inside. Peel and mash. Scald milk and add vanilla, sugar and butter and set aside. Add the orange juice and spices to the potatoes. Blend with a mixer, gradually adding the milk mixture. Blend until smooth. Place in a buttered casserole dish and bake at 350 degrees for 20 minutes. Place marshmallows on top and brown.

Sandy Baggett

You can microwave the potatoes instead of baking them.

Fancy Sweet Potatoes

YIELD: 8 servings
CALORIES: 402
CARBOHYDRATES: 75g

FAT: 12g
PROTEIN: 4g

4 or 5 fresh baked yams
2   apples, sliced

2   cups miniature
    marshmallows

TOPPING
1   teaspoon cinnamon
½ cup chopped pecans

¼ cup margarine

Slice sweet potatoes and mix with apples. Sprinkle topping on potatoes and bake at 350 degrees for 40 minutes. Add marshmallows on top and brown in oven.

Mary Jo Mason

Very good for Christmas Dinner.

Sweet Potatoes

YIELD: 4 to 6 servings
CALORIES: 335
CARBOHYDRATES: 70g

FAT: 7g
PROTEIN: 2g

6   medium yams
½ cup brown sugar, packed
3   tablespoons butter or
    margarine

3   tablespoons light cream or
    milk
½ teaspoon salt
marshmallows

Boil the yams in their skins until tender, drain and cool. Peel and cut in large pieces. Beat until smooth. Add the other ingredients except marshmallows and beat well. Pour into a baking dish and top with marshmallows. Bake until the marshmallows are golden brown at 350 degrees.

Karen Childress

Sweet Potato Casserole

YIELD: 8 servings
CALORIES: 547
CARBOHYDRATES: 95g

FAT: 18g
PROTEIN: 6g

3   cups mashed sweet
    potatoes
1   cup sugar
½   teaspoon salt

½   cup evaporated milk
1   teaspoon vanilla
2   eggs, beaten
⅓   stick of melted margarine

TOPPING
1   cup brown sugar
⅓   cup white sugar
⅓   cup flour

⅓   stick soft margarine
½   cup chopped nuts
½   cup shredded coconut

Mix all of the potato ingredients together and turn into a greased baking dish. Mix all of the topping ingredients together and spread on top. Bake at 350 degrees for 30 minutes.

Debbie Glasscock

Norfolk Noodles

YIELD: 12 to 14 servings
CALORIES: 274
CARBOHYDRATES: 27g

FAT: 13g
PROTEIN: 12g

1   12 ounce package noodles
1   cup fresh parsley, chopped
1   pint cottage cheese, large
    curd
1   pint sour cream
1   tablespoon Worcestershire
    sauce

1   bunch green onions,
    chopped with some green
    tops
½   cup cheese, grated
½   teaspoon paprika

Prepare noodles according to directions on package and drain. Mix remaining ingredients, except the cheese and paprika, with the hot noodles. Place in a shallow 9×13 inch baking dish. Refrigerate at least 1 hour. Top with cheese and paprika and bake uncovered at 350 degrees for 40 minutes.

Martha Henderson

Very good with beef or pork.

Creamy Macaroni and Cheese

YIELD: 6 servings
CALORIES: 561
CARBOHYDRATES: 27g

FAT: 41g
PROTEIN: 22g

1 12 ounce package macaroni
½ cup margarine
½ to 1 cup milk

16 ounces American cheese,
    grated
salt and pepper to taste

Boil the macaroni until tender and drain. Add margarine and milk, stir well. Add the cheese, mix well. Add salt and pepper. Serve hot.

Helen Bean

A great side dish for children.

Wild Rice Casserole

YIELD: 8 servings
CALORIES: 231
CARBOHYDRATES: 29g

FAT: 11g
PROTEIN: 4g

1 cup raw wild rice
3 cups boiling water
1 teaspoon salt
2 tablespoons butter
4 tablespoons onion, minced
2 tablespoons green pepper, chopped
1 8 ounce can sliced mushrooms, drained
1 10¾ ounce can cream of mushroom soup, undiluted

¾ cup half and half
¼ teaspoon dried marjoram
⅛ teaspoon dried basil
⅛ teaspoon dried tarragon
½ teaspoon curry
½ teaspoon salt
¼ teaspoon pepper
8 whole fresh buttered mushrooms, for garnish

Wash the rice in 3 or 4 changes of cold water. Then to the boiling water in a saucepan add the salt and then stir in the rice. Simmer, covered, for 30 minutes or until all of the water is absorbed. Preheat the oven to 350 degrees if serving immediately. While rice is cooking melt the butter and saute the onion, green pepper and mushrooms for about 5 minutes. Stir in the soup, half and half and the spices. Heat on low for about 10 minutes. When rice is done, rinse in a colander and add to sauce mixture. Pour into a greased 2 quart casserole dish and place in oven for 8 to 10 minutes. If serving later, refrigerate.

Mrs. C. Gary Garlitz (Jane Adams Garlitz)

This dish is better when prepared a day ahead so the herbs can blend.

Sweet Rice

YIELD: 4 servings
CALORIES: 337
CARBOHYDRATES: 65g

FAT: 7g
PROTEIN: 4g

2   cups cooked rice
¾   cup sugar

2   tablespoons butter
1   cup milk

Combine rice, sugar and butter in a saucepan. Add milk to the top of the rice mixture. Bring to a boil, stirring. Reduce heat and simmer until thickened.

Lou Deaton

A recipe from my German grandmother

Spanish Rice

YIELD: 8 servings
CALORIES: 170
CARBOHYDRATES: 16g

FAT: 10g
PROTEIN: 5g

3   tablespoons bacon grease
½   cup rice, uncooked
1   can Rotel tomatoes
1¼ cups water
1   medium onion, chopped
1   bell pepper, chopped

1   teaspoon salt
1   tablespoon sugar
1   bay leaf
⅛   teaspoon cayenne pepper
¼   teaspoon paprika
1   cup cheese, grated

Combine all ingredients except grated cheese. Mix and pour into a baking dish, top with cheese. Cover and bake at 350 degrees for 1 hour.

Paula Bailey

Rice Dish

YIELD: 8
CALORIES: 191
CARBOHYDRATES: 19G

FAT: 12G
PROTEIN: 2G

1   cup uncooked rice
1   cup water
1   can consomme beef soup
1   stick margarine, sliced

½   teaspoon pepper
1   teaspoon salt
¼   teaspoon garlic salt

Combine all ingredients in a baking dish. Cover. Bake at 350 degrees for 1 hour.

Jean North

Chinese Steamed Rice

YIELD: 6 servings
CALORIES: 223
CARBOHYDRATES: 50g

FAT: .3g
PROTEIN: 4g

2   cups long grain rice   water

In a tall, deep, heavy-bottomed pan equipped with a tight fitting lid, wash rice thoroughly in 4 to 5 changes of cold water, rubbing the rice between your hands until water is clear. Drain thoroughly and add water to 1 inch above the rice. Cover pan and bring to rolling boil. Continue until all of the water has evaporated, about 15 minutes. Turn heat as low as possible and steam for 15 minutes. The excess water absorbed by the rice during the vigorous boiling will evaporate leaving the rice tender and each grain separate. Fluff with fork before serving.

Paula D. Bailey

Fried Rice

YIELD: 4 servings
CALORIES: 132
CARBOHYDRATES: 14g

FAT: 6g
PROTEIN: 6g

3   slices bacon, halved
¼   cup green onion, diced
1   cup cooked rice

2   tablespoons soy sauce
2   eggs, slightly beaten
¼   cup water

Lay bacon slices in a wok and fry until crisp on medium heat for approximately 6 minutes. Crumble and set aside. Fry onion in the bacon drippings for 2 minutes, add rice and stir fry for 7 to 8 minutes. Add the soy sauce. Push the rice to the side, pour in the eggs and cook until eggs are set. Stir rice into egg and add bacon. Reduce heat to low for serving.

Tina Bean

Spanish Rice

YIELD: 4 to 6 servings
CALORIES: 283
CARBOHYDRATES: 57g

FAT: 3g
PROTEIN: 7g

4 strips of bacon
1 onion, chopped
1 bell pepper, chopped
1 to 2 cups rice
2 small cans tomato sauce

dash salt
chili powder to taste
garlic salt to taste
2 to 4 cups water

Fry bacon in saucepan until crisp, remove and set aside. Saute onion and pepper in saucepan for a few minutes and then add the rice and stir until it is browned. Add the seasonings and tomato sauce and simmer about 30 minutes or until all of the liquid is absorbed. Serve hot.

Karen Childress

Green Rice

YIELD: 10 servings
CALORIES: 359
CARBOHYDRATES: 33g

FAT: 21g
PROTEIN: 10g

2 cups rice, uncooked
1½ cups milk
½ cup salad oil
½ cup parsley, chopped
1 medium onion, chopped fine
8 ounces Velveeta cheese

1 small jar pimientos, chopped
2 eggs
garlic salt to taste
salt to taste
pinch of cayenne

Cook rice as directed on box. When it is done, add other ingredients, mixing well. Pour into 9×13 inch greased casserole and bake covered at 350 degrees for 30 minutes. Watch to see when it bubbles.

Susan Mertz Slaughter

Freezes well. This dish is especially good when served with ham.

Rice and Green Chili Casserole

YIELD: 6 servings
CALORIES: 425
CARBOHYDRATES: 13g

FAT: 36g
PROTEIN: 12g

1   cup rice, cooked
4   tablespoons butter
½   teaspoon salt
¼   teaspoon pepper
1   4 ounce can green chilies

2   cups sour cream
½   pound Monterey Jack
    cheese
1   cup grated sharp cheddar
    cheese

Season the cooked rice with 2 tablespoons of the butter, salt and pepper. Combine the green chilies and sour cream. Cut the Jack cheese into strips. Alternate layers of rice, sour cream mixture and strips of cheese in a buttered casserole dish, ending with a layer of the sour cream mixture. Dot with remaining 2 tablespoons of butter and sprinkle with grated cheddar cheese. Bake at 350 degrees for 30 minutes until browned.

Sandy Baggett

Green Chilies and Rice Casserole

YIELD: 8 servings
CALORIES: 340
CARBOHYDRATES: 22g

FAT: 25g
PROTEIN: 8g

1   cup rice, raw
½   cup butter or margarine
1½ cups Monterey Jack cheese,
    grated
1   cup sour cream

salt to taste
2   4 ounce cans chopped
    green chilies
paprika, optional

Cook the rice according to package directions and combine with 6 tablespoons of the butter or margarine. Add salt and 1 cup of the cheese, mix well. Add the sour cream and chilies. You may increase or decrease the amount of chilies according to taste. Place mixture in a greased casserole, top with remaining cheese and dot with remaining butter or margarine. Bake at 350 degrees for 30 minutes. Sprinkle with paprika before serving.

Lou Deaton

Baked Rice

YIELD: 4 to 6 servings
CALORIES: 243
CARBOHYDRATES: 51g

FAT: 1g
PROTEIN: 5g

1   cup rice

2   cans chicken broth

Butter a casserole dish and add raw rice and broth. Mix well. Bake at 350 degrees for 2 hours or until tender. Use more broth if necessary.

Helen Bean

Baked Rice Casserole

YIELD: 6 to 8 servings
CALORIES: 218
CARBOHYDRATES: 25g

FAT: 14g
PROTEIN: 4g

1   cup rice
½   cup margarine
½   pound mushrooms, sliced
1   clove garlic
2   tablespoons green onion or chives

2   tablespoons bell pepper, chopped
½   cup blanched almonds
3   cups chicken broth

Melt margarine in a saucepan. Add rice and brown. Add other ingredients except broth. Cook and stir about 5 minutes. Heat broth and add to rice. Turn into a buttered casserole dish and cover tightly and bake at 325 degrees for about 20 minutes.

Susan McMullan

A delicious zest for rice.

Herbed Rice

YIELD: 6 servings   FAT: 9g
CALORIES: 190   PROTEIN: 3g
CARBOHYDRATES: 26g

1	cup rice	½	teaspoon marjoram
2	cups chicken broth	½	teaspoon rosemary
½	stick margarine	½	teaspoon thyme
3	tablespoons dried onion flakes		

Place all ingredients in a large saucepan. Bring the mixture to a boil, stirring once. Cook the rice mixture 20 to 30 minutes, stir and serve.

Mary Jo Mason

Great side dish for chicken. Adds that extra zing to make an ordinary meal something special.

Ranch Vermicelli

YIELD: 6 servings   FAT: 7g
CALORIES: 114   PROTEIN: 2g
CARBOHYDRATES: 11g

1	5 ounce box vermicelli	3	tablespoons vegetable oil
1	8 ounce can tomato sauce	½	teaspoon ground comino
1	onion, chopped	1	cup hot water

Brown the vermicelli in the oil in a skillet. Add the remaining ingredients and bring to a boil. Reduce heat and simmer until vermicelli softens, approximately 20 minutes. Do not over cook. Do not cover.

Carmen Sutton

VARIATION: Add garlic salt and increase water to 3 cups and tomato sauce to two 8 ounce cans. Add black pepper. Continue as above.

Helen Bean

VARIATION: Decrease the onion by half and saute with 4 cloves of garlic and 3 slices of chopped bacon, before browning the vermicelli. Add 1 serrano pepper if you desire a hot flavor. Add 2 beef boullion cubes to the water. Omit tomato sauce. Continue as above.

Susan McMullan

Substitute rice for the vermicelli.

Peggy's Squash Medley

YIELD: 4-6 servings
CALORIES: 90
CARBOHYDRATES: 13g

FAT: 4g
PROTEIN: 3g

2	zucchini squash	2	tablespoons butter
2	yellow squash	½	teaspoon salt
3	carrots	¼	teaspoon pepper
2	onions	1	teaspoon thyme

Wash the squash, cut off the ends and cut into 2-inch cubes. Wash and peel the carrots, cut off the ends and cut into 1-inch rounds. Peel the onions and cut each into 6 pieces. Place all in a 2-quart saucepan and add enough water to cover one-fourth of the vegetables. Boil until tender crisp, aproximately 15 minutes. Drain well, add butter and seasonings.

Lou Deaton

Nannie Clayton's Squash

YIELD: 8 servings
CALORIES: 267
CARBOHYDRATES: 8g

FAT: 21g
PROTEIN: 11g

8-10 yellow squash
1 large yellow onion
1½ teaspoons bacon grease
dash salt, pepper and garlic
    salt
1½ teaspoons chicken broth

2 eggs, beaten
8 ounce carton sour cream
4 ounce can chopped green
    chilies
2 cups cheddar or monterey
    jack cheese

Slice squash and chop onion and grate cheese. Preheat oven to 350 degrees. Boil vegetables until tender. Drain, mash and drain again. Add rest of ingredients except cheese. Pour into buttered 2 quart casserole dish, top with cheese and bake for 30 minutes.

Sandy Baggett

Summer Squash Casserole

YIELD: 10 servings
CALORIES: 180
CARBOHYDRATES: 10g

FAT: 15g
PROTEIN: 3g

6   cups yellow summer
      squash, sliced
¼   cup onion, chopped
1   can condensed cream of
      chicken soup

1   cup sour cream
1   cup shredded carrots
1   8 ounce package herb
      seasoned stuffing mix
½   cup butter or margarine

In saucepan, cook squash and onion in salted, boiling water for 5 minutes, then drain. Combine soup and sour cream. Stir in shredded carrots, squash and onion. Combine stuffing mix and butter or margarine. Spread half of the stuffing mix in bottom of 8×12 inch baking dish. Spoon vegetable mixture on top and sprinkle remaining stuffing over vegetables. Bake in 350 degree oven for 25 to 30 minutes or in microwave oven for 10 minutes, rotating dish every 3 minutes.

Lou Deaton

Bernice Phillip's Yellow Squash
Casserole

YIELD: 10 servings
CALORIES: 200
CARBOHYDRATES: 9g

FAT: 17g
PROTEIN: 5g

8   yellow squash
salt and pepper to taste
½   stick butter
2-3 tablespoons milk

1   8 ounce package cream
      cheese
1   small package potato chips
      or cracker crumbs

Cut up the squash and simmer until tender, then mash and drain. Add the salt, pepper and milk. Break the cream cheese into chunks and add to the squash. Mix and pour into a casserole dish and crumble the potato chips or crumbs on top. Bake in 350 degree oven until bubbly.

Benny Gail Hunnicutt

Grated cheddar cheese on top is also good! Even if you don't like squash, you'll love this recipe.

Gladys Pierce's Squash Casserole

YIELD: 8 to 10 servings
CALORIES: 353
CARBOHYDRATES: 17g

FAT: 25g
PROTEIN: 16g

6   medium yellow squash, washed and sliced
2   cups cheese, grated

4   eggs, hard cooked and sliced
2   cups white sauce

WHITE SAUCE
2   cups milk, scalded
2-3 tablespoons flour
2   tablespoons butter or margarine

¼   teaspoon salt
⅛   teaspoon pepper
2   dashes garlic salt

Blend the flour and butter in a sauce pan over low heat. Add the milk and seasonings, stirring constantly. Cook and continue stirring until mixture thickens. Do not boil. Boil squash for 5 minutes and drain. Layer squash, eggs and 1 cup of the cheese in a casserole, ending with the eggs. Pour the white sauce over all and top with remaining cheese. Bake at 350 degrees for 30 minutes.

Shelley Conner

Parmesan Zucchini

YIELD: 4 servings
CALORIES: 86
CARBOHYDRATES: 7g

FAT: 6g
PROTEIN: 4g

2   8 to 10 inch zucchini squash
seasoned salt

4   teaspoons margarine
4   tablespoons Parmesan cheese, grated

Halve the zucchini lengthwise, scrape out seeds and discard. Place in 9×11 inch Pyrex dish, cut side up. Sprinkle liberally with seasoned salt. Spread 1 teaspoon margarine on each half and sprinkle with Parmesan cheese. Cover with plastic wrap and microwave 3 minutes. Rotate dish ¼ turn and microwave 3 more minutes or until tender.

Lou Deaton

Sauteed Zucchini

YIELD: 4 servings
CALORIES: 153
CARBOHYDRATES: 7g

FAT: 12g
PROTEIN: 8g

1 small onion
2 tablespoons safflower oil
1 cup fresh mushrooms, sliced
1 pound zucchini
1 teaspoon salt

¼ teaspoon pepper
½ teaspoon dried, whole thyme
¼ cup grated Parmesan cheese

Chop onion and slice the zucchini in a food processer. Saute onions in hot oil until tender. Add the next five ingredients and cook over low heat, stirring often, for 5 to 7 minutes or until squash is crisp and tender. Sprinkle with cheese and serve immediately.

Ann Childress

For a working girl it is a fast vegetable that has the qualities of hours to prepare.

Shredded Zucchini

YIELD: 4-6 servings
CALORIES: 73
CARBOHYDRATES: 5g

FAT: 6g
PROTEIN: 1g

2 medium sized zucchini
½ onion, chopped
1 tablespoon fresh parsley

2 tablespoons margarine
salt and pepper

Shred zucchini in a food processor or with a hand grater. Saute chopped onion in margarine for about 3 minutes. Add zucchini and salt and pepper to taste. Cook about 2-3 minutes. Sprinkle with parsley and serve.

Mary Jo Mason

German Squash

YIELD: 4 servings
CALORIES: 103
CARBOHYDRATES: 10g

FAT: 7g
PROTEIN: 3g

5   small yellow squash
2   tablespoons butter
½   teaspoon salt

½   teaspoon pepper
1   tablespoon sugar
½   cup milk

Wash squash, trim off ends and slice into ½ inch rounds. Place in a 2 quart saucepan, add water until you can see it and cook until a fork will pierce the edges. Drain in a colander and return to saucepan. Mash with a potato masher, add remaining ingredients and mix well. Reduce heat to low and simmer for 10 minutes.

Lou Deaton

Acorn Squash

YIELD: 6 servings
CALORIES: 227
CARBOHYDRATES: 28g

FAT: 12g
PROTEIN: 8g

3   10 to 12 ounce acorn
    squash
1   3 ounce package cream
    cheese
2   tablespoons milk
3   eggs, slightly beaten

2   tablespoons green onions,
    sliced
¼   teaspoon salt
⅛   teaspoon pepper
3   tablespoons almonds,
    toasted and chopped

Cut squash in halves and scoop out seeds. Trim bottom off to make it level. Place squash, hollowed side down, in a shallow baking pan. Bake at 375 degrees for 30 to 35 minutes until it is crisp-tender. Cut the cream cheese into chunks and beat until soft, add milk and continue beating until it is fluffy. Add remaining ingredients except almonds and beat well. Turn squash cut-side up and pour egg mixture into hollowed out squash. Sprinkle almonds on top. Bake at 375 degrees for 20 minutes. Let stand for 5 minutes before serving.

Benny Gail Hunnicutt

Neta Tillman's Squash Casserole

YIELD: 12 servings
CALORIES: 173
CARBOHYDRATES: 16g

FAT: 9g
PROTEIN: 10g

8 to 10 medium squash
1 medium onion, diced
2 to 3 tablespoons brown sugar
½ teaspoon black pepper
½ teaspoon garlic salt
1 4 ounce can chopped green
    chilies, drained

1 pound American or
    Velveeta cheese, grated
1 sleeve soda crackers,
    crushed

Slice squash, add onions. Cover with water and cook until tender. Drain and add other ingredients. Mix well and taste for salt tolerance. Bake in buttered 13×9×2 inch casserole dish for 30 minutes at 350 degrees.

Jean Read

Squash Saute

YIELD: 4 servings
CALORIES: 110
CARBOHYDRATES: 12g

FAT: 7g
PROTEIN: 3g

3 or 4 medium yellow or
    zucchini squash, diced
1 medium onion, chopped
1 clove garlic, minced
1 or 2 jalapeno peppers,
    minced

1 small bell pepper, chopped
2 tablespoons olive oil
salt and pepper

Saute the vegetables in the olive oil in a large skillet until just barely tender. Cover and cook for about 2 minutes. Add salt and pepper. For variety, after sauteing, add 10 to 12 crumbled crackers and 1 cup grated cheese. Pour into casserole dish and bake at 350 degrees until cheese bubbles.

Mary Jo Mason

Zucchini, Corn and Cheese

YIELD: 6 servings
CALORIES: 257
CARBOHYDRATES: 27g

FAT: 13g
PROTEIN: 11g

1 pound zucchini, sliced 1 inch thick
1 chopped onion
2 tablespoons butter, melted
2 eggs, beaten
1 10 ounce package frozen corn, or 2 cups fresh corn or 1 15 ounce can

whole kernel corn, drained
8 ounces grated cheddar cheese
¼ teaspoon salt
¼ cup fine, dry bread crumbs
2 tablespoons grated Parmesan cheese

Cook zucchini until tender. Drain and mash with a fork. Saute onion in 1 tablespoon butter until tender. Combine eggs, zucchini, onion, corn, cheddar cheese and salt. Put in a greased casserole. Mix the Parmesan cheese, bread crumbs and remaining tablespoon of butter and sprinkle on top of the first mixture. Bake at 350 degrees for 30 to 40 minutes.

Carol Hunnicutt

Zucchini Supreme

YIELD: 12 servings
CALORIES: 117
CARBOHYDRATES: 12g

FAT: 7g
PROTEIN: 3g

1 can creamy chicken mushroom soup
½ cup sour cream
4 cups sliced, cooked zucchini

1 cup shredded carrots
2 cups frozen peas, cooked
2 cups herb seasoned stuffing mix
¼ cup butter or margarine

In a 2 quart baking dish, combine all of the ingredients except the stuffing mix and butter which is sprinkled on top of the vegetables. Bake at 350 degrees for 30 minutes or until bubbly.

Cathy Carson

Stegemoller Sauerkraut

YIELD: 10 servings
CALORIES: 20
CARBOHYDRATES: 3g

FAT: 0g
PROTEIN: 1g

5 pounds cabbage, shredded   2 tablespoons salt

Weigh the cabbage after shredding to make 5 pounds. Place a couple of inches of cabbage in a large crock. Sprinkle with a little salt and mash. Repeat process until all of the cabbage has been layered into crock. It will begin making liquid and a little foam. Invert a glass plate on top of the cabbage. Fill plastic bags with water, doubling the bags to prevent breakage. Place bags on inverted plate forming a seal. Cover with a cup towel and tie with a string. Let stand in a cool, dark place for 14 days. Heat sauerkraut until very hot, pack in jars and seal.

Jane Richardson

Mixed Vegetable Casserole

YIELD: 10 to 12 servings
CALORIES: 287
CARBOHYDRATES: 7g

FAT: 25g
PROTEIN: 7g

1   10 ounce package frozen
    peas
1   10 ounce package frozen
    green beans
1   10 ounce package frozen
    lima beans

1½ small cartons sour cream
¾ cup real mayonnaise
2   cups grated cheese

Cook vegetables according to package directions. Mix together sour cream and mayonnaise. Drain vegetables and pour into casserole dish. Spread sour cream/mayonnaise mixture over vegetables. Top with grated cheese. Bake at 350 degrees for 25 minutes.

Susie Childress

Vegetable Casserole

YIELD: 15-20 SERVINGS
CALORIES: 102
CARBOHYDRATES: 7g

FAT: 6g
PROTEIN: 6g

1   10 ounce bag frozen
    broccoli
1   16 ounce can green beans
1   16 ounce can peas
1   10½ ounce can asparagus
1   4 ounce can water
    chestnuts

1   10¾ ounce can cream of
    mushroom soup
1   10¾ ounce can cream of
    chicken soup
1   16 ounce jar Jalapeno
    Cheez-Whiz
1   6 ounce can fried onion
    rings (save for last)

Mix first 8 ingredients together and bake at 350 degrees for 20 minutes. Top with onion rings and bake for 10 minutes.

Lee Allen

Great for a covered dish dinner.

Dixie's Spinach-Artichoke Casserole

YIELD: 8 to 10 servings
CALORIES: 246
CARBOHYDRATES: 12g

FAT: 20g
PROTEIN: 9g

2   10 ounce packages frozen
    chopped spinach
2   14 ounce cans artichoke
    hearts, drained and
    chopped
2   cups sour cream

½   cup margarine
½   cup onion, chopped
½   cup Parmesan cheese,
    grated
¼   teaspoon garlic powder
salt and pepper to taste

Cook spinach according to package directions and drain well. Saute the onions in the margarine. Add remaining ingredients, fold in the spinach and place in a 2 quart casserole dish. Bake at 325 degrees for 1 hour or 350 degrees for 30 minutes.

Ann Childress

A rich tasting dish. Serve with baked or broiled meat.

Spinach Loaf

YIELD: 8 to 10 servings
CALORIES: 53
CARBOHYDRATES: 4g

FAT: 3g
PROTEIN: 2g

2½ cups fresh or frozen spinach
1 cup cracker crumbs
2 tablespoons bacon drippings
1 tablespoon lemon juice
dash nutmeg
1 egg, beaten

1 medium clove garlic, crushed
2 tablespoons bell pepper, chopped
2 tablespoons pimiento, chopped
salt and pepper to taste

Cook and chop the spinach. Combine ingredients and place in a greased loaf pan and cover with foil. Place loaf pan in a pan of hot water. Bake at 325° for 1½ hours. **Susan McMullan**

Creme Fraiche

YIELD: 2 cups
CALORIES: 208
CARBOHYDRATES: 2g

FAT: 22g
PROTEIN: 1g

2 cups whipping cream

1 tablespoon buttermilk or sour cream

Combine cream and buttermilk or sour cream. Heat to a temperature of 85 degrees. Store in a 1 quart mason jar with lid. Let stand at room temperature until thickened, approximately 5 to 6 hours. Stir gently and refrigerate until ready to use. This tolerates higher temperatures in cooking than sour cream before it curdles. Use as a substitute for sour cream in vegetable and meat dishes, such as Spinach and Artichoke Casserole and Sour Cream Chicken found in this cookbook. **Camille Jones**

Mustard Sauce

YIELD: 1¼ cups, 5¼ cup servings
CALORIES: 139
CARBOHYDRATES: 7g

FAT: 11g
PROTEIN: 3g

1 cup sour cream
¼ cup milk
3 tablespoons onion soup mix

2 tablespoons prepared mustard

Combine all ingredients in a sauce pan. Heat through stirring often. Use as a sauce for vegetables such as broccoli and asparagus. **Mary Jo Mason**
Try this on beef fondue also.

Salads

Most everything has thorns, spines, burrs or stickers!

Guacamole Salad

YIELD: 10 servings
CALORIES: 252
CARBOHYDRATES: 7g

FAT: 24g
PROTEIN: 4g

12 ounces softened cream cheese
2 tablespoons picante sauce
2 tablespoons mayonnaise

3 average size avocados
½ onion
2 tomatoes

Combine cream cheese, mayonnaise and picante sauce. Mash avocados, add to the first mixture. Chop onion and tomatoes and mix with the avocado mixture. Serve as a salad or a dip.

Jeannine Henderson

Pico de Gallo Salad

YIELD: 10 servings
CALORIES: 249
CARBOHYDRATES: 14g

FAT: 22g
PROTEIN: 4g

6 peeled, chopped avocados
3 coarsely chopped tomatoes
2 chopped onions

2 tablespoons jalapeno juice
juice from 2 limes
salt and pepper

Combine first 3 ingredients, toss lightly with lime juice and jalapeno juice. Adjust amounts according to taste. Season with salt and pepper. Do not over toss. Chopped fresh jalapeno could be added for those who like it hot.

Sandy Baggett

Can be served as dip with tortilla chips.

Broccoli Salad

YIELD: 8 servings
CALORIES: 238
CARBOHYDRATES: 20g

FAT: 16g
PROTEIN: 5g

8 slices bacon
½ cup raisins
1 small onion
3 tablespoons vinegar

2 tablespoons sugar
1 cup mayonnaise
4 cups fresh broccoli

Fry bacon until crisp. Boil raisins in water. Crumble bacon into a jar, add drained raisins, diced onion, vinegar, sugar and mayonnaise. Store in refrigerator overnight. Pour over fresh broccoli and serve.

Luann Pierce

Broccoli-Cauliflower Salad

YIELD: 10 to 12 servings
CALORIES: 151
CARBOHYDRATES: 12g

FAT: 10g
PROTEIN: 4g

1   bunch broccoli
1   head cauliflower
tomatoes to taste

1   bunch green onions,
    chopped

DRESSING
1   cup mayonnaise
½   cup sour cream
1   tablespoon vinegar

2   tablespoons sugar
salt and pepper

Use only flowerettes from broccoli and cauliflower. Place them in a large covered bowl. Mix dressing and pour over flowerettes and let marinate overnight. Before serving, add tomatoes and onions.

Teri Jackson

Cauliflower Salad Bowl

YIELD: 8 to 10 servings
CALORIES: 143
CARBOHYDRATES: 6g

FAT: 14g
PROTEIN: 1g

4   cups thinly sliced raw
    cauliflower
1   cup chopped ripe olives
⅔   cup chopped bell pepper

½   cup chopped onion
½   cup chopped pimiento

DRESSING:
½   cup salad or olive oil
3   tablespoons lemon juice
3   tablespoons wine vinegar
2   teaspoons salt

1   teaspoon to 1 tablespoon
    sugar
¼   teaspoon pepper

In medium bowl combine first 5 ingredients. Blend dressing ingredients and pour over cauliflower mixture. Refrigerate covered until well chilled, 4 hours or overnight. It's good served with hot bread for lunch.

Sharon Forehand

German Cabbage Slaw

YIELD: 4 servings
CALORIES: 186
CARBOHYDRATES: 17g

FAT: 13g
PROTEIN: 2g

½ large head of cabbage
1 medium onion
2 tablespoons sugar
½ teaspoon salt

½ teaspoon pepper
¼ cup vinegar
¼ cup oil

Grate cabbage and onion on small grater or process small amounts at a time in food processor. In 1 cup measure mix next 5 ingredients. Pour over cabbage and onions and mix well. Chill and serve.

Lou Deaton

My grandmother Rosenow served this with her beans and cornbread.

Cabbage/Onion Salad

YIELD: 12 cups
CALORIES: 259
CARBOHYDRATES: 26g

FAT: 18g
PROTEIN: 2g

1 large head shredded cabbage
2 large onions
1 cup sugar
1 cup vinegar

1 teaspoon salt
1 teaspoon celery seeds
1 teaspoon dry mustard
¼ teaspoon pepper
1 cup salad oil

Shred cabbage. Slice onions thin and separate into rings. Arrange cabbage and onions in layers in a gallon jar or tupperware container. Combine next 6 ingredients and bring to a boil. Remove from heat and add oil. Drip hot mixture over cabbage and onions. DO NOT STIR. Cover and refrigerate 24 hours.

Nancy Vannoy

This salad goes well with barbeque and pinto beans and will keep for several days in refrigerator.

Charlotte B's Sauerkraut Salad

YIELD: 10 to 12 servings
CALORIES: 53

CARBOHYDRATES: 14g
PROTEIN: 1g

1   #2 can sauerkraut
1   cup celery
1   large white onion
1   bell pepper

1   3 ounce jar pimientos
½   cup wine vinegar
½   cup sugar

Drain sauerkraut, mince vegetables, mix and set aside. Bring the vinegar and sugar to a boil, cool. Add to salad ingredients and serve. This salad will keep indefinitely in a closed container in the refrigerator.

Benny Gail Hunnicutt

Cucumbers with Sour Cream

CALORIES: 128
CARBOHYDRATES: 9g

FAT: 9g
PROTEIN: 2g

3   cucumbers
1   onion
1   cup sour cream
2   tablespoons chopped pecans

2   tablespoons lemon juice
1   teaspoon salt
1   tablespoon sugar

Peel and slice cucumbers, add onion sliced into rings. Combine next 5 ingredients and pour over cucumbers and onions. Stir and chill before serving. Best the second day.

Lou Deaton

Corn Salad

YIELD: 8 to 10 servings
CALORIES: 103
CARBOHYDRATES: 19g

FAT: 3g
PROTEIN: 2g

1   16 ounce can white corn, whole kernel
1   16 ounce can yellow corn, whole kernel
1   cup chopped onion
1   cup chopped sweet pickles
1   cup chopped green pepper
1   cup chopped celery
1   cup chopped cucumbers
1   small jar pimientos, chopped
¼   cup mayonnaise (do not substitute)
¼   cup sweet pickle juice
salt and pepper to taste

Combine vegetables. Stir together mayonnaise, juice and seasonings. Pour dressing over salad and store in covered bowl in refrigerator overnight.

Nancy Vannoy

This will keep for several days.

Daisy's Potato Salad

YIELD: 6 servings
CALORIES: 314
CARBOHYDRATES: 24g

FAT: 21g
PROTEIN: 5g

5   medium potatoes
1   medium onion, chopped
4   hard cooked eggs, chopped
1   cup coarsely chopped dill pickles
1   teaspoon salt
½   teaspoon pepper
1½ cups mayonnaise type salad dressing
1½ teaspoons mustard

Cook potatoes until fork tender. Cool, peel and cube potatoes. Add eggs, onion, pickles, salt and pepper. Toss together. Add salad dressing and mix, being careful not to mash potatoes. Chill for at least 2 hours or better overnight.

Cathy Carson

Great for picnics!

Yummy Potato Salad

YIELD: 8 to 12 servings
CALORIES: 313
CARBOHYDRATES: 17g

FAT: 25g
PROTEIN: 5g

8   cups diced cooked potatoes
1½ cups celery slices
6   hard boiled eggs, chopped
⅔   cup radish slices
½   cup green onion slices
1   cup chopped bell pepper

1   teaspoon salt
dash of pepper
1½ cups salad dressing
2   tablespoons prepared
    mustard
cherry tomato halves

Combine all ingredients except the last 3 in a large bowl. Mix salad dressing and mustard. Pour over first ingredients and mix lightly. Chill and garnish with tomato halves.

Nancy Vannoy

Rice Salad

YIELD: 8 servings
CALORIES: 129
CARBOHYDRATES: 15g

FAT: 6g
PROTEIN: 1g

2   ribs of celery, minced
2   green onions tops, minced
2   tablespoons chopped ripe
    olives
½   bell pepper, chopped

2   cups cooked rice, chilled
½   cup mayonnaise
1   tablespoon soy sauce
½   teaspoon lemon juice
¼   teaspoon curry powder

Mix rice and vegetables together. Combine last 4 ingredients and pour over rice. Garnish with tomato wedges.

Jo Nel Stokes

Pickled Bean Salad

YIELD: 8 servings
CALORIES: 233
CARBOHYDRATES: 36g

FAT: 9g
PROTEIN: 5g

1   can green beans
1   can yellow wax beans
1   can kidney beans
½   green pepper
½   cup onion

¾   cup sugar
⅔   cup vinegar
⅓   cup salad oil
1   teaspoon salt
1   teaspoon pepper

Drain and rinse canned beans, chop onion, and green pepper, mix with the beans. Mix remaining ingredients and pour over beans. Cover and refrigerate overnight.

Cathy Carson

Vegetable Medley

YIELD: 12 to 16 servings
CALORIES: 265
CARBOHYDRATES: 20g

FAT: 21g
PROTEIN: 3g

1 head cauliflower
1 bunch broccoli
8 ounces fresh mushrooms
4 ribs celery

6 carrots
2 zucchini
2 yellow squash

MARINADE
¾ cup sugar
2 teaspoons dry mustard
1 teaspoon salt
½ cup vinegar

1½ cups salad oil
1 small onion, quartered
2 to 3 tablespoons poppy
seeds

Use flowerettes of cauliflower and broccoli, slice all other vegetables and combine. Blend marinade ingredients until smooth.
Pour over vegetables and chill overnight before serving.

Marilyn Chalmers

Marinated Vegetable Medley

YIELD: 12 cups
CALORIES: 184
CARBOHYDRATES: 17g

FAT: 12g
PROTEIN: 3g

1 can Mexicorn
1 small jar artichoke hearts,
drained
1 zucchini
1 yellow squash
12 cherry tomatoes

1 bunch green onions
2 cucumbers
1 bunch broccoli
fresh mushrooms

DRESSING:
⅓ cup brown sugar
⅔ cup tarragon vinegar
⅔ cup salad oil

½ teaspoon dill weed
garlic salt to taste
1 tablespoon lemon pepper
marinade

Slice all vegetables and combine. Layer in a 3 quart dish or jar.
Mix all dressing ingredients together, pour over vegetables. Refrigerate 24 hours before serving. To double recipe you will
need to triple dressing recipe.

Elizabeth Upham

Potato Salad

YIELD: 10 to 12 servings
CALORIES: 188
CARBOHYDRATES: 20g

FAT: 10g
PROTEIN: 4g

6 large potatoes, boiled
4 eggs, hard boiled
1 small onion
1 small bell pepper
½ cup celery
3 medium dill pickles

3 medium sweet pickles
1-2 ounce jar pimientos
2 tablepoons mustard
1 cup salad dressing
2 tablespoons sugar
sweet pickle juice

Peel potatoes, dice in one inch squares. Salt liberally and set aside. In another bowl place the next seven ingredients, which have been chopped fine. Add mustard, salad dressing and sugar. Mix together and add pickle juice until mix is runny. Pour this mixture over potatoes. Stir gently so potatoes will retain shape. Taste to see if more salt is needed. Let set and chill for 4 to 6 hours.

Lou Deaton

I haven't found a man yet who doesn't try to eat it all.

Apple Tree Marinated Vegetable Salad

YIELD: 50 2-ounce servings
CALORIES: 88
CARBOHYDRATES: 3g
FAT: 9g
PROTEIN: 1g

4 cups sliced zucchini
2 cups sliced yellow squash
2 cups broccoli flowerettes and chopped stems
1½ cups bite size cauliflower flowerettes

1 cup sliced carrots
1 cup sliced purple onion
1 cup whole or halved cherry tomatoes

DRESSING
2 cups vegetable oil
1 cup white vinegar
½ cup wine vinegar
½ cup lemon juice
¼ cup salt
1 teaspoon oregano

1 teaspoon dry mustard
1 teaspoon dehydrated onion
1 teaspoon granulated garlic
½ teaspoon beau monde
1 tablespoon sugar

Combine dressing ingredients in a large jar. Mix well. Combine vegetables in a large container (2 gallon Tupperware container). Pour approximately 2 cups dressing over vegetables and refrigerate overnight or several hours. Stir occasionally. Store remaining dressing in refrigerator. Salad will keep indefinitely.

Nancy Vannoy

Great for family reunions, picnics, church dinners, etc.

Strawberry-Spinach Salad

YIELD: 8 to 10 servings
CALORIES: 148
CARBOHYDRATES: 15g
FAT: 11g
PROTEIN: 2g

⅓ cup sugar
2 green onions, with tops
dash of Tabasco sauce
½ teaspoon Worcestershire sauce
¼ teaspoon paprika

¼ cup apple cider vinegar
½ cup salad oil
fresh spinach, thoroughly washed, and torn
pint fresh strawberries, sliced
2 to 3 fresh kiwi fruit, sliced

Combine first 6 ingredients in food processor. Using steel blade, process 20 seconds or until blended. With machine running continuously, add the oil in a slow stream. Store in an airtight container in the refrigerator. Before serving, toss spinach, strawberries and kiwi. Add dressing and toss gently.

Ann Childress

Tossed Vegetable Salad

YIELD: 12 servings
CALORIES: 361
CARBOHYDRATES: 26g

FAT: 24g
PROTEIN: 12g

1   head lettuce
celery
bell pepper
cucumber
cauliflower
onion
carrots

broccoli
tomatoes
15 ounce can Ranch Style
    Beans
¾ pound cheddar cheese
Catalina dressing by Kraft
small bag corn chips

Use any or all of these vegetables, diced to desired size, holding lettuce and tomatoes until serving time. Drain and rinse beans, then grate the cheese. Combine the vegetables, beans, cheese and dressing. Toss lightly and marinate in refrigerator for 1 hour. Before serving, add cut up tomatoes, lettuce and corn chips. Toss and serve.

Benny Gail Hunnicutt

Great light summer meal.

Fiesta Salad

YIELD: 6 servings
CALORIES: 619
CARBOHYDRATES: 30g

FAT: 36g
PROTEIN: 26g

1   head lettuce
½ onion
2   tomatoes
1   pound cheddar cheese
1   15 ounce can ranch style
    beans

¾ of 8 ounce bottle Catalina
    Salad Dressing
3   cups corn chips, broken

Chop lettuce, onion and tomatoes and combine in a mixing bowl. Add grated cheese and drained beans. Add dressing and chips just before serving.

Jeannine Henderson

Great with Mexican food.

Wilted Lettuce or Spinach Salad

YIELD: 6 servings
CALORIES: 198
CARBOHYDRATES: 4g

FAT: 17g
PROTEIN: 6g

4 cups leaf lettuce (Romaine, Curly or Redtipped) or spinach
8 green onions and tops
8 slices bacon

3 eggs, hard boiled
salt and pepper
vinegar
3 teaspoons sugar

Chop or tear up lettuce, slice onions and tops. Fry bacon crisp, drain and reserve drippings. Crumble bacon and add to lettuce and onion. Slice 2 eggs and add to mixture. Pour drippings into a 1 cup measure, add enough vinegar to fill. Add salt, pepper and sugar. Return to skillet, heat and pour over lettuce. Garnish with remaining egg slices. Serve immediately. If using spinach, add 1 cup sliced fresh mushrooms.

Lou Deaton

Cranberry Salad

YIELD:
CALORIES: 305
CARBOHYDRATES: 31g

FAT: 20g
PROTEIN: 2g

2 3 ounce packages cream cheese
2 tablespoons mayonnaise
2 tablespoons sugar
1 can whole cranberry sauce

½ cup chopped nuts
1 cup whipping cream
1 teaspoon vanilla
½ cup powdered sugar

Soften cream cheese and blend in mayonnaise and sugar. Add fruits and nuts. Add powdered sugar and vanilla to cream while whipping. Fold into first mixture. Pour into mold and freeze for 6 hours before serving.

Lee Allen

German Apple and Pecan Salad

YIELD: 8 servings
CALORIES: 307
CARBOHYDRATES: 47g

FAT: 14g
PROTEIN: 2g

8   tart apples, cubed
1   cup pecans
1   cup sugar
1   egg

3   tablespoons cream
1   tablespoon vinegar
pinch of salt
1   teaspoon prepared mustard

Beat sugar, egg, cream, vinegar and salt in saucepan and place over low heat. Stir and boil for ½ to 1 minute, add mustard and cool. Toss over cubed apples and pecans. Chill and serve.

Sandy Baggett

My Grandmother Schmidt of Yoakum, Texas served this at Thanksgiving.

Snapp Salad

YIELD: 12 servings
CALORIES: 413
CARBOHYDRATES: 44g

FAT: 28g
PROTEIN: 2g

2   pints fresh strawberries
4   nectarines
3   avocados

1   16 ounce can pineapple
4   pears

POPPY SEED DRESSING
1   cup salad oil
1½ tablespoons poppy seeds
1   tablespoon grated onion
1   teaspoon dry mustard

⅓   cup cider vinegar
¾   cup sugar
½   teaspoon salt

Blend dressing and chill. Slice fruit into a large bowl, stir in dressing and serve.

Susan McMullan

Marka's Salad

YIELD: 4 to 8 servings
CALORIES: 266
CARBOHYDRATES: 19g

FAT: 21g
PROTEIN: 4g

lettuce
⅔ cup mozzarella cheese
 pieces

½ cup chopped celery
11 ounce can mandarin
 oranges

DRESSING
½ cup sugar
1 teaspoon dry mustard
⅓ cup salad vinegar

1 teaspoon onion flakes
⅔ cup oil
¼ teaspoon salt

Tear up lettuce, add next three ingredients, mix dressing ingredients and pour over salad. Amount of lettuce determines the number of servings.

Cynthia Berry

Easy Sunday Salad

YIELD: 12 servings
CALORIES: 231
CARBOHYDRATES: 28g

FAT: 13g
PROTEIN: 2g

1 16 ounce can sliced peaches
3 bananas, sliced
1 carton sliced frozen
 strawberries

1 cup chopped pecans
1 12 ounce carton non-dairy
 whipped topping

Pour drained peaches into a large bowl. Add strawberries and bananas. Stir in whipped topping, reserving a small amount for garnish. Stir in ¾ cup of the nuts. Cover top with reserved topping and sprinkle with remaining nuts. Place in refrigerator to chill. Excellent when served on angel food cake.

Judy Probst

This can be served in pastry cups as dessert.

Easy Fruit Salad

YIELD: 4 servings
CALORIES: 355
CARBOHYDRATES: 34g

FAT: 19g
PROTEIN: 3g

11 ounce can mandarin
   oranges
13½ ounce can pineapple
   chunks

1½ cups miniature
   marshmallows
1   cup canned coconut
1   cup sour cream

Drain fruit well. Mix together, add marshmallows and coconut. Stir in sour cream. Will be better if made a day or two before serving. Keep in refrigerator.

Susan Mertz Slaughter

1 cup chopped pecans can be added.

Fruit Salad

CALORIES: 255
CARBOHYDRATES: 44g

FAT: 10g
PROTEIN: 3g

3   apples
3   oranges
2   bananas
1   cup green grapes

½   cup raisins
½   cup coconut
½   cup chopped pecans

Peel and dice apples and oranges, slice bananas. Combine all ingredients and refrigerate until ready to serve.

Barbara Malone

Cool Whip Fruit Salad

YIELD:
CALORIES: 360
CARBOHYDRATES: 54g

FAT: 15g
PROTEIN: 4g

1   can condensed milk
1   can cherry pie filling
12 ounce carton Cool Whip
10½ ounce can pineapple
   chunks

17 ounce can fruit cocktail
1   cup pecans

Drain pineapple and fruit cocktail. Mix condensed milk and pie filling. Fold in Cool Whip. Add othe ingredients. Mix well. Serve as is, or freeze and cut in squares to serve.

Benny Gail Hunnicutt

Gail Hunnicutt won the 4-H District Food Show with this recipe.

Cherry Pie Filling Salad

YIELD: 10 servings
CALORIES: 215
CARBOHYDRATES: 45g

FAT: 4g
PROTEIN: 1g

1   can cherry pie filling
1   small can pineapple
    chunks, drained

2   bananas, sliced
½   cup pecans, broken
    handful marshmallows

Mix all ingredients together and serve.

Nancy Miller Johnson

Great when you are in a hurry.

Frozen Fruit Salad

YIELD:
CALORIES: 243
CARBOHYDRATES: 31g

FAT: 13g
PROTEIN: 3g

8   ounces cream cheese
10 ounces frozen sweetened
    strawberries
16 ounce can apricots
9   ounce can crushed
    pineapple

8   ounce carton sour cream
¼   cup sugar
½   teaspoon salt
2   cups miniature
    marshmallows
3   drops red food coloring

Soften cream cheese, thaw strawberries, drain apricots and chop and drain pineapple. Beat cream cheese until fluffy, stir in sour cream, sugar and salt. Add fruits, marshmallows and red food coloring. Pour into 9×9 inch pan and freeze. Cut in squares to serve. This will keep in freezer up to 3 weeks. May also be frozen in lined muffin tins.

Helen Bean

Blueberry Salad

YIELD: 10 to 15 servings
CALORIES: 182
CARBOHYDRATES: 182g

FAT: 19g
PROTEIN: 2g

2   3-ounce packages raspberry jello
2   cups boiling water
1   15-ounce can blueberries, drained
1   8¼-ounce can crushed pineapple, drained

1   8-ounce package cream cheese
½   cup sugar
½   pint sour cream
½   teaspoon vanilla
½   cup chopped pecans

Dissolve jello in the boiling water. Measure liquid from berries and pineapple, add enough water to make 1 cup and add to dissolved jello mixture. Stir in drained fruit. Pour into 2-quart flat pan, cover and refrigerate until firm. Combine cream cheese, sour cream, sugar and vanilla. Spread over congealed salad and sprinkle with pecans.

Charlotte Williams

Keep well chilled

Sherry's Lime Delight

YIELD: 12 to 18 servings
CALORIES: 175
CARBOHYDRATES: 12g

FAT: 14g
PROTEIN: 2g

1   box lime Jello
1   cup boiling water
½   envelope unflavored gelatin
8   ounces cream cheese
1   #2 can crushed pineapple, drained

2   cups small marshmallows
1   cup chopped pecans
1   cup whipping cream, whipped

Dissolve Jello in hot water. Mix unflavored gelatin in a little cold water and add to Jello. Mash the cream cheese, add pineapple and stir well. Add to Jello mixture and blend well. Add marshmallows and pecans.Pour into a 9×13 inch pan. Refrigerate until slightly set, add whipped cream, folding gently. Chill until firm. Cut into squares. Nice served on lettuce leaf.

Sherry Scott

Strawberry Nut Salad

YIELD: 10 to 12 servings
CALORIES: 278
CARBOHYDRATES: 36g

FAT: 15g
PROTEIN: 3g

2 3 ounce packages
   strawberry gelatin
1 cup boiling water
2 10 ounce packages frozen
   sliced strawberries
1 20 ounce can crushed
   pineapple, drained

3 medium bananas, mashed
1 cup coarsely chopped
   pecans or walnuts
2 cups sour cream

Thaw strawberries, drain and reserve juice. Combine gelatin with boiling water and stir until dissolved. Fold in bananas, strawberries, pineapple and nuts. Pour mixture into a 9 × 13 inch baking dish and chill until firm. Spread top with sour cream and return to refrigerator. Cut into squares and serve on bed of lettuce.

Barbara Malone

Orange Mist

YIELD: 8 servings
CALORIES: 175
CARBOHYDRATES: 23g

FAT: 7g
PROTEIN: 1g

2 tablespoons gelatin
¼ cup cold water
1½ cups sugar
1¼ cups orange juice

¼ cup lemon juice
3 packages non-dairy
   whipped topping mix.

Whip topping mix and set aside. Soak gelatin in cold water. Add sugar, orange juice and lemon juice. Fold topping into orange mixture, pour into molds and chill until set. If desired, top with orange slices and whipped cream when serving.

Marolyn Bean

Orange Gelatin Salad

YIELD: 10
CALORIES: 142
CARBOHYDRATES: 35g

FAT: 0g
PROTEIN: 2g

1   6 ounce package orange
    gelatin
1   cup boiling water
1   6 ounce can frozen orange
    juice concentrate

1½ cups cold water
1   20 ounce can crushed
    pineapple, with juice
1   11 ounce can mandarin
    oranges, drained

Dissolve gelatin in boiling water. Mix orange juice with cold water and combine. Add rest of ingredients, mix well and refrigerate until set. Serve on bed of lettuce and garnish with slice of kiwi and strawberry.

Susan McMullan

Costs $3.25

Orange Apricot Salad

YIELD: 8 to 10 servings
CALORIES: 271
CARBOHYDRATES: 42g

FAT: 9g
PROTEIN: 6g

2   3 ounce packages orange
    gelatin
3   cups boiling water
2   cups miniature
    marshmallows
1   12 ounce can apricot nectar
1   15 ounce can crushed
    pineapple

3   heaping teaspoons flour
1   egg, beaten
½   cup sugar
2   tablespoons butter
1   cup whipped topping
5   ounces cheddar cheese,
    grated

Drain pineapple, reserving juice. Mix boiling water, gelatin and marshmallows and stir until marshmallows are melted. Set aside ½ cup nectar and ½ cup reserved pineapple juice for topping. Add remaining juices and pineapple to gelatin. Pour into a 2 quart dish and refrigerate until set. Cook the flour, egg, sugar, butter and reserved juices over low heat until thick, stirring constantly. It scorches easily. When cooled, fold in the whipped topping. Spread over gelatin just before serving and top with grated cheese.

Barbara Malone

Apricot Salad

YIELD: 12 servings
CALORIES: 280
CARBOHYDRATES: 30g

FAT: 16g
PROTEIN: 5g

1   3 ounce package apricot
    gelatin
⅔ cup sugar
⅔ cup water
1   14 ounce can sweetened
    condensed milk
1   8 ounce package cream
    cheese

2   4½ ounce jars apricot baby
    food
1   10½ ounce can crushed
    pineapple
1   cup chopped pecans

Combine gelatin, sugar and water in saucepan and bring to boil stirring until dissolved. Set aside to cool. Combine condensed milk and cream cheese, beat with electric mixer until smooth. Stir in gelatin mixture, baby food, undrained pineapple and nuts. Pour into 11×7 inch Pyrex dish and refrigerate until set.

Elizabeth Upham

Quick and Easy Salad

YIELD: 8 to 10 servings
CALORIES: 291
CARBOHYDRATES: 26g

FAT: 17g
PROTEIN: 10g

24 ounces cottage cheese
9   ounces whipped dessert
    topping
15½ ounce can crushed
    pineapple
11 ounce can mandarin
    oranges

4   ounce can coconut
½ cup chopped nuts
3   ounce package orange
    gelatin

Drain pineapple and oranges. Add all other ingredients. Do not add water for gelatin. Place in refrigerator for at least 4 hours before serving. Substitute cherry or strawberry gelatin for Christmas.

Belinda Wilkins

Pineapple Banana Salad

YIELD: 12 to 15 servings
CALORIES: 214
CARBOHYDRATES: 32g

FAT: 9g
PROTEIN: 3g

2   3½ ounce packages lemon
    gelatin
½   cup miniature
    marshmallows
4   cups hot water
15½ ounce can crushed
    pineapple
4   bananas, sliced

2   tablespoons flour
2   eggs, beaten
1   cup whipping cream
½   cup sugar
½   cup chopped pecans

Dissolve jello and marshmallows in hot water. Drain pineapple, reserving 1 cup juice. Add pineapple and sliced bananas to jello mixture. Chill until firm. Combine sugar, flour, eggs and reserved pineapple juice and cook until thickened. Cool. Whip cream and fold in cooled mixture and spread over salad. Sprinkle with nuts.

Wanda Bunger

Cranberry Salad

YIELD: 8 to 10 servings
CALORIES: 215
CARBOHYDRATES: 35g

FAT: 8g
PROTEIN: 3g

1   3 ounce package cherry
    jello
1   cup sugar
1   cup boiling water
1   medium orange
rind of ¼ orange
2   cups raw cranberries

1   cup crushed pineapple
1   cup chopped pecans
2   packages Knox gelatin
½   cup water
lemon juice to taste

Mix jello, sugar, and boiling water in saucepan and bring to a boil. Let cool. Grind orange rind and cranberries. Combine jello mixture, ground mixture, pineapple and pecans. Mix well. Add lemon juice to taste. Dissolve gelatin in water and add last. Pour into 2 quart dish and chill. Cut in squares and serve on lettuce leaves.

Mary Jo Mason

This was Mrs. Mason's recipe and is especially good.

Frozen Banana Salad

YIELD: 4 to 6 servings
CALORIES: 169
CARBOHYDRATES: 35g

FAT: 3g
PROTEIN: 1g

1 cup sugar
1 cup buttermilk
1 medium can crushed
   pineapple

3 bananas, mashed
8 ounce package non-dairy
   topping
maraschino cherries, optional

Mix sugar and buttermilk together. Add crushed pineapple and bananas and mix. Stir in topping. Pour into 9×13 inch pan. Freeze, cut into squares or freeze in muffin pan. Garnish with cherry halves if desired.

Jeannine Henderson

Avocado and Ham Salad

YIELD: 8 servings
CALORIES: 989
CARBOHYDRATES: 25g

FAT: 84g
PROTEIN: 421g

1 cup lemon juice
¼ cup water
4 avocados
2 heads red leaf or Boston
   lettuce
3 pounds ham, baked
8 tomatoes, quartered

1 purple onion
1 cup Lemon Vinaigrette
   (recipe follows)
salt and fresh ground pepper
   to taste
¼ cup parsley, chopped

LEMON VINAIGRETTE:
1 cup olive oil
⅔ cup lemon juice
½ cup snipped fresh chives
2 tablespoons finely minced
   shallots

2 tablespoon prepared Dijon
   style mustard
salt and fresh ground pepper
   to taste

Combine all ingredients with seasonings in a covered container and shake well until blended.

Dip avocado slices into the mixture of lemon juice and water, then drain. Line a large serving platter with lettuce leaves. Slice ham into ¼ by 2 inch strips and arrange on platter along with avocados, tomatoes and thinly sliced onion rings in a decorative spiral. Drizzle salad with vinaigrette, salt and pepper and sprinkle with parsley. Serve immediately.

Sandy Baggett

May substitute turkey for ham. Very festive for buffet table.

Mandarin Shrimp Salad

YIELD: 4 servings
CALORIES: 822
CARBOHYDRATES: 31g

FAT: 57g
PROTEIN: 48g

2   11 ounce cans mandarin
    oranges
1½ pounds cooked deveined
    shrimp
1½ cups celery, finely sliced

1   cup salad dressing
1   tablespoon curry powder
2   tablespoons lemon juice
1½ cups broken pecans
Romaine or Belgian endive

Drain oranges, reserving ¼ cup syrup. Mix with shrimp and celery. Into salad dressing stir curry powder, lemon juice, and reserved syrup. Pour dressing over shrimp mixture, toss and refrigerate. Just before serving, add nuts and toss. Serve individually on beds of romaine or endive.

Darla Jones

2 cups crab meat may be substituted for shrimp.

Charlotte Phillip's Salmon and Tuna Spread

YIELD: 2 DOZEN SANDWICHES
CALORIES: 254
CARBOHYDRATES: 32g

FAT: 9g
PROTEIN: 11g

15½ ounce can red salmon
10 ounce can white tuna in
    oil
8   ounce jar pickle relish
3   hard boiled eggs, diced

1   medium onion, minced
salad dressing to mix
lemon juice to mix

Drain salmon and tuna, add other ingredients. Mix well and spread on thin sliced bread, trim off crusts and cut in halves or triangles. Can be served on lettuce leaves.

Benny Gail Hunnicutt

Shrimp Ritz

YIELD: 4 to 6 servings
CALORIES: 298
CARBOHYDRATES: 10g

FAT: 19g
PROTEIN: 18g

1 pound cooked, peeled shrimp, split in half lengthwise
juice of one lemon
black pepper, freshly ground
lettuce leaves
paprika
¼ cup tomato sauce

1 cup mayonnaise
1 celery heart, chopped
½ green bell pepper, minced
1½ tablespoons horseradish
1 clove of garlic, crushed
2 to 3 tablespoons heavy cream
few drops of Tabasco sauce

Place the shrimp in a bowl and sprinkle with lemon juice and pepper. Cover and set aside for 30 minutes. Mix the remaining ingredients except lettuce and paprika. Mix well. Taste and adjust seasonings. Drain the shrimp. Pour sauce over the shrimp. Serve on lettuce leaves and sprinkle with paprika.

Paula Bailey

Seafood does not need salt. Try to avoid adding it.

Hot Chicken Salad

YIELD: 8 to 10 servings
CALORIES: 324
CARBOHYDRATES: 15g

FAT: 22g
PROTEIN: 15g

3 cups cooked, diced chicken breasts
3 hard boiled eggs, finely chopped
2 tablespoons chopped onion
1½ cups finely chopped celery
8 ounce can water chestnuts, sliced
1 cup cooked rice

1 tablespoon lemon juice
¾ cup mayonnaise
10¾ ounce can cream of chicken soup
⅛ teaspoon salt
⅛ teaspoon pepper
1 cup cornflake crumbs
butter
½ cup sliced almonds

Mix all ingredients except last 3 together. Place in a greased 2 quart casserole. Top with cornflake crumbs, dot with bits of butter all over. Sprinkle almonds over top. Bake at 350 degrees until thoroughly heated.

Marilyn Chalmers

Salmon Outrigger

YIELD: 6
CALORIES: 256
CARBOHYDRATES: 6g

FAT: 18g
PROTEIN: 16g

15½ ounce can pink salmon, drained and flaked
1 cup celery slices
½ cup chopped and toasted walnuts or almonds

2 to 3 green onions, sliced
½ cup mayonnaise
1 teaspoon lemon juice
¼ teaspoon dill weed
⅛ teaspoon pepper

Combine mayonnaise, lemon juice, dill weed and pepper. Stir in salmon, celery, nuts, and green onions. Mix lightly and chill. Serve in quartered pineapple shells, leaf lettuce, avocado halves, or cantaloupe halves.

Marilyn Chalmers

Chicken Salad Supreme

YIELD: 8 servings
CALORIES: 411
CARBOHYDRATES: 9g

FAT: 32g
PROTEIN: 20g

2½ cups diced cold cooked chicken
1 cup finely chopped celery
1 cup sliced white grapes
½ cup almonds, shredded and toasted

2 tablespoons minced parsley (optional)
1 teaspoon salt
1 cup mayonnaise
½ cup cream, whipped

Combine ingredients and chill. This can be served in lettuce cups with thin slices of chicken on top or garnished with stuffed olives, sliced thin, or chopped ripe olives.

Nancy Vannoy

Meme's Supper Salad

YIELD: 20 servings
CALORIES: 129
CARBOHYDRATES: 4g

FAT: 10g
PROTEIN: 6g

1   6 ounce package lemon jello
1   cup hot water
½   teaspoon salt
1   tablespoon grated onion
½   cup mayonnaise
½   cup heavy cream
3   hard boiled eggs, sliced
½   pound coarsely grated cheese

1   small can chopped pimiento
1   small chopped green pepper
3   cups chopped celery
5   ounce can tuna, chicken or crab

Mix jello, hot water, salt, onion and let cool. Add mayonnaise, whipped cream, eggs, cheese, pimiento, pepper, celery, and meat. Pour into mold and chill thoroughly.

Jeannine Henderson

Oriental Salad

CALORIES: 247
CARBOHYDRATES: 14g

FAT: 17g
PROTEIN: 8g

2   cups chopped cooked chicken or shrimp
1   can bean sprouts, drained and chilled
1   cup chow-mein noodles

SOY MAYONNAISE:
¾   cup mayonnaise
1   tablespoon lemon juice
1   tablespoon soy sauce

5   ounce can sliced water chestnuts, drained and chilled
¼   cup chopped green onions
¼   cup chopped celery

⅜   teaspoon ground ginger
½   teaspoon Accent

Combine and mix with soy mayonnaise and serve on lettuce leaves.

Susan McMullan

Avocado Dressing

YIELD: 1 cup
CALORIES: 300g
CARBOHYDRATES: 8g

FAT: 30g
PROTEIN: 2g

1   egg
½   teaspoon dry mustard
4   ounces salad oil
½   teaspoon Tabasco Sauce
2   large lemons
1   teaspoon Worcestershire
    Sauce
½   teaspoon salt

½   teaspoon white pepper
2   avocados
3   fresh shallots, minced
garlic to taste
1   ounce anchovy fillets or
    paste
4   ounces mayonnaise
½   teaspoon saffron

Blend egg and mustard, add oil and blend thoroughly. Add Tabasco, juice of lemons, salt and pepper, and remaining ingredients and blend on medium speed. Chill for 2 hours before serving.

Lee Allen

Buttermilk Dressing

YIELD: 8 servings at 2 tablespoons
        per serving
CALORIES: 15

CARBOHYDRATES: 2g
PROTEIN: 1g

1   cup buttermilk
1   tablespoon mayonnaise,
    reduced calorie type
1   tablespoon chopped fresh
    parsley

1   small clove garlic, minced
½   teaspoon dried rosemary
⅛   teaspoon pepper

Place all ingredients in a jar with a tight fitting lid. Shake well for 2 minutes. Refrigerate at least 2 hours before serving. This dressing does not thicken.   Cathy Carson
Calcium rich and best on dark green salads.

Italian Dressing

YIELD: 1¼ cups
CALORIES: 321

FAT: 36g

1   cup salad or olive oil
¼   cup red wine vinegar
1   teaspoon salt
½   teaspoon pepper
½   teaspoon celery salt

¼   teaspoon cayenne
¼   teaspoon dry mustard
1   clove garlic, minced
dash of Tabasco

Combine ingredients in cruet or jar. Shake well and refrigerate. Shake again before serving.   Cathy Carson

Poppy Seed Dressing

YIELD: 2 cups
CALORIES: 125
CARBOHYDRATES: 8g

FAT: 11g

3/4 cup sugar
1 teaspoon salt
1 teaspoon mustard
1/3 cup vinegar

1 tablespoon onion juice
1 cup salad oil
1 teaspoon poppy seeds

Mix together sugar, salt, mustard, vinegar and onion juice. Add the oil gradually, beating constantly. Add poppy seed. Great over fresh fruit.

Jeannine Henderson

Vinaigrette Dressing

YIELD: 1/2 cup
CALORIES: 241

FAT: 27g

1 clove garlic
1 1/2 teaspoons Dijon mustard
2 tablespoons red wine
   vinegar
1/2 cup olive oil

3/4 teaspoon salt
1 tablespoon fresh herbs,
   minced, in season
black pepper, to taste, freshly
   ground

Crush the garlic either in a garlic press or with tines of a fork against a plate. Mix the garlic, mustard and vinegar thoroughly with a fork. Slowly dribble in the oil, drop by drop, stirring constantly so that the dressing will stay creamy and not separate. Season with salt and pepper and the fresh herbs in summertime. For warm vinaigrette, place the mixing bowl of dressing in a pan of simmering water until it has warmed and serve immediately over spinach or favorite greens.

Sandy Baggett

May be made in food processor

Fresh Tomato Vinaigrette

YIELD: 4 cups
CALORIES: 265
CARBOHYDRATES: 7g

FAT: 27g
PROTEIN: 1g

4 large, ripe tomatoes
1 cup basil, chopped or ⅓ cup dried basil
8 tablespoons red wine vinegar

1 cup light olive oil
4 tablespoons Dijon mustard
salt and pepper

Peel, seed and dice the tomatoes. Combine all ingredients in a saucepan and simmer 6 to 8 minutes. Set aside. Spoon warm dressing over salad of tomato and avocado slices on lettuce leaves.

                                                              Lou Deaton

Use with avocado and tomato salad.

Spinach Salad Dressing

YIELD: 1⅓ cups
CALORIES: 349
CARBOHYDRATES: 7g

FAT: 37g

1 cup salad oil
⅓ cup apple cider vinegar
1½ teaspoons salt
3 tablespoons sugar

1 tablespoon Parmesan cheese
¼ teaspoon garlic salt

Mix well in a fruit jar. Shake before using on spinach, red onion, mushrooms, boiled eggs, bacon and sesame seeds.

                                                    Nancy Miller Johnson

Used at the Jones House Restaurant.

Jill Seahorn's Thousand Island Dressing

YIELD: 1¾ quarts
CALORIES: 206
CARBOHYDRATES: 9g

FAT: 17g
PROTEIN: 2g

1   quart mayonnaise
1   cup Velveeta or American cheese
1   large can chopped ripe olives, drained
1½ teaspoons garlic powder

1½ teaspoons paprika
4   tablespoons sugar
½   cup water, optional
½   cup catsup
½   cup grated sweet pickle

Grind all ingredients together except for mayonnaise. Add mayonnaise and mix well. Keeps well.

Jean Read

Is better after sitting 24 hours.

Thousand Island Dressing

YIELD: 1½ cups
CALORIES: 205
CARBOHYDRATES: 7g

FAT: 18g
PROTEIN: 2g

1   cup mayonnaise
2   eggs, hard cooked and chopped
2   tablespoons chopped green pepper
2   tablespoons chopped dill pickles

1½ tablespoons finely minced onion
1   tablespoon paprika
½   teaspoon salt
¼   cup chili sauce

Combine all ingredients. Mix well and store covered in refrigerator.

Cathy Carson

Mayonnaise

YIELD: 2 cups
CALORIES: 245
CARBOHYDRATES:

FAT: 28g

1 egg yolk
juice from ½ lemon
¼ teaspoon cayenne
2 cups vegetable oil

1 teaspoon vinegar
½ teaspoon salt
2 tablespoons boiling water

Start beating egg yolk, lemon juice and cayenne. Slowly add ½ of the oil. Check to see if it's getting thick. Add vinegar and continue beating, adding ¾ of the remaining oil. Add salt and rest of oil, continuing to beat. Then add boiling water which keeps it from turning back to oil.

Susan Slaughter

David West's Mayonnaise

YIELD: 4½ cups
CALORIES: 225

FAT: 25g

6 egg yolks
3 tablespoons vinegar
1½ teaspoons salt
½ teaspoon paprika

½ teaspoon cayenne pepper
1 tablespoon grated onion
4 cups oil

Blend egg yolks and vinegar, add salt, paprika, cayenne and onion with blender running all the while. Slowly add all of the oil. Blend until smooth. If using a food processor, do not use oil dripper as it is too slow and mayonnaise will liquify.

Lockie Sue Bissett

Salad Dressing Plus for Pasta

YIELD: 1 cup
CALORIES: 193
CARBOHYDRATES: 10g

FAT: 18g

½ cup salad oil
½ cup garlic-wine vinegar
¼ cup sugar
1 tablespoon seasoned salt
1 tablespoon lemon juice
pepper to taste

pasta shells, any variety, cooked
tomatoes, chopped
onions, chopped
cucumbers, chopped
fresh mushrooms

Combine the first 6 ingredients and shake well. Store in the refrigerator. Combine remaining ingredients in amounts desired and toss with the dressing.

Carol Hunnicutt

Good on green salads also.

Dressing for Slaw

YIELD: 1 cup
CALORIES: 137
CARBOHYDRATES: 6g

FAT: 12g

¾ cup mayonnaise
3 tablespoons vinegar
½ teaspoon salt
1 tablespoon sugar to taste

½ teaspoon paprika
½ teaspoon pepper
½ teaspoon celery seed

Combine ingredients thoroughly in a blender or with a whisk. Pour over slaw and mix well.

Mary Jo Mason

Diet Mayonnaise

YIELD: 1 cup
CALORIES: 95

FAT: 10g

1 egg
pinch salt
⅛ teaspoon dry mustard
⅛ teaspoon white pepper
dash paprika

2 tablespoons apple cider vinegar
¾ cup safflower oil
garlic and onion powder to taste

Place all ingredients except oil in a blender and blend at high speed for 5 seconds. Add the oil in a slow steady stream. If the mayonnaise becomes too thick add a few extra drops of vinegar. Store in a tightly covered container and chill well.

Ann Childress

Desserts

Windmill — pumping water for a thirsty land.

Apricot Pound Cake

YIELD: 12 to 16 servings
CALORIES: 319
CARBOHYDRATES: 38g

FAT: 17g
PROTEIN: 4g

1   box pound cake mix
1   box apricot or orange
    gelatin
½ cup salad oil

¾ cup canned apricots with
    juice
3   to 4 eggs

Stir the cake mix and the gelatin together. Add the oil and the apricots to the mixture and mix well. Add the eggs one at a time to the mixture beating well after each. Bake in greased and floured layer pans or in a greased and floured loaf pan at 325 degrees for one hour and fifteen minutes. Glaze the cake after it has cooled.

GLAZE:
1   cup powdered sugar   ¼ cup apricot juice

Blend the powdered sugar and the apricot juice together.

Sherry Scott

Almond Cake Squares

YIELD: 20 squares
CALORIES: 216
CARBOHYDRATES: 20g

FAT: 15g
PROTEIN: 3g

3   eggs
1   cup sugar

1   cup flour
1   cup butter, melted

Combine eggs and sugar, beat with electric mixer until thick and lemon colored. Stir in flour and butter. Pour into a greased and floured 9×13 inch pan. Bake at 350 degrees for 30 minutes.

TOPPING
½ cup butter
½ cup sugar
½ cup slivered almonds

1   tablespoon flour
1   tablespoon milk

Combine ingredients in a small saucepan and cook over low heat, stirring constantly until thickened. Spread on cake and broil about 5 minutes or until golden and bubbly.

Mary Hufstedler

Fresh Apple Cake

YIELD: 12 servings
CALORIES: 495
CARBOHYDRATES: 62g

FAT: 27g
PROTEIN: 5g

1	cup cooking oil	1	teaspoon cinnamon
2	cups sugar	½	teaspoon cloves
2	eggs, well beaten	½	teaspoon nutmeg
3	cups flour	2	teaspoons vanilla
1	teaspoon soda	1	cup chopped nuts
½	teaspoon salt	3	cups fresh apples, chopped

Combine the oil and sugar. Add the eggs. Sift dry ingredients together and add to egg mixture. Add remaining ingredients and mix well. Bake in a greased and floured bundt pan at 300 degrees for 55 minutes.

Judy Reagor

Banana Nut Rum Cake

YIELD: 12 servings
CALORIES: 773
CARBOHYDRATES: 85g

FAT: 45g
PROTEIN: 8g

1	cup margarine	¼	cup dark rum
2	cups sugar	1	teaspoon baking soda
2	eggs, beaten	1	teaspoon vanilla
3	ripe bananas, mashed	½	teaspoon lemon extract
2½	cups unsifted flour	1	teaspoon brandy
1	teaspoon cinnamon	1	cup chopped pecans
1	cup buttermilk		

ICING

8	ounces cream cheese, softened	1 pound powdered sugar	
¼	cup margarine	1 cup chopped pecans	
1	teaspoon vanilla		

Cake: Cream margarine and sugar. Add eggs and bananas and beat until well blended. Sift dry ingredients together and add to creamed mixture alternately with buttermilk. Blend well, add brandy, rum and extracts. Beat well and gently stir in the pecans. Pour batter into a well greased and floured bundt pan and bake at 325 degrees for 1 hour or until toothpick inserted into center comes out clean. Cool for 1 hour and ice. Icing: Beat cream cheese and margarine until smooth. Add powdered sugar and vanilla and mix well. Sprinkle pecans over iced cake.

Karen Childress

Brownstone Front Cake

YIELD: 18 to 20 servings
CALORIES: 460
CARBOHYDRATES: 59g

FAT: 24g
PROTEIN: 4g

1 cup buttermilk
1 teaspoon baking soda
1 cup margarine
2 cups sugar
3 egg yolks

2 1 ounce squares chocolate, unsweetened and melted
3 cups cake flour, sifted
½ teaspoon salt
1 teaspoon vanilla
3 egg whites, stiffly beaten

ICING
1 cup margarine
2 cups sugar

1 5⅓ ounce can evaporated milk
1½ teaspoon vanilla

Mix buttermilk and soda together, let stand to expand. Cream margarine and sugar, add egg yolks and chocolate. Mix. Add buttermilk mixture alternately with the sifted dry ingredients. Add vanilla and beat well. Fold in egg whites. Bake in a greased and floured tube pan at 300 degrees for 1 hour. Icing: Combine margarine, sugar and milk in a saucepan. Dissolve over low heat. Bring to a boil and simmer for 45 minutes uncovered. Remove from heat, add vanilla, cool to room temperature, then beat with a wire whip. Do not use electric mixer. Spread on cooled cake. **Ann Childress**

Buttermilk Cake

YIELD: 8 to 12 servings
CALORIES: 451
CARBOHYDRATES: 53g

FAT: 25g
PROTEIN: 5g

2 cups flour
½ teaspoon soda
½ teaspoon baking powder
pinch of salt
1 cup butter
2 cups plus 2½ tablespoons sugar, divided

4 eggs
1 teaspoon vanilla
1 cup buttermilk
1 cup heavy cream

Sift together dry ingredients. Cream butter with 2 cups sugar and add eggs, one at a time, beating until smooth. Add flour mixture alternately with the buttermilk and vanilla. Pour into a 9×13 inch pan and bake at 350 degrees for 45 minutes. Combine cream and remaining sugar in a saucepan and heat but do not let it boil. Pour over warm cake. This cake must be served from the baking dish. Special! **Jane Richardson**

Mother's Mahogany Cake

YIELD: 20 servings
CALORIES: 349
CARBOHYDRATES: 56g

FAT: 14g
PROTEIN: 4g

½ cup cocoa
½ cup hot water
1 teaspoon baking soda
2 cups sugar

¾ cup shortening
2 eggs
1 cup buttermilk
3 cups flour

FROSTING
1½ boxes powdered sugar
6 tablespoons cocoa
6 tablespoons hot coffee

1 egg
1 tablespoon butter or
   margarine

Cake: Mix the first three ingredients and set aside for 30 minutes. Cream the sugar and the shortening, add eggs, one at a time, beating well after each addition. Add the buttermilk alternately with the flour stirring until well blended. Add the cocoa mixture and beat well. Bake in three greased and floured 9-inch layer cake pans at 350 degrees for 25 to 30 minutes. Frosting: Mix all of the ingredients together, beat until smooth. Add more powdered sugar if too thin and cream if too thick. Spread over cooled cake.

Norma Champion Carson

This cake keeps well and is even better a day or two after it has been baked.

Hester's Bohemian Coffee Cake

YIELD: 10 to 20 servings
CALORIES: 549
CARBOHYDRATES: 61g

FAT: 33g
PROTEIN: 5g

2½ cups flour
1 cup vegetable oil
1 cup sugar
1 cup brown sugar
1 cup buttermilk
2 eggs

1 teaspoon soda
1 teaspoon salt
1 can coconut
1 cup chopped pecans
1 tablespoon vanilla

CREAM CHEESE ICING
8 ounces cream cheese, softened
¼ cup margarine

2 teaspoons vanilla
4 cups powdered sugar
1 cup chopped pecans

Cake: Mix all ingredients in the order given, beating well. Bake in a greased, floured tube pan at 350 degrees for 1 hour. Icing: Mix cream cheese, margarine and vanilla well, add powdered sugar until mixture reaches spreading consistancy. Add pecans, stir. When cake has cooled, spread icing over cake.

Helen Bean

Trinity River Mud Cake

YIELD: 20 servings
CALORIES: 516
CARBOHYDRATES: 53g

FAT: 34g
PROTEIN: 6g

4 eggs
2 cups sugar
1 cup margarine,melted
1½ cups flour
⅓ cup cocoa

1 teaspoon vanilla
1 cup coconut
2 cups pecans
7 ounces marshmallow creme

ICING
½ cup margarine
6 tablespoons milk
⅓ cup cocoa

1 pound powdered sugar
1 teaspoon vanilla
2 cups chopped pecans

Cake: Combine eggs and sugar, blend for 5 minutes at high speed. Combine remaining ingredients except the marshmallow creme. Mix well with first two ingredients. Pour into a 9×13 inch greased and floured pan. Bake at 350 degrees for 30 minutes. Remove from oven and spread marshmallow creme on the cake. Let stand for a few minutes then frost while cake is warm. Frosting: Combine all ingredients. Mix well and spread over the marshmallow creme.

Barbara Malone

Mom's Eggnog Cake

YIELD: 12 to 16 servings
CALORIES: 205
CARBOHYDRATES: 28g

FAT: 10g
PROTEIN: 3g

2 cups flour, sifted
1¼ cups sugar
1 teaspoon salt
2 teaspoons baking powder
1 to 2 teaspoons nutmeg

3 eggs
1½ cups whipping cream
2 to 3 teaspoons rum or orange
flavoring

Sift dry ingredients into large bowl. Add eggs, whipping cream and flavoring. Blend for about 30 seconds at low speed of electric mixer. Beat 3 minutes at medium speed. Pour into a greased and floured 9×5-inch loaf pan. Bake at 350 degrees for 60 to 70 minutes. Remove from pan immediately and cool on a rack.

Sherry Scott

Divinity Cake

YIELD: 24 servings
CALORIES: 239
CARBOHYDRATES: 44g

FAT: 6g
PROTEIN: 3g

1½ cups sugar
¾ cup butter
3 eggs, separated
2⅔ cups flour
3 teaspoons baking powder

1 teaspoon baking soda
¼ teaspoon salt
2 cups buttermilk
1 teaspoon vanilla

Cream butter and sugar, add beaten egg yolks. Sift together dry ingredients and add alternately with buttermilk to creamed mixture, beating well. Stir in vanilla. Pour into a greased and floured 9×13 inch pan. Bake at 350 degrees for 30 minutes.

DIVINITY ICING:
3 egg whites
10 tablespoons sugar
½ teaspoon vanilla

1½ cups light corn syrup
¼ teaspoon salt

Beat egg whites until stiff, slowly add 4 tablespoons sugar and the vanilla. Bring to a boil the syrup, 6 tablespoons of sugar and the salt. Count to 15 while mixture boils. Remove from heat and slowly add to egg whites. Beat well and spread on cool cake.

Elizabeth Clark

Chocolate Chip Cake

YIELD: 12 servings
CALORIES: 257
CARBOHYDRATES: 69g

FAT: 17g
PROTEIN: 6g

1 box yellow cake mix
1 3½ ounce box instant chocolate pudding
1 3½ ounce box instant vanilla pudding

5 eggs
1½ cups water
6 or 12 ounce package semi-sweet chocolate chips

Mix all ingredients except chocolate chips. Do not overbeat. Stir in chocolate chips. Bake in a greased and floured tube pan at 350 degrees for 50 to 60 minutes.

Benny Gail Hunnicutt

Four Day Coconut Cake

YIELD: 12 servings
CALORIES: 448
CARBOHYDRATES: 73g

FAT: 16g
PROTEIN: 3g

2 cups sugar
2 cups sour cream
12 ounces frozen coconut

1 butter cake mix
1½ cups frozen whipped topping

The night before baking cake, mix sugar, sour cream, and thawed coconut. Blend well and chill overnight. Prepare cake mix according to package directions. Cool. Split each layer in two. Assemble cake with layers cut side up. Divide and spread sour cream mixture between layers and on top. Frost with thawed whipped topping. Seal cake in airtight container and refrigerate 3 days before serving.

Lockie Sue Bissett

Fresh Coconut Orange Cake

YIELD: 16 servings
CALORIES: 640
CARBOHYDRATES: 77g

FAT: 35g
PROTEIN: 9g

1   cup butter
2   cups sugar
4   egg yolks, well beaten
1   teaspoon orange juice
1   tablespoon orange rind, grated
2½ cups all purpose flour
½   teaspoon soda

¼   teaspoon salt
1   cup buttermilk
¼   teaspoon vanilla
7   stiffly beaten egg whites
1   cup fresh coconut, grated

Cream together butter and sugar. Add egg yolks, orange juice, grated orange rind. Sift together flour, soda and salt. Add alternately with buttermilk and vanilla. Fold in coconut and egg whites. Bake in three 8 inch greased and floured cake pans at 350 degrees for 30 minutes. Cool, then fill between layers and frost with seven minute frosting.

FILLING FOR FRESH COCONUT ORANGE CAKE
1   cup evaporated milk
1   cup sugar
3   egg yolks

½   cup butter
1   teaspoon orange peel, grated
1   cup fresh coconut, grated

Combine first 4 ingredients and cook for 12 minutes until thick. Then add orange rind and coconut. Fill between layers. Cover top and sides with 7 minute frosting.

Tina Bean

Seven Minute Frosting

2   egg whites
1½ cups sugar
¼   teaspoon cream of tartar

⅓   cup water
1½ teaspoons vanilla
¾   cup fresh grated coconut

Combine in top of double boiler: egg whites, sugar, cream of tartar and water. Place over boiling water and beat with rotary beater until mixture holds its shape. Fold in vanilla. Spread on cooled cake and sprinkle top and sides with coconut.

Tina Bean

Rosalie's Chocolate Cake

YIELD: 16 to 20 servings
CALORIES: 402
CARBOHYDRATES: 55g

FAT: 20g
PROTEIN: 4g

2 cups flour	1 cup water
2 cups sugar	2 eggs
1 teaspoon salt	½ cup buttermilk
½ cup cocoa	1 teaspoon soda
½ cup butter	1 teaspoon vanilla
½ cup oil	

Preheat oven to 325 degrees. Combine flour, sugar and salt in a mixing bowl. Combine cocoa, butter, oil and water in a saucepan and bring to a boil. With an electric mixer, beat the dry ingredients while adding the contents of the saucepan. Add remaining ingredients and beat on high until very smooth. Bake in a greased and floured 9×13 inch baking pan for 30 to 35 minutes.

ICING

½ cup butter	1 pound powdered sugar
½ cup cocoa	1 teaspoon vanilla
⅓ cup milk	1 cup chopped pecans

Prepare icing 10 minutes before cake is done. Melt butter, add cocoa and milk. Stir constantly until it boils. Add powdered sugar and vanilla and beat well. Fold in nuts. Ice cake 5 minutes after taking it out of the oven.

Sandy Baggett

Also known as Cocoa Sheath Cake: 1 teaspoon cinnamon can be added.

VARIATION: In place of the cocoa, use 4 tablespoons Nestle's Quick Chocolate Drink Mix in the cake as well as the icing and proceed with the recipe as above. Add 6 tablespoons of buttermilk to the icing in place of the milk.

Shawn Mitchell

Coconut Cream Cheese Pound Cake

YIELD: 14 servings
CALORIES: 528
CARBOHYDRATES: 69g

FAT: 26g
PROTEIN: 7g

½ cup butter or margarine, softened
½ cup shortening
8 ounce package cream cheese, softened
3 cups sugar
6 eggs

3 cups flour
¼ teaspoon baking soda
¼ teaspoon salt
6 ounce package frozen coconut, thawed
1 teaspoon vanilla
1 teaspoon coconut flavoring

Cream margarine, shortening and cream cheese, gradually add sugar, beating at medium speed until light and fluffy. Add eggs one at a time. Combine flour, soda and salt. Add to creamed mixture, stirring just until blended. Stir in coconut and flavorings. Spoon batter into a greased and floured 10 inch tube pan. Bake in an oven preheated to 350 degrees for 1 hour. Cool for 10 to 15 minutes, then remove.

Karen Huffman

Fig Preserve Cake

YIELD: 20 servings
CALORIES: 424
CARBOHYDRATES: 68g

FAT: 13g
PROTEIN: 5g

2½ cups sugar
¾ cup butter
4 eggs
1 cup buttermilk
1 teaspoon baking soda
3 cups flour

2 cups fig preserves
1 teaspoon nutmeg
1 teaspoon cloves
1 teaspoon cinnamon
1 teaspoon vanilla
1 cup nuts

Cream sugar and butter, add well beaten eggs. Mix soda into buttermilk and add gradually to the creamed mixture. Add dry ingredients and mix. Add preserves, vanilla and nuts. Bake in a 10 inch tube pan or two loaf pans at 300 degrees for 1 hour.

ICING
1 cup brown sugar
1 5 ounce can evaporated milk

1 tablespoon margarine
1 tablespoon vanilla

Boil sugar and milk until it reaches the soft ball stage. Add the butter and vanilla. Beat well and spread over cooled cake.

Barbara Malone

Sock-It-To-Me-Cake

YIELD: 12 servings
CALORIES: 512
CARBOHYDRATES: 59g

FAT: 29g
PROTEIN: 5g

1 box All Butter Cake mix
4 eggs
¾ cup buttery flavor oil
1 cup sour cream

½ cup sugar
3 tablespoons brown sugar
2 teaspoons cinnamon
½ cup chopped nuts

Mix together cake mix, eggs, oil, sour cream and sugar. Mix brown sugar, cinnamon, and nuts separately. Layer batter, then cinnamon mixture, 3 times and bake in a greased and floured bundt pan at 350 degrees for 1 hour.

GLAZE:
1 cup powdered sugar
2 tablespoons butter

3 tablespoons milk

Glaze: mix ingredients together and pour over warm cake.

Sandy Baggett

Girdle Buster Cake

YIELD: 20 servings
CALORIES: 280
CARBOHYDRATES: 32g

FAT: 16g
PROTEIN: 3g

1 box Duncan Hines Butter cake mix
4 eggs
½ cup margarine, melted

1 8 ounce package cream cheese, softened
1 box powdered sugar
1 cup chopped pecans

Mix the cake mix, 2 eggs and margarine. Pat out in greased and floured 9×13 inch pan. Mix the cream cheese, 2 eggs and powdered sugar. Pour over the first mixture in the pan. Sprinkle top with chopped pecans. Bake at 350 degrees for 45 minutes.

Barbara Malone

Easy Amaretto Cake

YIELD: 12 servings
CALORIES: 448
CARBOHYDRATES: 55g

FAT: 19g
PROTEIN: 5g

1½ cups chopped pecans
1 yellow cake mix, not pudding type
1 3½ ounce package vanilla instant pudding mix
4 eggs
½ cup oil

½ cup amaretto
1 teaspoon almond extract
½ cup sugar
¼ cup water
2 tablespoons margarine
¼ cup amaretto
½ teaspoon almond extract

Sprinkle 1 cup pecans into the bottom of a well greased and floured 10 inch tube pan and set aside. Combine next 6 ingredients in a mixing bowl and beat on low speed until dry ingredients are moistened. Beat for 4 minutes at medium speed. Stir in remaining nuts and pour batter into the prepared pan. Bake at 325 degrees for 1 hour. Cool cake in baking pan for 10 minutes. Remove to serving plate and cool completely. For glaze, combine sugar and ¼ cup water and margarine in a small pan. Bring to a boil, reduce heat and boil until sugar dissolves. Remove from heat and cool for 15 minutes. Stir in amaretto and extract. Poke holes in top of cake with a wooden pick and slowly spoon glaze over cake, allowing it to absorb into the crust of cake.

Barbara Malone

Harvey Wallbanger Cake

YIELD: 18 servings
CALORIES: 179
CARBOHYDRATES: 38g

FAT: 4g
PROTEIN: 4g

1   box orange supreme cake
    mix
1   3 ounce package instant
    vanilla pudding mix
4   ounce frozen orange juice
    concentrate, thawed

½   cup water
4   eggs
3   ounces Galliano
1   ounce Vodka or white rum

Mix all ingredients in large mixer bowl for 5 minutes at medium speed. Pour into a greased and floured tube pan. Bake at 350 degrees for 40 to 55 minutes. Cool in pan 15 minutes before removing.

GLAZE:
1   cup powdered sugar
1   ounce orange juice
    concentrate

1½ tablespoons Galliano
1   tablespoon Vodka or white
    rum

Blend ingredients together and spread over top of cake.

Lisa Wagoner

Freezes well.

Baptist Pound Cake

YIELD: 20 servings
CALORIES: 277
CARBOHYDRATES: 42g

FAT: 11g
PROTEIN: 3g

3   cups cake flour
½   teaspoon baking powder
3   cups sugar
½   teaspoon salt
5   eggs, room temperature

1   cup milk
1   teaspoon vanilla
1   cup butter, room
    temperature

Sift the dry ingredients in a large mixing bowl. Add all other ingredients and mix well. Pour into a greased and floured 10 inch tube pan. Bake at 325 degrees for 1 hour and 20 minutes.

Ann Mayfield Murrah

Serve with fruit and whipped cream

Kahlua Cake

YIELD: 15 servings
CALORIES: 616
CARBOHYDRATES: 63g

FAT: 43g
PROTEIN: 8g

18 ounce box white or yellow cake mix
3½ ounce box vanilla instant pudding
¾ cup oil

1 cup water
¼ cup Kahlua
1 teaspoon vanilla
1 teaspoon instant coffee
4 eggs, separated

Combine cake mix, pudding mix, oil, water, Kahlua, vanilla, instant coffee and egg yolks. Beat 4 minutes. Fold in stiffly beaten egg whites. Pour batter into 3 greased and floured cake pans. Bake at 350 degrees for 30 to 40 minutes.

ICING:
2 cups whipping cream
1 to 2 tablespoons sugar
1 to 2 tablsepoons Kahlua

1 tablespoon vanilla
shaved chocolate
slivered almonds

Whip the cream. Add the sugar, Kahlua, and vanilla, mixing well. Ice the cake and garnish with chocolate and almonds. Chill the cake 30 to 45 minutes before serving.

Virginia Henderson Howell

Sherry Cake

YIELD: 18 to 20 slices
CALORIES: 263
CARBOHYDRATES: 26g

FAT: 16g
PROTEIN: 3g

1 cup chopped pecans
1 18½ ounce box yellow cake mix
1 3¾ ounce package vanilla instant pudding mix

4 eggs
½ cup cold water
½ cup oil
½ cup sherry

Preheat oven to 325 degrees. Grease and flour 12 cup bundt pan. Sprinkle pecans over bottom of pan. Mix all cake ingredients together and pour over nuts. Bake 1 hour.

GLAZE:
¼ cup butter
⅛ cup water

½ cup sugar
¼ cup sherry

Melt butter in saucepan, stir in water and sugar. Boil 5 minutes, stirring constantly. Remove from heat and stir in sherry. Brush on warm cake.

Benny Gail Hunnicutt

Also may be made using rum.

Buttermilk Pound Cake

YIELD: 20 servings
CALORIES: 285
CARBOHYDRATES: 42g

FAT: 12g
PROTEIN: 3g

1 cup vegetable shortening
3 cups sugar
6 eggs
3 cups cake flour

½ teaspoon salt
¼ teaspoon baking soda
1 cup buttermilk
2 teaspoons orange extract

Cream the shortening and sugar until fluffy. Add the eggs, one at a time, beating well after each. Combine the dry ingredients and add alternately with the buttermilk to the creamed mixture. Add the extract and mix. Pour the batter into a large tube pan that has been lined on the bottom with waxed paper. Bake at 350 degrees for 1 hour or until cake tests done with a wooden pick. Cool in the pan for 15 minutes. Invert onto a serving plate.

Luann Pierce

Plum Jam Cake

YIELD: 20 servings
CALORIES: 290
CARBOHYDRATES: 34g

FAT: 16g
PROTEIN: 4g

1 cup margarine
1 cup sugar
1 cup buttermilk
⅔ cup plum jam
3 eggs
1 tablespoon allspice
1 teaspoon cloves

½ teaspoon nutmeg
1 teaspoon cinnamon
1 teaspoon baking soda
3 cups flour
1 cup chopped pecans
1 cup coconut

Cream margarine and sugar. Add eggs and jams. Dissolve soda in buttermilk, Combine dry ingredients, and add alternately. Add the pecans and coconut. Stir well. Pour into a greased and floured tube pan. Bake at 350 degrees for one hour.

Barbara Malone

Red Velvet Pound Cake

YIELD: 18
CALORIES: 523
CARBOHYDRATES: 64g

FAT: 29g
PROTEIN: 5g

1 cup softened butter
½ cup shortening
3 cups sugar
7 eggs
2 teaspoons vanilla
1 ounce bottle red food coloring

1 cup milk
3 cups cake flour
2 tablespoons cocoa
½ teaspoon baking powder
¼ teaspoon salt

ICING:
½ cup butter
2 3 ounce packages cream cheese, softened

1 teaspoon vanilla
1 pound powdered sugar
1 to 2 tablespoons milk

Cream butter, shortening and sugar. Add eggs one at a time, beating well. Stir in vanilla and food coloring. Sift flour, cocoa, baking powder and salt. Add alternately with milk to creamed mixture. Pour into greased and floured tube pan. Bake at 325 degrees for 1 hour and 20 minutes. Cool completely. Icing: Mix all ingredients until easy to spread. Ice cooled cake.

Jann Miller

Million Dollar Pound Cake

YIELD: 20 servings
CALORIES: 399
CARBOHYDRATES: 50g

FAT: 21g
PROTEIN: 5g

3 cups sugar
1 pound butter
6 eggs
¾ cup milk
4 cups flour

¾ teaspoon baking powder
1 teaspoon vanilla
1 teaspoon lemon or almond extract

Cream the sugar and butter until fluffy. Add the eggs, one at a time, beating well after each. Add the milk and flour alternately to the creamed mixture. Fold in the baking powder, vanilla and extracts. Pour into a greased and floured tube pan. Bake at 300 degrees for 1 hour and 40 minutes.

Belinda Wilkins

Potato Cake

YIELD: 14 servings
CALORIES: 808
CARBOHYDRATES: 94g

FAT: 50g
PROTEIN: 8g

4 eggs,beaten
1 cup butter
1 cup mashed potatoes
2 teaspoons baking powder
½ teaspoon cloves
½ teaspoon nutmeg

¾ cup cocoa
½ cup milk
2 cups sugar
2 cups flour
1 cup pecans, chopped
½ tsp. cinnamon

Mix all ingredients well. Pour into a greased and floured tube pan. Bake at 350 degrees for 45 minutes or until it tests done.

Teri Jackson

Cream Cheese Pound Cake

YIELD: 20 servings
CALORIES: 389
CARBOHYDRATES: 47g

FAT: 21g
PROTEIN: 5g

1   cup margarine, softened
½   cup butter, softened
1   8 ounce package cream
    cheese, softened
3   cups sugar

¼   teaspoon salt
2   teaspoons vanilla
6   large eggs
3   cups cake flour

Combine margarine, sugar, butter and cream cheese and beat well. Add salt and vanilla. Add eggs one at a time, then flour, and mix well. Pour batter into a greased and floured 10 inch tube pan. Place in a cold oven and set at 275 degrees. Bake for 1½ hours, remove from oven and cool in the pan. Glaze when cool if desired.

Tina Bean

This would be good with mid-morning coffee.

Praline Cake

YIELD: 12 servings
CALORIES: 254
CARBOHYDRATES: 31g

FAT: 14g
PROTEIN: 3g

2   eggs
1   cup sugar
1   cup cake flour
1   teaspoon baking powder

¼   teaspoon salt
½   cup milk, scalded
2   tablespoons butter

Beat eggs well, add sugar slowly until well mixed. Sift flour, baking powder and salt, add to the egg mixture, beating well. Scald milk and butter, add and mix well. Pour into a greased and floured 9×9 inch pan. Bake at 350 degrees preheated oven for 30 minutes.

ICING:
5   tablespoons brown sugar
3   tablespoons butter

2   tablespoons cream
1   cup chopped pecans

Melt brown sugar, butter, and cream. Sprinkle coarsely chopped pecans on cake, then cover with sugar mixture. Place under broiler for a few minutes. Do not burn pecans.

Shawn Mitchell

Very Quick, my grandmother baked this in her new range 50 years ago.

Hubbard Pound Cake

YIELD: 14 servings
CALORIES: 207
CARBOHYDRATES: 28g

FAT: 9g
PROTEIN: 4g

1   cup margarine
2   cups sugar
5   eggs

2   cups flour
1   teaspoon lemon flavoring
1   teaspoon vanilla

Cream margarine and sugar. Add eggs one at a time, beating well after each. Batter will be very creamy. Beat in flour, a little at a time. Add flavorings. Pour into a greased and floured tube pan. Place in cold oven. Turn oven to 350 degrees and bake for 1 hour. Test for doneness.

Sherry Scott

Very easy, freezes well. There is no liquid in this cake.

Oatmeal Cake

YIELD: 12 servings
CALORIES: 496
CARBOHYDRATES: 61g

FAT: 28g
PROTEIN: 4g

1¼ cups boiling water
½ cup margarine
1   cup oatmeal
1   cup sugar
1   cup brown sugar

1¼ cups flour
2   eggs
1   teaspoon soda
1   teaspoon cinnamon

Combine boiling water, margarine and oatmeal and let stand 20 minutes. Add to this mixture, sugar, flour and eggs with soda and cinnamon. Pour into a greased and floured 9 × 13 inch baking pan and bake at 350 degrees for 35 minutes.

ICING:
½ cup margarine
¼ cup cream
¾ cup sugar

1   teaspoon vanilla
1   cup coconut
1   cup pecans

Mix margarine, milk and sugar in a saucepan and bring to a boil over medium heat. Stir in vanilla, coconut and pecans. Spread over cake in pan and place under the broiler for 1 minute.

Barbara Malone

This is a very easy and nutritious cake.

Orange Slice Cake

YIELD: 20 slices
CALORIES: 609
CARBOHYDRATES: 77g

FAT: 32g
PROTEIN: 7g

2 cups sugar
1 cup butter or margarine
4 eggs, separated
1 teaspoon baking soda
1½ cups buttermilk

4 cups sifted flour
3 to 4 cups chopped pecans
1 1 pound bag orange slice
candy

Separate eggs, beat egg whites stiff and reserve. Add soda to buttermilk. Cream butter and sugar, add beaten egg yolks. Add buttermilk alternately with flour. Add pecan and chopped orange slice candy. Fold in egg whites. Pour into a greased and floured tube pan. Bake at 300 degrees for 1½ hours.

GLAZE:
½ cup butter
1⅓ cups sugar

⅔ cup orange juice

Heat mixture until sugar is dissolved. Do not boil. Pour over cake slowly.

Teri Jackson

Freezes well.

7-UP Pound Cake

YIELD: 20 servings
CALORIES: 337
CARBOHYDRATES: 46g

FAT: 16g
PROTEIN: 4g

3 cups sugar
½ cup shortening
1 cup margarine
5 eggs
3 cups flour

10 ounces 7-Up
3 teaspoons vanilla
1 teaspoon almond or lemon
extract

Cream the sugar, shortening and margarine. Add eggs one at a time beating well after each. Add flour alternately with the 7-Up. Add the flavorings and bake in a greased and floured tube pan for 1 hour and 20 minutes at 350 degrees.

Helen Bean

An excellent cake to freeze.

Alleane's Rum Cake

YIELD: 12
CALORIES: 489
CARBOHYDRATES: 73g

FAT: 20g
PROTEIN: 6g

1 cup shortening	3 cups flour
2 cups sugar	½ teaspoon baking powder
1 teaspoon rum extract	½ teaspoon salt
1 teapoon lemon extract	½ teaspoon soda
4 eggs	1 cup plus 2 tablespoons buttermilk

Cream the shortening and sugar well. Add the lemon and rum extracts to the creamed mixture. Add the eggs to the mixture one at a time, beating well after each addition. Add the flour, baking powder and salt to the mixture and beat well. Mix the soda with the buttermilk and then add to the mixture, beating well. Pour into a greased and floured tube pan and bake at 325 degrees for one hour and ten minutes. Do not open oven during the cooking time.

GLAZE:
1 cup sugar
½ cup water

1 tablespoon butter or margarine
1 teaspoon rum extract

Bring the sugar and the water to a rolling boil. Add the butter and the rum extract to the sugar and water mixture. Pour this glaze over the cake as soon as it comes out of the oven.

Helen Bean

Fruitcake

YIELD: 4 loaves-45 slices
CALORIES: 194
CARBOHYDRATES: 22g

FAT: 12g
PROTEIN: 2g

1 pound candied cherries	1 cup flour
1 pound candied pineapple	4 eggs
1 pound dates	½ cup orange or pineapple juice
1 cup flour	1 teaspoon salt
8 cups pecans	
1 cup sugar	

Cut up fruits, mix with pecans and sprinkle with 1 cup flour and salt mixed. Mix batter of the next 4 ingredients. Pour over fruit and mix well. Pour into 4 greased and wax paper-lined loaf pans. Place a pan of water on bottom shelf of oven. Bake at 200 degrees for 4 hours.

Tammy Bunger

Mahogany Pound Cake

YIELD: 12 to 16 servings
CALORIES: 537
CARBOHYDRATES: 74g

FAT: 25g
PROTEIN: 6g

2½ cups flour
½ cup cocoa
1 cup butter, softened
2 cups sugar
1 cup brown sugar

6 eggs, separated
1 teaspoon vanilla
1 cup sour cream
¼ teaspoon baking soda

Sift together flour and cocoa; set aside. In large mixer bowl, combine butter and sugars and beat until light and fluffy. Add egg yolks, one at a time, beating well after each addition. Stir in vanilla. Combine sour cream and baking soda and add to creamed mixture alternately with dry ingredients. Beat egg whites until stiff; fold into batter. Pour batter into a well-greased and floured tube pan. Bake at 325 degrees for 1½ hours or until a toothpick inserted into center of cake comes out clean. Cool slightly and remove from pan. Dust with powdered sugar.

Sherry Scott

Coconut Sour Cream Cake

YIELD: 12 servings
CALORIES: 443
CARBOHYDRATES: 62g

FAT: 20g
PROTEIN: 6g

1 box white cake mix
1 cup sour cream
3 eggs

ICING
1 8 ounce package cream cheese
1 1 pound box powdered sugar

1 9½ ounce can cream of coconut
¼ cup cold water

1 teaspoon vanilla
1 teaspoon milk

Mix ingredients together on medium speed with the electric mixer until smooth. Pour into a greased 9 × 13 inch pan Bake at 350 degrees for 50 to 55 minutes. ICING: soften cream cheese and then beat until fluffy. Beat in the sugar until smooth. Add the vanilla and milk and mix well. Spread on cooled cake. Sprinkle with grated coconut, if desired.

May Lay

Pina Colada Cake

YIELD: 16 to 18 servings
CALORIES: 414
CARBOHYDRATES: 47g

FAT: 25g
PROTEIN: 5g

1 box white cake mix
½ cup oil
½ cup pineapple juice

2 cups cream of coconut
1 cup sour cream
3 eggs

Mix in order given, beat 4 minutes and pour into 3 well greased and floured cake pans. Bake at 325 degrees for 30 minutes; or bake in 9×13 inch pan for 45 minutes.

ICING

1 8 ounce package cream cheese
2 tablespoons milk
1 teaspoon vanilla

1 box powdered sugar
½ cup flaked coconut, or fresh

Soften cream cheese, mix with sugar, vanilla and milk. Beat well. Add coconut. Spread between layers, sides and top. Top may also be sprinkled with coconut.

Barbara Malone

Vanilla Wafer Cake

YIELD: 20 servings
CALORIES: 287
CARBOHYDRATES: 29g

FAT: 18g
PROTEIN: 3g

2 cups sugar
1 cup butter or margarine
6 eggs
1 12 ounce box vanilla wafers, crushed

½ cup milk
7 ounces flaked coconut
1 cup pecans

Cream margarine and sugar. Add eggs one at a time beating well after each. Add vanilla wafers and milk. Beat well. Add coconut and pecans. Pour into a greased and floured 10 inch tube pan. Bake for 1 hour and 15 minutes at 275 degrees.

Barbara Malone

Hummingbird Cake

YIELD: 16 servings
CALORIES: 573
CARBOHYDRATES: 62g

FAT: 22g
PROTEIN: 4g

3 cups flour
2 cups sugar
1 teaspoon salt
1 teaspoon cinnamon
1 teaspoon baking soda
3 eggs, beaten

1 cup salad oil
1½ teaspoons vanilla
1 8 ounce can crushed
  pineapple
1 cup chopped pecans
2 chopped bananas

Combine flour, sugar, salt, cinnamon and soda. Add eggs and salad oil and stir until moistened. Do not overbeat. Stir in vanilla, pineapple, pecans and bananas. Pour batter into three well greased and floured cake pans. Bake at 350 degrees for 25 to 30 minutes or until cake tests done. Cool in pans for 10 minutes, remove from pans and cool thoroughly.

ICING
4½ ounces cream cheese,
  softened
1 cup butter or margarine,
  softened

1½ pounds powdered sugar
2 teaspoons vanilla

Blend cream cheese, butter and cream until smooth. Add the powdered sugar and beat until light and fluffy. Stir in vanilla and spread over cooled cake layers and on sides.

Karen Huffman

Chocolate Icing

YIELD: 2½ cups or 20 servings
CALORIES: 94g
CARBOHYDRATES: 14g

FAT: 5g

6 tablespoons butter or
  margarine
⅓ cup evaporated milk
1 teaspoon vanilla

2⅔ cups powdered sugar
Cocoa: ⅓ cup for light flavor
  ½ cup for medium
  flavor
  ¾ cup for rich flavor

Cream the butter, add cocoa and powdered sugar alternately with milk. Beat to spreading consistency. Add additional milk if you desire a thinner icing. Blend in vanilla.

Karen Childress

Chocolate Icing

YIELD: 20 servings
CALORIES: 90
CARBOHYDRATES: 13g

FAT: 5g

1 pound box powdered
  sugar, sifted
¼ cup butter

2 tablespoons cocoa
1 teaspoon vanilla
whipping cream

Melt butter with the cocoa. Add the sugar and beat. Add the vanilla and enough whipping cream to make it the consistency you want. Beat well. Spread on cake.

Jane Richardson

Creamy Cake Icing

YIELD: 20 servings
CALORIES: 190
CARBOHYDRATES: 27g

FAT: 10g

2 cups sugar
½ cup butter or margarine
½ cup light corn syrup

½ cup half and half
1 tablespoon vanilla
1 cup chopped pecans

Mix sugar, butter, syrup and cream. Boil to soft ball stage or 238 degrees on candy thermometer. Cool. Add vanilla and pecans. Beat until slightly creamy and spread on cake.

Helen Bean

This is good on plain cakes

Vanilla Glaze

YIELD: 20 servings
CALORIES: 85
CARBOHYDRATES: 11g

FAT: 5g

½ cup buttermilk
1 cup sugar
1 tablespoon corn syrup

½ cup margarine
½ teaspoon baking soda
½ teaspoon vanilla

Combine first 5 ingredients in a saucepan. Stir slowly until mixture comes to a boil and let boil for about 3 minutes. Remove from heat and add vanilla. Pour over cake while glaze is warm.

Tina Bean

Deluxe Cheesecake

YIELD: 8 servings
CALORIES: 715
CARBOHYDRATES: 53g

FAT: 52g
PROTEIN: 12g

CRUST:
1 package graham crackers, crushed
½ cup butter, melted

¼ cup sugar
¼ teaspoon cinnamon

Mix all ingredients together until moistened. Press into 10 inch spring form pan. Bake at 375 degrees for 5 minutes. Cool.

FILLING:
24 ounces cream cheese, softened
1 cup sugar

4 eggs
1 teaspoon vanilla

Beat cream cheese until fluffy. Add sugar and beat until smooth. Add eggs one at a time beating well after each. Stir in vanilla. Pour over crust. Bake at 350 degrees for 50 to 55 minutes or until it tests done.

TOPPING:
2 cups sour cream
2 tablespoons sugar

1 teaspoon vanilla

Mix all ingredients together by hand. Spread over baked cheesecake, then place in oven for 5 minutes. Remove from oven. Cool well before cutting. Flavor actually improves if refrigerated overnight before serving.

Karen Huffman

May top with your favorite glaze.

Creamy Cheesecake with Blueberry Topping

YIELD: 12 servings
CALORIES: 593
CARBOHYDRATES: 53g

FAT: 40g
PROTEIN: 8g

CRUST

16 graham crackers, crushed
2 tablespoons sugar

6 tablespoons melted butter
1½ teaspoons cinnamon

Mix all ingredients and press into a large and deep spring-form pie pan. Refrigerate until ready to fill.

CHEESE CAKE

3 8 ounce packages cream cheese
3 eggs
1 cup sugar

1½ pints sour cream
3 tablespoons sugar

Beat cream cheese until soft. Beat eggs in another bowl until fluffy. Add sugar to eggs gradually. Beat until pale yellow color and smooth, about 10 minutes. Combine cheese and egg mixtures and mix thoroughly. Pour into crust and bake at 375 degrees for 20 to 30 minutes. Remove from oven and while hot pour sour cream mixed with sugar over top. Bake at 500 degrees for 3 to 5 minutes with a cookie sheet placed underneath.

TOPPING

1 16 ounce can blueberries, drained, reserve liquid
¼ cup plus 2 tablespoons cornstarch

liquid from blueberries, plus water to make one cup
1 cup sugar

Make a paste of corn starch and 2 tablespoon of juice. Add remaining juice and sugar. Cook until thick, about 10 minutes, on medium heat. After juice cools, add berries. Spoon carefully on top of cheese cake and chill overnight.

Sandy Baggett

This is a New York style cheese cake, very rich and delicious.

David's Cherry Cheesecake

YIELD: 12 servings
CALORIES: 430
CARBOHYDRATES: 57g

FAT: 21g
PROTEIN: 4g

CRUST
1½ cups flour
2 tablespoons sugar

1½ sticks plus 1 teaspoon
  margarine
¾ cup Rice Krispies

Combine first 3 ingredients with a pastry cutter or in a blender. Add cereal and stir. Pat into a Pyrex dish and bake at 350 degrees for 20 minutes. Let cool.

FILLING
1 8 ounce package cream
  cheese
2 cups powdered sugar

2 packages non-dairy
  whipped topping
2 cans cherry pie filling

Combine cream cheese and powdered sugar and beat until smooth. Fold in whipped topping. Pour into cooled crust, top with cherry pie filling. Chill.

Helen Bean

Gail's Quick Cheesecake

YIELD: 6 servings
CALORIES: 344
CARBOHYDRATES: 41g

FAT: 18g
PROTEIN: 8g

8 ounces cream cheese
1 cup sweetened condensed
  milk
⅓ cup lemon juice

1 teaspoon vanilla
graham cracker pie shell
1 cup cherry pie filling

Mix first four ingredients listed and pour into a graham cracker pie shell. Chill at least 2 hours. Top with cherry pie filling. Blueberry or strawberry filling can be substituted.

Benny Gail Hunnicutt

Fresh Strawberry Cheesecake

YIELD: 16 servings
CALORIES: 504
CARBOHYDRATES: 52g

FAT: 31g
PROTEIN: 7g

FILLING:
32 ounces cream cheese
1½ cups sugar
8 ounces sour cream

4 eggs
3 teaspoons vanilla
1½ teaspoons almond extract

CRUST:
2¼ cups graham cracker
    crumbs

¾ cup sugar
½ cup margarine

TOPPING AND GLAZE:
1 cup sliced fresh
   strawberries

2 tablespoons orange juice
8 ounces apricot preserves

Filling: With electric mixer, blend cream cheese. Slowly add sugar until well blended. Then mix in sour cream and eggs one at a time. Mix in extracts. Chill while preparing crust. Crust: Mix crumbs and sugar, add margarine and blend. Grease the rim of a spring form pan. Place crumb mixture in pan and press firmly into the bottom and up the sides. Fill with chilled filling. Bake at 350 degrees for 50 to 55 minutes until golden brown or until knife inserted into the center comes out clean. Let cool for about 30 minutes before glazing. Topping: Place strawberry slices on top and sides of cake. Bring orange juice and preserves to a boil. Cool and pour over strawberries on the cake.

Carmen Sutton

Stefny Sutton won 4-H district food show in the Dessert Division with this recipe.

Cherry Cream Cheese Muffins

YIELD: 24
CALORIES: 158
CARBOHYDRATES: 21g

FAT: 8g
PROTEIN: 2g

2 8 ounce packages cream
   cheese, softened
¾ cup sugar
2 large eggs

1 teaspoon vanilla
1 16 ounce can cherry pie
   filling
24 vanilla wafers

Beat cream cheese and sugar together until well mixed. Add eggs, one at a time and beat well. Add vanilla and beat until light and fluffy. Place liners in muffin pans. Put a vanilla wafer in the bottom of each. Fill ¾ full of creamed mixture. Bake in a 350 degree oven for 15 minutes. Cool completely. Top each muffin with a little of the cherry pie filling.

Nancy Miller Johnson

Cherry Pie Supreme

YIELD: 8 to 12 servings
CALORIES: 280
CARBOHYDRATES: 24g

FAT: 19g
PROTEIN: 5g

9   inch pie shell, unbaked
1   22 ounce can cherry pie
    filling
12 ounces cream cheese,
    softened

½   cup sugar
2   eggs
½   teaspoon vanilla
1   cup sour cream

Preheat oven to 425 degrees. Spread half of the pie filling in bottom of pie shell. Save remaining filling. Bake for approximately 15 minutes. Crust should be golden brown. Reduce oven temperature to 350 degrees. Cream the cheese with sugar, eggs and vanilla until smooth. Pour over hot cherry pie filling and bake for 25 minutes. (Filling will be slightly soft in center) Cool completely on a wire rack, spread sour cream on top of pie and spoon pie filling in center. Chill.

Sherry Scott

Blueberry pie filling may be substituted.

Tassos Praline Cheesecake

YIELD: 10 to 12 servings
CALORIES: 468
CARBOHYDRATES: 41g

FAT: 32g
PROTEIN: 7g

1   cup graham cracker crumbs
3   tablespoons sugar
3   tablespoons melted butter
24   ounces cream cheese, at
     room temperature
1½   cups brown sugar, packed

3   eggs
1½   teaspoons vanilla
½   cup chopped pecans
maple syrup
whole pecans for garnish

Combine the crumbs, sugar and butter and press into bottom of a spring form pan. Bake at 350 degrees for 10 minutes. Combine the cream cheese and brown sugar. Beat at medium speed until well blended. Add the eggs, one at a time, beating well after each. Blend in vanilla and pecans. Bake at 350 degrees for 50 to 55 minutes. Loosen the rim of pan and cool at room temperature before removing. Chill, brush top of cheesecake with maple syrup and garnish with pecan halves.

The Barn Door Restaurant, San Antonio, Texas

Buttermilk Pie

YIELD: 8 servings
CALORIES: 391
CARBOHYDRATES: 46g

FAT: 22g
PROTEIN: 5g

1 9 inch pie shell, unbaked	3 eggs, beaten
½ cup softened butter	1 cup buttermilk
1¼ cups sugar	1 teaspoon vanilla
3 rounded tablespoons flour	¼ teaspoon nutmeg

Preheat oven to 350 degrees. Cream butter and sugar well, add flour and beaten eggs. Stir in buttermilk and vanilla. Pour into pie shell. Sprinkle with nutmeg. Bake 40 to 50 minutes or until knife inserted in center comes out clean.

Sue Arledge

VARIATION: Mix 3¾ cup sugar, ½ cup flour and 4 tablespoons powdered buttermilk. Pour into 1 cup less 1 tablespoon melted butter. Add 6 eggs, 1½ teaspoons vanilla and 1 cup of water. Beat well and pour into 2 unbaked pie shells. Continue as above.

Kay Stewart

VARIATION: Increase the sugar to 3 cups, decrease flour to 2 tablespoons, increase eggs to 6, add a dash of salt and and omit nutmeg. Beat the eggs until fluffy. Add the sugar and flour, beating well. Add the buttermilk, butter, salt and 1 tablespoon vanilla, beating continuously to keep mixture from separating. Bake at 400 degrees for 10 minutes, then at 350 degrees for 20 minutes.

Janie Chandler

Chocolate-Coconut Cream Pie

YIELD: 8 to 10 servings
CALORIES: 533
CARBOHYDRATES: 60g

FAT: 34g
PROTEIN: 6g

CRUST
2   ounces unsweetened
    chocolate
2   tablespoons butter or
    margarine

2   tablespoons hot milk or
    water
⅔   cup sifted powdered sugar
1½ cups coconut

Melt chocolate and butter in double boiler. Combine hot milk and sugar, stir into first mixture. Add coconut and stir. Press into bottom and sides of a 9 inch pie pan and refrigerate.

FILLING:
24 large marshmallows
½   cup milk
1   ounce unsweetened
    chocolate

1   cup heavy cream
additional chocolate for
    garnish

FILLING: Melt marshmallows in milk and stir well. Cool. Chip chocolate. Whip the cream, add to cold marshmallow mixture. Then add chipped chocolate. Pour into prepared crust and top with chipped chocolate or chocolate curls. Refrigerate 4 hours or more before serving.

Sherry Scott

Better made a day earlier.

Coconut Cream Pie

YIELD: 6 to 8 servings
CALORIES: 466
CARBOHYDRATES: 59g

FAT: 22g
PROTEIN: 9g

½ cup flour
1 cup sugar
⅜ teaspoon salt
3 cups milk

5 egg yolks, beaten
3 tablespoons margarine
¾ teaspoon vanilla
1 3½ ounce can coconut

MERINGUE:
5 egg whites
9 tablespoons sugar

1 baked pie shell

In a saucepan, mix flour, sugar and salt, gradually add milk. Stirring constantly, cook over moderate heat until mixture thickens, cook two minutes. Remove from heat. Add a small amount of hot mixture to beaten egg yolks. Add egg mixture to the hot mixture, cook one minute more. Remove from heat, stir in butter and vanilla. Cool slightly. Add ½ can coconut to filling. Pour into baked pie shell.

Beat egg whites until stiff but not dry. Add sugar, 1 tablespoon at a time. Cover pie with meringue. Sprinkle with remaining coconut. Bake at 350 degrees for 15 to 20 minutes.

Jeannine Henderson

To make into chocolate cream pie, add ⅓ cup more sugar and 4 tablespoons cocoa and leave out the coconut.

Pineapple Coconut Pie

YIELD: 8 servings
CALORIES: 438
CARBOHYDRATES: 54g

FAT: 25g
PROTEIN: 4g

5 eggs, slightly beaten
3 cups sugar
2 tablespoons flour
2 cups flaked coconut

2 pound can pineapple, crushed
1 cup margarine, melted
2 unbaked pie crusts

Add sugar to slightly beaten eggs, then add flour, coconut, pineapple and margarine. Mix well and pour into unbaked pie crusts. Bake at 350 degrees for 45 minutes.

Teri Jackson

Elfreda's Apple Pie

YIELD: 8 to 10 servings
CALORIES: 794
CARBOHYDRATES: 113g

FAT: 40g
PROTEIN: 3g

12 to 20 Winesap apples,
  small, firm and very dark
1 cup butter or margarine,
  melted
1 recipe for a double crust
  pie

cinnamon to taste
brown sugar to taste (can use
  white sugar)

Peel the apples and put in a cool place. Place bottom crust in a large glass pie plate, with plenty of overhang. Spread a little of the melted butter evenly over the bottom crust. Generously sprinkle part of the brown sugar and part of the cinnamon over the butter. Make a nice layer of this. Slice the apples parallel to the core, thinly. Layer apples in the crust 3 slices deep. Pour a small amount of butter over apples. Sprinkle with cinnamon and sugar to taste. Layer apples, cinnamon and sugar again. Continue layers until they are 2 to 3 inches above the pie plate. This will settle during baking. Press layers gently to allow more room. Pour the remaining butter on last layer and make a generous layer of cinnamon and sugar on top. Cover the pie with a lattice crust. Place pie pan into a larger pan. Bake at 350-400 degrees for 30 to 45 minutes until the juices begin to boil. Reduce the heat to 300-325 degrees and bake for 1 to 2 hours, until the crust is nicely browned and the apples are permeated with the cinnamon and sugar.

Mary Jo Mason

This recipe pre–dates the Civil War, and should be tried when you have time to experiment.

Mamie's Butterscotch Cream Pie

YIELD: 8 servings
CALORIES: 410
CARBOHYDRATES: 64g

FAT: 15g
PROTEIN: 6g

1¼ cups brown sugar
5   tablespoons flour
pinch of salt
2   cups milk
3   egg yolks, beaten
1   tablespoon butter

1   teaspoon vanilla
¼   teaspoon maple flavor
3   egg whites
¼   cup sugar
vanilla wafers

Mix sugar, flour and salt in a saucepan, add milk and cook until thick. Remove from heat. Beat egg yolks then add a little of the hot mixture, stirring well. Then add egg mixture to the saucepan and return to heat. Add butter and flavorings and bring to a full boil. Cook until thick. Line bottom and sides of a pie plate with whole vanilla wafers and fill with custard. Cool. Beat egg whites until stiff, slowly adding sugar until glossy. Top pie with meringue and brown in a 350 degree oven. Refrigerate to set.

Shawn Mitchell

Jo Neville's Chocolate Pie

YIELD: 6 to 8 servings
CALORIES: 301
CARBOHYDRATES: 36g

FAT: 16g
PROTEIN: 5g

2   cups milk
2   egg yolks
¼   cup plus 1 tablespoon flour
¾   cup sugar

3   tablespoons cocoa
2   tablespoons butter
1   teaspoon vanilla

Place dry ingredients into saucepan. Combine milk and slightly beaten egg yolks and stir into flour mixture. Cook over medium heat, stirring constantly, boiling for 1 minute. Remove from heat, add butter, cool 5 minutes and add vanilla. Stir well. Pour into a baked 9 inch pie shell. May top with whipped cream or meringue.

Jane Richardson

Milk Chocolate Pie

YIELD: 8 servings
CALORIES: 434
CARBOHYDRATES: 59g

FAT: 21g
PROTEIN: 6g

1½ cups sugar
½ teaspoon salt
3 cups milk
2 squares semi-sweet chocolate
½ square unsweetened chocolate

2½ tablespoons cornstarch
1 tablespoon flour
3 egg yolks
3 tablespoons butter or margarine

Combine flour, sugar, cornstarch and salt in saucepan. Add milk and cook until thick stirring constantly. Beat egg yolks in a small bowl and add a spoonful of the hot mixture to them and stir well. Keep adding the hot mixture to the egg mixture until you have about 1 cup, then return all to saucepan and stir until blended over low heat. Add chocolate and continue to cook, stirring constantly until thick. Add vanilla and butter and pour into baked pie shell.

Janie Chandler

Candy Bar Pie

YIELD: 8 to 12 servings
CALORIES: 449
CARBOHYDRATES: 36g

FAT: 34g
PROTEIN: 4g

1⅓ cups grated coconut
2 tablespoons butter or margarine, melted
1 teaspoon instant coffee powder
2 tablespoons water

1 7½ ounce milk chocolate candy bar with almonds or 6 regular candy bars
4 cups whipped topping, thawed

Combine coconut and butter and press into bottom and sides of an 8 inch pie pan. Bake at 325 degrees for approximately 10 minutes. Coconut should be golden brown. Set aside to cool. In small saucepan dissolve coffee powder in water, stir in candy bars, which have been broken up. Stir over low heat until melted, set aside to cool. Fold in whipped topping and pile into prepared crust. Place in freezer overnight or at least several hours. It will not freeze solid. Garnish with chocolate curls.

Sherry Scott

4-H Award winner! Men love it.

German Buttermilk Pie

YIELD: 8 to 12 servings
CALORIES: 274
CARBOHYDRATES: 33g

FAT: 14g
PROTEIN: 5g

3 tablespoons butter, softened
¾ cups sugar
2 tablespoons flour
2 eggs, separated

¼ teaspoon salt
2 cups buttermilk
1 teaspoon vanilla or lemon extract
1 10 inch pie shell, unbaked

Cream butter and sugar, add flour and then egg yolks and salt. Add buttermilk and vanilla or lemon extract and mix well. Beat egg whites until soft peaks form and fold gently into creamed mixture. Pour into pie shell and bake at 350 degrees for 1 hour or until brown. Cool before serving.

Sherry Scott

Martha's Pumpkin Pie

YIELD: 6 to 8 servings
CALORIES: 353
CARBOHYDRATES: 40g

FAT: 20g
PROTEIN: 6g

3 eggs
1 cup sugar
1 cup canned pumpkin
½ teaspoon pumpkin pie spice

2 teaspoons vanilla
1 pint Half and Half
2 tablespoons butter
1 unbaked pie shell

Mix eggs, sugar, pumpkin, spice and vanilla. Stir in Half and Half. Pour into pie shell. Dot with butter. Bake at 400 degrees for 50 minutes.

Martha Henderson

Gooder Pies

YIELD: 16
CALORIES: 393
CARBOHYDRATES: 40g

FAT: 24g
PROTEIN: 4g

2 graham cracker pie crusts
1 can sweetened condensed milk
1 large can crushed pineapple, drained well

1 large carton non-dairy whipped topping
1 cup chopped pecans

Mix milk, pineapple, whipped topping and pecans in bowl. Pour into pie shells and freeze for 1 hour. Pies may be left in freezer until ½ hour before serving.

Teri Jackson

Jeff Davis Pie

YIELD: 8-10 servings
CALORIES: 287
CARBOHYDRATES: 38g

FAT: 13g
PROTEIN: 6g

9 inch pie shell, uncooked
1 cup sugar
¼ teaspoon cloves
¼ teaspoon allspice

½ teaspoon cinnamon
4 eggs
1½ cups milk
¼ cup Half and Half

Mix sugar and spices thoroughly. Add remaining ingredients until it is a creamy consistency. Pour into pie shell, bake at 400 degrees for 30 to 40 minutes, or until crust is brown and filling is set. Cover with foil if crust is browning too much.

Carmen Sutton

Pinto Bean Pie

YIELD: 8-12 servings
CALORIES: 521
CARBOHYDRATES: 65g

FAT: 29g
PROTEIN: 6g

1 cup cooked pinto beans
4 eggs
2 cups sugar
¾ cup margarine or butter

1 teaspoon vanilla
1 unbaked 9-10 inch pie shell

Mash beans well. Beat eggs and sugar, add butter, vanilla and beans. Mix well. Pour into unbaked pie shell. Bake at 350 degrees until firm.

Sherry Scott

Peanut Butter Pie

YIELD: 6 to 8 servings
CALORIES: 333
CARBOHYDRATES: 29g

FAT: 22g
PROTEIN: 7g

3   ounces cream cheese,
    softened
1   cup powdered sugar
½   cup milk

½   cup peanut butter
9   ounces non-dairy whipped
    topping

Mix cream cheese, sugar, milk and peanut butter until well blended. Add whipped topping. Pour into a baked pie crust or a graham cracker crust. Freeze. Sprinkle with chopped peanuts for garnish. Serve frozen.

Sharon Forehand

Pecan Pie

YIELD: 8 servings
CALORIES: 485
CARBOHYDRATES: 67g

FAT: 23g
PROTEIN: 5g

3   eggs
1   teaspoon vanilla
1   cup pecans

1   cup white Karo Syrup
2   tablespoons butter
1   cup sugar

Beat eggs and add a dash of salt. Mix in vanilla, sugar, syrup and melted butter into eggs. Pour over pecans in an unbaked pie shell. Bake at 350 degrees for 45 to 55 minutes.

Benny Gail Hunnicutt

This recipe is so simple that even a child can make it.

Sour Cream Raisin Pie

YIELD: 8 servings
CALORIES: 442
CARBOHYDRATES: 66g

FAT: 19g
PROTEIN: 5g

3   eggs
1½ cups brown sugar
1½ cups sour cream
1   teaspoon vanilla

pinch of salt
1   cup raisins
1   unbaked pie shell

Combine eggs and brown sugar, beat well. Add sour cream, vanilla and salt. Mix well. Stir in raisins. Pour into pie shell. Bake at 450 degrees for 10 minutes; reduce to 350 degrees and bake about 30 minutes or until filling is set.

Jeannine Henderson

Strawberry Pie

YIELD: 8 servings
CALORIES: 708
CARBOHYDRATES: 64g

FAT: 52g
PROTEIN: 5g

1   baked pie crust
3   pints fresh strawberries
1   cup sugar or more to taste

2   pints whipping cream
1   teaspoon vanilla
sugar to taste

Ahead of time, wash and slice the strawberries, add sugar and set aside. Whip cream, adding 2 tablespoons sugar or more to taste and vanilla. Place strawberries in crust and top with cream. Serve immediately.

Mary Jo Mason

Mincemeat Cream Pie

YIELD: 6 to 8 pieces
CALORIES: 392
CARBOHYDRATES: 59g

FAT: 16g
PROTEIN: 4g

1   9 inch pie shell, baked
1¼ cups water
½   package mincemeat (9
    ounce size)

3   egg yolks, slightly beaten
1   cup sugar
¼   cup flour
¼   cup butter

MERINGUE:
3   egg whites
⅛   teaspoon cream of tartar
¼   teaspoon salt

½   teaspoon vanilla
6   tablespoons sugar, added
    gradually

Bring water to boil in saucepan, add mincemeat, breaking up with fork. Sift flour into sugar and add gradually to mincemeat, stirring constantly. Cool mixture slightly before adding egg yolks, cook over medium low heat until thickened, stirring constantly. Add butter and stir until melted. Pour into prepared pie crust. Cover with meringue and brown in 400 degrees oven 8 to 10 minutes.

Jann Miller

Frozen Lime Cream Pie

YIELD: 8 servings
CALORIES: 384
CARBOHYDRATES: 34g

FAT: 27g
PROTEIN: 5g

CRUST
1¼ cups graham cracker crumbs
6 tablespoons butter, softened

¼ cup sugar
⅓ cup finely chopped pecans
¼ teaspoon cinnamon

FILLING
3 eggs, separated
½ cup sugar
⅛ teaspoon salt

1 tablespoon grated lime rind
¼ cup fresh lime juice
1 cup heavy cream, whipped

Mix ingredients for crust and press into a 9 inch pie pan. Bake at 325 degrees for 10 minutes. Cool.

Filling: In top of a double boiler, combine egg yolks, ¼ cup sugar, salt, lime rind and juice and blend well. Cook over hot water, stirring until mixture coats a metal spoon and is smooth and thickened. Chill thoroughly. Whip egg whites and remaining ¼ cup sugar until stiff. Fold into cooled lime mixture. Add whipped cream and blend well. Turn into cooled crust and freeze until firm, about 4 hours. May be kept frozen 6 to 7 weeks if wrapped in foil and tightly sealed.

Mary Jo Mason

Grandmother Bunger's Lemon Pie

YIELD: 8 servings
CALORIES: 286
CARBOHYDRATES: 46g

FAT: 11g
PROTEIN: 3g

1¼ cups sugar
⅓ cup flour
4 egg yolks
1 cup boiling water

dash of salt
¼ cup lemon juice
rind of one lemon, grated
1 baked 8 inch pie shell

Cook all ingredients in double boiler until thick. Fill pie shell.

MERINGUE
4 egg whites
¼ teaspoon cream of tartar

½ teaspoon vanilla
6 tablespoons sugar

Meringue: Beat the egg whites with cream of tartar and vanilla until soft peaks form. Gradually add the sugar, beating until stiff peaks form. Spread on the pie. Bake at 350 degrees for 12 to 15 minutes or until golden.

Tammy Bunger

Pie Crust

YIELD: 2 crusts (16 slices)
CALORIES: 204
CARBOHYDRATES: 19g

FAT: 13g
PROTEIN: 3g

3 cups flour	⅓ cup water
1 teaspoon salt	1 egg, well beaten
1 tablespoon sugar	1 tablespoon vinegar
1 cup shortening	

Combine flour, salt and sugar. Cut shortening in with pastry blender or 2 knives. Combine egg, water, and vinegar. Add to flour and blend until it forms a ball. Divide and roll into 2 pie crusts. Prick with fork and bake at 425 degrees about 12 minutes or until lightly browned. May be stored uncovered in plastic bag in refrigerator or freezer for several days. Let warm to room temperature before rolling.

Tina Bean

VARIATION: Use 1¼ cups of shortening and 5 tablespoons of water. Omit the sugar. Mix as above. Divide into thirds and continue as above.

Kay Stewart

VARIATION: Use 4 cups of flour, 1 teaspoon baking powder, 1¾ cups shortening and ½ cup cold water. Mix as above and divide into 5 equal parts.

Lou Deaton

Fruit Cobbler

YIELD: 8-10 servings
CALORIES: 298
CARBOHYDRATES: 44g

FAT: 13g
PROTEIN: 3g

½ cup butter or margarine	1 cup milk
1 cup flour	3 cups peaches, apricots,
1 cup sugar	cherries or blackberries
1 tablespoon baking powder	1 cup sugar
½ teaspoon salt	1 teaspoon cinnamon

Preheat oven to 350 degrees. Melt margarine in 9×13×2 baking dish. Stir flour, sugar, baking powder and salt together, add milk. Blend. Pour mixture over melted margarine. Mix together fruit, sugar and cinnamon. Add ½ cup water if not very juicy. Pour over dough mixture. Bake 1 hour. Crust will magically appear and cover entire surface of cobbler.

Lou Deaton

Peach Cobbler Supreme

YIELD: 8 to 10 servings
CALORIES: 599
CARBOHYDRATES: 88g

FAT: 27g
PROTEIN: 4g

8 cups sliced peaches
2 cups sugar
2 to 4 tablespoons flour
½ teaspoon nutmeg

1 teaspoon almond extract
⅓ cup margarine, melted
pastry for 9-inch, double crust
pie

Combine peaches, sugar, flour and nutmeg in saucepan; set aside until syrup forms. Bring to a boil and cook over low heat for 10 minutes. Remove from heat. Add almond extract and margarine, stirring well. Roll out half of pastry and cut into a 10×8 inch rectangle. Place in bottom of 10×8 inch baking dish. Spoon peaches over pastry. Roll remaining pastry and cut into ½ inch strips. Arrange in lattice design over peaches. Bake at 350 degrees for 30 minutes or until top is lightly browned.

Barbara Malone

Peach Cobbler

YIELD: 8 servings
CALORIES: 451
CARBOHYDRATES: 18g

FAT: 7g
PROTEIN: 4g

pastry for double crust pie
5 cups sliced peaches
¼ cup water
3 tablespoons flour
1 cup sugar

¼ cup sugar
⅛ teaspoon salt
½ teaspoon almond flavoring
butter

Roll half of the pastry very thin and line a 2 inch deep baking dish. Roll and cut other half into strips. Bake half of the strips at 375 degrees until light brown. Mix fruit, 1 cup sugar and water in saucepan and cook until fruit is soft. Mix flour, ¼ cup sugar and salt and add to fruit. Cook, stirring until slightly thickened. Stir in flavoring and cooked pastry strips. Spoon into crust lined dish, dot with butter and cover with uncooked pastry strips. Bake at 400 degrees until brown.

Karen Childress

Cobbler, The Easy Way

YIELD: 10 servings
CALORIES: 381
CARBOHYDRATES: 52g

FAT: 19g
PROTEIN: 3g

fruit, your choice, fresh, frozen
   or canned
frozen, use 2-10 ounce
   packages, thawed
canned, use 2-16 ounce cans
fresh, use enough to half fill a
   9×13 inch pan

2 cups flour
1 cup sugar
1 cup butter, sliced into
    pieces

Place fruit in 9×13 baking dish. In a food processor bowl combine flour, sugar and butter. Process until dough is formed, about 1 minute. Crumble dough over fruit. Bake at 350 degrees for about 40 minutes or until crust is golden brown.

Elizabeth Upham

Quick and Easy Apple Crisp

YIELD: 4-6
CALORIES: 596
CARBOHYDRATES: 114g

FAT: 16g
PROTEIN: 3g

4 apples, tart and firm
⅔ cup sugar
½ teaspoon salt
¼ teaspoon cinnamon
2 tablespoons lemon juice

3 tablespoons butter
1 cup flour
½ cup brown sugar
¼ cup butter, melted

Preheat oven to 400 degrees. Peel and slice apples into a small deep baking dish. Mix sugar, salt, cinnamon and lemon juice. Sprinkle over apples. Dot with 3 tablespoons butter. Blend flour, brown sugar and melted butter to crumb like consistency. Sprinkle over apples. Bake 30-40 minutes. Serve warm with soft vanilla ice cream.

Sandy Baggett

Date Coconut Balls

YIELD: 24 pieces
CALORIES: 118
CARBOHYDRATES: 18g

FAT: 5g
PROTEIN: 1g

1 egg	½ cup butter
1 cup sugar	4 cups Rice Krispies
1 package dates, chopped	1 can coconut

Combine egg, sugar, dates and butter in a saucepan. Cook 10 minutes or until sugar is dissolved. Add cereal. Coat your hands with butter. Form small balls and roll in coconut. Mixture will be hot. Set on wax paper to cool.

Jeannine Henderson

Good on a Christmas Holiday snack plate.

Caramel Brownies

YIELD: 4 dozen bars
CALORIES: 143
CARBOHYDRATES: 18g

FAT: 7g
PROTEIN: 1g

14 ounces caramels	¾ cup butter, melted
⅔ cup evaporated milk	1 cup chopped pecans
1 box German Chocolate cake mix	6 ounces chocolate chips

Pre-heat the oven to 350 degrees. Melt caramels with ⅓ cup evaporated milk in a double boiler. Stir cake mix, butter, remaining milk and pecans until mixed well. Pat half of this mixture into a greased and floured 9 × 13 inch pan. Bake for 6 minutes and then pour caramel mixture over cake. Sprinkle chocolate chips over the caramel mixture. Pat remainder of cake mixture to cover. Bake at 350 degrees for 16 to 18 minutes. Refrigerate for 30 minutes before cutting.

Karen Huffman

Brownie Cupcakes

YIELD: 12 servings
CALORIES: 462
CARBOHYDRATES: 42g

FAT: 33g
PROTEIN: 5g

1¾ cups sugar
1 cup flour
4 eggs
4 ounces baking chocolate

1 cup margarine
1½ cups nuts, chopped
1 teaspoon vanilla

Blend sugar, flour and eggs together by hand. Melt chocolate squares and margarine in a saucepan. Stir in the sugar mixture. Add nuts and vanilla. Pour into cupcake papers in muffin tin and bake at 325 degrees for 30 minutes.

Helen Bean

VARIATION: Use semi-sweet chocolate and add ¼ teaspoon butter flavoring with the nuts and vanilla. Miniature baking cups can also be used. Reduce cooking time to 15 minutes.

Carol Hunnicutt

Toffee Cookies

YIELD: 3 dozen
CALORIES: 129
CARBOHYDRATES: 12g

FAT: 9g
PROTEIN· 1g

1 package cinnamon graham crackers
1 cup butter

1 cup brown sugar
1½ cup pecans

Line jelly-roll pan with crackers. Boil remaining ingredients together and pour over crackers. Bake at 350 degrees for 10 minutes. Cool and slice.

Patti May

Tasty and quick

Banana Cookies

YIELD: 5 dozen cookies
CALORIES: 53 per cookie
CARBOHYDRATES: 7g

FAT: 3g
PROTEIN: 1g

¾ cup shortening
¾ cup brown sugar
1 egg
½ teaspoon vanilla

2 bananas, mashed
1 teaspoon salt
1 teaspoon soda
2 cups flour

Cream the shortening and sugar. Add the egg, vanilla and bananas. Beat well. Add the dry ingredients, mixing well. Drop by teaspoon on a greased cookie sheet. Bake at 350 degrees for 8 to 10 minutes. Cookies will be soft and puffy.

Carmen Sutton

Try a vanilla glaze on these cookies.

Chocolate Drop Cookies

YIELD: 5 dozen cookies
CALORIES: 46 per cookie
CARBOHYDRATES: 5

FAT: 3
PROTEIN: 1

½ cup margarine
¾ cup sugar
1 egg
4 tablespoons cocoa
1½ cups flour, sifted

½ teaspoon soda
dash of salt
½ cup milk
1 teaspoon vanilla
½ cup chopped pecans

Cream the margarine and sugar. Add the egg and beat well. Combine the dry ingredients. Combine the milk and vanilla. Add the last 2 mixtures alternately to the creamed mixture. Stir in pecans. Drop by teaspoon on a lightly greased baking sheet. Bake at 400 degrees for 6 to 8 minutes.

Jean North

Chocolate Peanut Butter Cookies

YIELD: 4 dozen
CALORIES: 78
CARBOHYDRATES: 10g

FAT: 4g
PROTEIN: 1g

2   cups sugar
½   cup margarine
4   tablespoons cocoa
½   cup milk

½   cup peanut butter
2½ cups oatmeal, quick
1   cup pecans
1   teaspoon vanilla

Combine sugar, margarine, cocoa and milk in saucepan and bring to a full boil. Boil 1½ minutes. Test by dropping a morsel in cold water until it forms a soft ball. Remove from heat and add peanut butter, quick oats, vanilla and nuts. Stir well and drop by teaspoons on wax paper.

Barbara Malone

Cocoa Kiss Cookies

YIELD: 4½ dozen
CALORIES: 99
CARBOHYDRATES: 10g

FAT: 6g
PROTEIN: 1g

1   cup butter
⅔   cup sugar
1   teaspoon vanilla
1⅔ cups flour
¼   cup cocoa

1   cup chopped pecans, (optional)
9   ounce package chocolate kisses

Cream butter and sugar, add vanilla. Gradually add dry ingredients and nuts. Chill. Wrap 1 teaspoon dough around each kiss and roll into a ball until completely covered. Place on a cookie sheet and bake at 375 degrees for 8 to 10 minutes. Cool slightly on the pan, then on a rack. Dust with powdered sugar if desired.

Lou Deaton and Suzy Black

Aunt Hester's Date Nut Cookies

YIELD: 6 to 7 dozen
CALORIES: 155
CARBOHYDRATES: 16

FAT: 10
PROTEIN: 2

1 cup butter or vegetable shortening	1½ teaspoon soda
	½ teaspoon cloves
2⅓ cups brown sugar, packed	2 teaspoons cinnamon
4 eggs	3 tablespoons buttermilk
3½ cups unsifted flour	2 cups chopped dates
½ teaspoon salt	6 cups chopped pecans

Cream butter and sugar, add eggs. Add flour, salt, soda and spices, alternating with buttermilk and mixing well. Add dates and pecans. Cover dough with wax paper. Store in refrigerator overnight or can be stored for several days. When ready to cook make into 1 inch balls. Bake on greased cookie sheet at 350 degrees for 12 to 15 minutes. Place pan of water on bottom shelf to prevent burning. Store in cans or plastic containers.

Helen Bean

These freeze well. Flavor improves whether frozen or stored in airtight containers. This is my great aunt's recipe.

Forgotten Cookies

YIELD: 2 dozen
CALORIES: 104
CARBOHYDRATES: 13

FAT: 6
PROTEIN: 1

2 egg whites	1 cup chocolate chips
¾ cup sugar	2 cups Post Toasties
1 cup chopped pecans	

Preheat oven to 350 degrees. Beat egg whites until stiff, gradually add sugar and beat until very stiff. Add nuts, chocolate chips, and Post Toasties. Drop by teaspoon onto wax paper-lined cookie sheet. Place in oven and turn off heat. Leave 3 to 4 hours or overnight.

Barbara Malone

Ginger Cream Cookies

YIELD: 100 - 2 inch cookies
CALORIES: 49
CARBOHYDRATES: 8

FAT: 2
PROTEIN: 1

½ cup vegetable shortening
1 cup sugar
1 egg
1 cup molasses
4 cups flour, sifted
1 teaspoon nutmeg

2 teaspoons ginger
1 teaspoon cloves
1 teaspoon cinnamon
½ teaspoon salt
1 cup hot water
2 teaspoons soda

Cream shortening, add sugar, egg, molasses. Sift flour and spices together. Dissolve soda in water. Add alternately to creamed mixture. Drop by teaspoon on cookie sheet and bake at 350 degrees for 8 minutes.

ICING
2 cups powdered sugar
1 tablespoon butter

3 or 4 tablespoons cream
1 teaspoon vanilla

Combine ingredients and beat until smooth. Spread on cooled cookies.

Tammy Bunger

Kentucky Thumbprint Cookies

YIELD: 6 dozen
CALORIES: 62
CARBOHYDRATES: 6g

FAT: 4g
PROTEIN: 1g

1 cup butter
½ cup brown sugar
2 egg yolks
1 cup chopped nuts

1 teaspoon vanilla
2 cups flour
½ teaspoon salt
jelly

Cream butter and sugar, then add egg yolks and vanilla. Add flour, salt and pecans. Drop or shape in round nickel size and press thumb into middle. Add dab of grape or strawberry jelly in the middle. Bake at 350 degrees for 10 to 12 minutes until golden brown.

Lorelei McMullan

May use other jellies or sauces for filling. Store in tins in refrigerator or freezer.

Lace Cookies

YIELD: 5 to 6 dozen
CALORIES: 44
CARBOHYDRATES: 5

FAT: 3
PROTEIN: .34

¼ cup butter
¼ cup shortening
⅔ cup firmly packed brown sugar
½ cup light corn syrup
1 cup flour

2 tablespoon quick cooking oatmeal
or 4 tablespoons regular oatmeal
1 cup chopped pecans or almonds

Melt butter and shortening in a sauce pan and stir in sugar and corn syrup. Bring to a boil, stirring frequently. Remove from heat and stir in flour, oatmeal and nuts. Drop by half teaspoon 3 inches apart onto oiled baking sheets. Bake at 325 degrees for 8 to 10 minutes. Let cool 1 minute and lift off.

Paula Bailey and Tammy Bunger

Melt Away Cookies

YIELD: 4 dozen (48)
CALORIES: 75 per cookie
CARBOHYDRATES: 7

FAT: 5
PROTEIN: .56

1 cup butter
¾ cup cornstarch

⅓ cup powdered sugar
1 cup flour

FROSTING
6 ounces cream cheese
2 teaspoons vanilla

2 cups powdered sugar

Beat butter until creamy. Add other 3 ingredients, beating until smooth. Roll dough into small balls and press down like thumb-print cookies. Bake on ungreased cookie sheet at 350 degrees for 12 minutes; cool. Mix together cream cheese, vanilla and powdered sugar. Beat until smooth and frost cookies.

Patti May

Do not make on a humid day. A great tea cookie. You can use food coloring to color frosting.

Oatmeal Cookies

YIELD: 6 dozen
CALORIES: 97
CARBOHYDRATES: 11

FAT: 6
PROTEIN: 1

1	cup shortening	1	teaspoon salt
2	cups brown sugar	1	teaspoon soda
2	eggs, well beaten	1	teaspoon cinnamon
1	cup milk	1	teaspoon nutmeg
1	tablespoon vanilla	2	cups chopped pecans
3	cups flour	3	cups rolled oats

Cream sugar and shortening. Stir in the eggs. Mix milk and vanilla. Mix together flour, soda and spices. Add milk and flour mixture alternately to creamed mixture. Stir in oats and pecans. Drop by teaspoons on cookie sheet. Bake at 350 degrees for 15 to 20 minutes.

Mary Jo Mason

Nutritious snack for the children.

Oatmeal Cookies

YIELD: 10 dozen
CALORIES: 51
CARBOHYDRATES: 5

FAT: 4
PROTEIN: .59

1	cup margarine	1	teaspoon soda
1	cup sugar	½	teaspoon salt
1	cup brown sugar	1½	cups flour
2	eggs, beaten	3	cups 3 Minute Oats
1	teaspoon vanilla	2	cups pecans (optional)

Cream margarine and sugar; mix well. Add eggs one at a time, then vanilla. Stir in sifted soda, salt and flour, then add oats. Drop by small spoonfuls onto cookie sheet. Bake at 375 degrees for 5 to 10 minutes.

Kay Stewart

These cookies are chewy and lacy.

Oatmeal Cookies

YIELD: 7-8 dozen
CALORIES: 119
CARBOHYDRATES: 13

FAT: 8
PROTEIN: 1

4	eggs	2	teaspoons baking powder
2	cups sugar	2	teaspoons baking soda
2	cups brown sugar	2	teaspoons vanilla
2	cups butter, margarine, or shortening	2	cups coconut
		2	cups oatmeal
4	cups flour	2-3	cups chopped pecans

Beat eggs, sugars, and butter together. Sift flour, baking powder and soda, add to first mixture. Add vanilla, coconut, oatmeal and pecans. Mix well. Drop by teaspoons onto cookie sheet. Bake at 350 degrees until light brown, 6-8 minutes. Remove from oven and let fall on cookie sheet. Remove and cool on wax paper.

Jane Richardson

Grandmother Stegemoller passed this recipe down.

Ritz Cracker, Peanut Butter Cookies

YIELD: 30 Cookies

White chocolate
1   large jar crunchy peanut
butter

1   large box Ritz crackers

Make sandwiches of crackers and peanut butter. Melt chocolate in microwave. Dip sandwiches, using tongs, in melted chocolate. Place on wax paper to dry.

Benny Gail Hunnicutt

Microwave

Toll Cookies

YIELD: 48 small cookies
CALORIES: 137 per cookie
CARBOHYDRATES: 17g

FAT: 8g
PROTEIN: 1g

1 cup shortening
½ cup brown sugar
½ cup sugar
2 egg yolks
1 teaspoon soda in 1 tablespoon water
2 cups flour

1 12 ounce package chocolate morsels
2 egg whites
1 cup brown sugar
1 teaspoon vanilla
1 cup chopped pecans

Mix together the first 6 ingredients. Pat into a 11 × 15 inch pan. Sprinkle the chocolate morsels over the mixture. Beat the egg whites, brown sugar and vanilla. Spread over the morsels. Sprinkle pecans on top and press down. Bake at 325 degrees for 20 to 25 minutes. Cut into squares to serve. The secret is not to overbake.

Martha Henderson

The perfect cookie for a picnic.

Double Chocolate Brownies

YIELD: 12 to 16 servings
CALORIES: 314
CARBOHYDRATES: 38g

FAT: 20g
PROTEIN: 4g

6 ounces unsweetened chocolate
¾ cup butter
3 large eggs
2¼ cups sugar

1 cup flour
¼ teaspoon salt
2 teaspoons vanilla
¾ cup chopped walnuts or pecans

Preheat oven to 375 degrees. Grease and flour a 9 inch square pan. Melt chocolate and butter in a heavy sauce pan over low heat, stirring until smooth. Let mixture cool completely. In mixer bowl, beat eggs, add sugar gradually, beating at high speed until thick and pale, 7 or 8 minutes. Stir in chocolate mixture, flour, salt and vanilla. Blend well. Stir in nuts. Pour into pan, smoothing top. Bake 30 to 40 minutes, until batter pulls away from sides of pan or wooden pick inserted in center comes out with crumbs adhering to it. Do not overcook. Let cool completely before cutting.

Mary Jo Mason

These are sinfully rich and delicious.

Honey Bars

YIELD: 32
CALORIES: 160
CARBOHYDRATES: 20

FAT: 9
PROTEIN: 1

¾ cup oil
½ cup honey
1 cup sugar
1 egg
2 cups flour

1 teaspoon soda
1½ teaspoons cinnamon
pinch of salt
1 cup chopped nuts

GLAZE
1 cup powdered sugar
1 tablespoon water

2 tablespoons mayonnaise
1 teaspoon vanilla

Mix ingredients in the order given. Spread on greased cookie sheet. Bake at 350 degrees for 15 minutes. Mix all ingredients for glaze together until smooth. Spread on hot cookie bars. Allow to cool and then cut in squares.

Patti May

Lemon Squares

YIELD: 24 to 36
CALORIES: 180
CARBOHYDRATES: 29

FAT: 10
PROTEIN: 2

1 box lemon cake mix
½ cup melted margarine
3 eggs

1 8 ounce package cream cheese, softened
1 box powdered sugar

Mix cake mix, margarine, and 1 egg. Press into 9×13 inch pan. Beat together well, cream cheese, sugar and 2 eggs. Spread on top of cake mixture. Bake at 350 degrees for 40 to 50 minutes until top is golden brown.

Marilyn Chalmers

Praline Squares

YIELD: 3 dozen
CALORIES: 137
CARBOHYDRATES: 16g

FAT: 8g
PROTEIN: 1g

2   eggs
2   cups light brown sugar
1   cup melted butter or
    margarine

1½ cups flour
1   teaspoon vanilla
1   cup chopped pecans

Beat eggs, blend with sugar and stir in butter. Add flour gradually. Add vanilla and pecans. Pour into a greased 8×12 inch pan. Bake at 350 degrees for 40 minutes. Cool and cut into squares.

Shirley Kirby

Pumpkin-Pecan Bars

YIELD: 24
CALORIES: 172 per cookie
CARBOHYDRATES: 20g

FAT: 10g
PROTEIN: 3g

½   cup margarine
1   cup firmly packed brown
    sugar
1½ cups flour
1   cup oatmeal
1   teaspoon baking powder
1   teaspoon salt
1   16 ounce can pumpkin

1   14 ounce can sweetened
    condensed milk
2   eggs, beaten
2   teaspoons pumpkin pie
    spice
1½ teaspoons vanilla
1   cup chopped pecans

Preheat oven to 350 degrees. Beat margarine and sugar until fluffy; add flour, oatmeal, baking powder and ½ teaspoon salt. Mix until crumbly. Reserve ½ cup crumble mixture, press remainder on bottom of 10×15 inch jellyroll pan. Bake 20 minutes. Combine pumpkin, condensed milk, eggs, pumpkin pie spice, vanilla and ½ teaspoon salt. Spread over crust. Combine reserved crumble mixture and pecans and sprinkle over pumpkin mixture. Bake 30-35 minutes. Cool thoroughly. Dust with powdered sugar. Cut into bars. Store covered in refrigerator.

Barbara Malone

English Toffee Bars

YIELD: 5-6 dozen
CALORIES: 75 per cookie
CARBOHYDRATES: 7g

FAT: 5g
PROTEIN: 1g

1 cup butter
1 cup sugar
1 egg yolk
2 cups sifted flour
1 teaspoon cinnamon

1 egg white, slightly beaten
1 cup chopped pecans
2 ounces semi-sweet
  chocolate, melted

Cream butter, add sugar gradually beating until fluffy. Beat in egg yolk. Sift flour and cinnamon together; gradually add to creamed mixture, beating until blended. Turn into a greased 10 x 15 inch jelly roll pan and press evenly. Brush top with egg white. Sprinkle with pecans and press lightly into dough. Bake at 275 degrees for 1 hour. While still hot cut into 1½ inch squares. Drizzle with melted chocolate. Cool on wire racks.

Martha Gries

Aunt Hester's Fruit Cake Cookies

YIELD: 5 dozen
CALORIES: 130
CARBOHYDRATES: 15g

FAT: 6g
PROTEIN: 2g

½ cup shortening or butter
1½ cups brown sugar, packed
4 eggs
¾ cup whiskey
3 cups flour
3 teaspoons baking soda
½ teaspoon nutmeg
1 teaspoon cloves
1 teaspoon cinnamon

½ teaspoon allspice
1 tablespoon milk
½ pound white raisins
½ pound dates, chopped
1 pound candied pineapple, chopped
1 pound candied cherries, chopped
3 cups chopped pecans

Cream sugar and shortening, add 2 eggs at at time, beating well. Add whiskey and let set 10 minutes. Sift 2 cups of flour with soda and spices, set aside other cup of flour. Add flour mixture to egg mixture and add milk. Dredge the fruit in the cup of flour that was set aside, add to mixture. Add pecans. Mix well, cover with wax paper and chill. Can be stored in refrigerator for several days. Drop by teaspoonful on a greased cookie sheet, shape into small balls. Bake in 275 degree oven for 15 to 20 minutes. Place pan of water on lower shelf to prevent burning. Store in bags or air tight containers. The flavor improves with storage.

Helen Bean

VARIATION: Increase to 3 tablespoons milk, 1 teaspoon nutmeg, 1 teaspoon allspice, 1½ pounds candied cherries, 1½ pounds candied pineapple, 1 box white raisins, 1 box chopped dates, and 6 cups chopped pecans.

Mary Jo Mason

Kathryn Richardson's Candy

YIELD: 12 servings
CALORIES: 117
CARBOHYDRATES: 11g

FAT: 8g
PROTEIN: 2g

6 ounces butterscotch chips
2 tablespoons crunchy peanut butter

1¾ ounce can shoestring potatoes

Melt butterscotch chips in double boiler and stir in peanut butter. Remove from heat and add the potatoes which have been broken into approximately ½ inch lengths. Drop mixture by spoon onto wax paper covered cookie sheet. Refrigerate until hardened.

Lockie Sue Bissett

Unusual and good!

Pecan Pralines

YIELD: 25 to 30 pieces
CALORIES: 134
CARBOHYDRATES: 17g

FAT: 7g
PROTEIN: 1g

1½ cups sugar
½ cup brown sugar
¾ cup evaporated milk
3 tablespoons light corn syrup

2 cups pecan halves
¼ cup margarine
1 teaspoon vanilla

Mix sugars, milk and syrup in saucepan and bring to boil, stirring constantly. Add pecans and continue cooking to soft ball stage, 240 degrees on candy thermometer. For soft ball test when not using thermometer, drop a small amount of the mixture into a glass of ice water, if it forms a soft ball at the bottom of the glass, you know that the proper stage has been reached. Remove from heat, add vanilla and margarine. Stir until candy takes on a dull appearance, and drop by spoon onto wax paper.

Susan McMullan

Peanut Clusters

YIELD: 5 to 6 dozen
CALORIES: 226
CARBOHYDRATES: 19g

FAT: 16g
PROTEIN: 5g

12 ounces milk chocolate chips

14 ounces almond bark
16 ounces cocktail peanuts

Combine first two ingredients and microwave for six minutes, stirring until well blended. Pour in peanuts and mix well. Drop by teaspoon onto wax paper.

Benny Gail Hunnicutt

Peanut Brittle

YIELD: 40 servings
CALORIES: 147
CARBOHYDRATES: 23g

FAT: 6g
PROTEIN: 3g

3 cups sugar
½ cup water
1 cup light corn syrup
1 teaspoon salt

3 cups raw peanuts
3 teaspoons butter
3 teaspoons baking soda
3 teaspoons vanilla

Mix sugar, water and syrup in 3 quart heavy saucepan. Cook until mixture threads when spoonful is held above pan and tipped toward pan. Add peanuts and cook stirring constantly until temperature reaches 300 degrees on candy thermometer. Remove from fire. Stirring quickly, add soda, vanilla, salt and butter. Mix well and pour onto a buttered 14×16 inch cookie sheet or into five 9 inch buttered aluminum foil pie pans.

Jean Read

Old Fashioned Peanut Brittle

YIELD: 15 pieces
CALORIES: 125
CARBOHYDRATES: 19g

FAT: 5g
PROTEIN: 2g

1   cup raw peanuts
1   cup sugar
½   cup light corn syrup
⅛   teaspoon salt

1   teaspoon baking soda
1   teaspoon vanilla
1   teaspoon butter

In a 2 quart casserole, stir together peanuts, sugar, syrup and salt. Cook 8 minutes at high, stirring well after 4 minutes. Add butter and vanilla. Cook one minute longer. Add baking soda and quickly stir until light and foamy. Immediately pour onto a lightly buttered baking sheet. Spread out thin and even. When it has cooled, break into serving pieces.

Barbara Malone

This is a microwave recipe.

Jeanette Bailey's Great Toffee

YIELD: 30 pieces
CALORIES: 215
CARBOHYDRATES: 16g

FAT: 17g

1   pound butter
2   cups sugar

3   1½ ounce Hershey candy
    bars
½   cup pecans, finely ground

Cook butter and sugar to 300 degrees on candy thermometer (hard crack stage). Stir constantly until it darkens to caramel color. Pour into foil lined 9×11 inch pan. Place Hershey bars on top and spread out to evenly distribute chocolate. Sprinkle finely ground nuts on top. When it has hardened, break into serving size pieces.

Benny Gail Hunnicutt and Paula D. Bailey

Jeanette traditionally gave this for Christmas gifts.

Magic Toffee Brittle

YIELD: 48 pieces
CALORIES: 88
CARBOHYDRATES: 8g

FAT: 6g

40 saltine crackers
1 cup brown sugar
1 cup butter

6 ounces chocolate chips
½ cup chopped pecans

Place layer of crackers on 11×16×1 inch foil lined pan. Boil butter and sugar for 3 minutes. Pour over crackers. Bake at 350 degrees for 5 minutes or until crackers float to top. Sprinkle chips on top and when the chocolate is melted, spread it out evenly. Top with nuts, cool and cut into bars.

Katharine Russell

Bon Bons

YIELD: 200 to 220 pieces
CALORIES: 51
CARBOHYDRATES: 5g

FAT: 3g

1 can sweetened condensed milk
2 boxes powdered sugar
1 cup butter or margarine
2 teaspoons vanilla

2 teaspoons rum extract
4 cups finely chopped pecans
¾ bar paraffin, shaved
3 8 ounce Hershey bars

Mix first 6 ingredients well in a large bowl. Roll into small balls approximately 1 heaping teaspoon in size or smaller. Place on wax paper lined cookie sheet and chill until firm. In top of double boiler, melt 1 chocolate bar and ⅓ of the paraffin. Stir well. Remove 2 or 3 balls at a time, insert a toothpick into the center to hold by and either dip into the melted chocolate or pour chocolate over each ball, as you prefer. Place each one back onto the wax paper to harden. This recipe halves easily. ½ can of sweetened condensed milk equals 5 ounces.

Lockie Sue Bissett

Great Grandmother's Butter Divinity

YIELD: 3 dozen
CALORIES: 170
CARBOHYDRATES: 29g

FAT: 6g
PROTEIN: 1g

4	egg whites		pinch salt
4	cups sugar	¼	cup butter, do not
1	cup water		substitute margarine
1	cup light corn syrup	2	cups pecans

Beat egg whites until stiff. Cook sugar, water, syrup and salt until it reaches firm ball stage. A dribble of the mixture will form a firm ball when dropped into ice water. Be sure to cook long enough to reach this stage. With electric mixer on medium high speed, pour hot mixture in a steady stream into beaten egg whites. Immediately add the butter and continue beating with mixer until the butter melts. Add pecans. Beat by hand until smooth and thick enough not to run when spooned onto waxed paper.

Jane Richardson

Two people spooning is much easier.

Microwave Divinity

YIELD: 36 pieces
CALORIES: 75
CARBOHYDRATES: 13g

FAT: 2g

2	cups sugar	2	egg whites
½	cup water	1	teaspoon vanilla
⅓	cup light corn syrup	1	cup chopped pecans
½	teaspoon salt		

Combine sugar, water, corn syrup and salt in a 4 cup measure. Microwave, uncovered, 3 minutes. Stir. Microwave, uncovered 6 to 8 minutes or until 260 degrees on candy thermometer is reached, checking temperature during last few minutes. Meanwhile, beat egg whites in large bowl of electric mixer until they form stiff peaks. Pour hot syrup in thin stream over egg whites while beating at high speed. Continue beating until mixture holds its shape and starts to lose gloss. Beating time is long. Add vanilla, fold in nuts. Spoon onto waxed paper. When set, remove from paper and store in tightly covered container.

Lou Deaton

Fire Stick Crystal Candy

YIELD: 12   CARBOHYDRATES: 86g
CALORIES: 337

4   cups sugar   5   drops red food coloring
1   cup water   ¾   teaspoon oil of cinnamon
1   cup light corn syrup

Combine sugar, water and syrup in heavy pan. Bring to a boil over medium heat, stirring constantly. Stir in food coloring and continue to cook without stirring until mixture reaches hard crack stage, or 300 degrees on a candy thermometer. Remove from heat, stir in oil of cinnamon, and spread on an oiled pan. Cool and break into pieces.

Brenda Comer

Store in airtight container.

Good Fudge

YIELD: 5 pounds   FAT: 6g
CALORIES: 164   PROTEIN: 1g
CARBOHYDRATES: 28g

3-6 ounce packages chocolate   4½ cups sugar
    chips   12 ounce can evaporated milk
2   cups marshmallow cream   2   cups chopped pecans
¾   cup butter

Mix chocolate chips, marshmallow cream and butter and set aside. Cook sugar and evaporated milk on medium heat, stirring constantly, to 240 degrees on a candy thermometer. Stir in chocolate mixture, stirring until melted. Add pecans, then drop by teaspoons onto waxed paper.

Benny Gail Hunnicutt

Microwave Fudge

YIELD: 32 pieces
CALORIES: 97
CARBOHYDRATES: 11g

FAT: 6g

1 pound powdered sugar	½ cup margarine
¼ to ½ cup cocoa	1 teaspoon vanilla
¼ cup milk	½ cup chopped pecans

Blend sugar and cocoa, then add milk and margarine. Do not stir. Cook on high heat in microwave for 2 minutes. Remove and stir well to mix. Add pecans and vanilla then stir until blended. Pour into greased oblong pan. Put in freezer for 20 minutes or in the refrigerator for 1 hour.

Benny Gail Hunnicutt

Velveeta Cheese Fudge

YIELD: 48 pieces
CALORIES: 244
CARBOHYDRATES: 26g

FAT: 16g
PROTEIN: 2g

2 cups butter or margarine	2 cups chopped pecans
4 pounds powdered sugar	1 cup cocoa
1 pound Velveeta cheese	2 teaspoons vanilla

Melt margarine and cheese, then add remaining ingredients. Mix well. Spread in pan or cookie sheet. Cut in squares and keep in refrigerator.

Carolyn Stuart Wilson

Minted Pecans

YIELD: 20 servings
CALORIES: 181
CARBOHYDRATES: 18g

FAT: 12g
PROTEIN: 2g

¼ cup light corn syrup	1 teaspoon essence of
1 cup sugar	peppermint
½ cup water	10 marshmallows
	3 cups pecan halves

Combine first 3 ingredients in saucepan. Cook over medium heat stirring constantly until mixture boils and reaches the soft ball stage, 238 degrees on a candy thermometer. Remove from heat and add peppermint and marshmallows. Stir until dissolved and add nuts. Stir until nuts are well coated and pour onto wax paper. Separate while warm.

Barbara Malone

This recipe makes a great Christmas gift.

Brazo De Gitano

YIELD: 10 servings
CALORIES: 249
CARBOHYDRATES: 37g

FAT: 9g
PROTEIN: 7g

¾ teaspoon baking powder
½ teaspoon salt
4 eggs, room temperature
¾ cup sugar
½ cup flour

¼ cup cocoa
1 teaspoon vanilla
powdered sugar
almonds, slivered and toasted

CREMA AL RON
2 cups milk
¼ teaspoon cinnamon
1 teaspoon vanilla
¼ cup sugar

1 egg, beaten
1 teaspoon rum extract or
rum to taste
¼ cup flour

Cake: Preheat oven to 400 degrees. Line a 16×10×1 inch jelly-roll pan with wax paper and grease thoroughly. Place baking powder, salt and eggs in a medium bowl. Beat at high speed, adding sugar 2 tablespoons at a time until mixture is thick and lemon colored. Fold in flour, cocoa and vanilla. Pour into prepared pan spreading batter evenly. Bake for approximately 13 minutes or until cake tests done with a toothpick. Loosen edges of cake with a knife and quickly invert cake onto a clean linen towel that has been sprinkled with powdered sugar. Peel waxed paper off slowly. Roll cake with towel from the short end. Let stand for at least 30 minutes. Unroll cake and spread with Crema Al Ron (custard). Re-roll cake, removing linen towel and place on serving plate. Sprinkle with powdered sugar and almonds. Serve with sweetened whipped cream, if desired. Crema Al Ron: In a heavy 1 quart saucepan, stir the milk, sugar, flour and cinnamon together. Cook over low heat until thickened. Beat 2 tablespoons of the hot mixture into the beaten egg, then put egg mixture into the saucepan, beating constantly. Cook until the mixture comes to a boil and is thick. Remove from heat, add flavoring and cool completely before filling the Brazo De Gitano.

Cathy Carson

The perfect ending to a Mexican meal.

Noel Log

YIELD: 10 servings
CALORIES: 301
CARBOHYDRATES: 26g

FAT: 21g
PROTEIN: 5g

6   eggs, separated and whites
     at room temperature
¾   cup sugar
⅓   cup unsweetened cocoa

1½ teaspoon vanilla
dash of salt
powdered sugar

FILLING
1½ cups heavy cream, chilled
½ cup powdered sugar
¼ cup unsweetened cocoa
2 teaspoons instant coffee

1   teaspoon vanilla extract
candied cherries
angelica

Grease the bottom of a 15×10×1 inch jelly roll pan. Line the pan with wax paper and grease the paper lightly. Pre-heat the oven to 375 degrees. Beat the egg whites in a large mixing bowl with an electric mixer at high speed until soft peaks form. Add the ¼ cup sugar, 2 tablespoons at a time. Beat until stiff peaks form. With the same beaters, beat the yolks at high speed, adding the remaining ½ cups sugar, 2 tablespoons at a time. Beat until mixture is very thick or about 4 minutes. Beat cocoa, vanilla and salt into yolk mixture at low speed until smooth. Using a wire whisk or rubber scraper, fold cocoa mixture into egg whites gently, just until no whites show. Spread evenly in prepared pan and bake for 15 minutes. The surface of the cake will spring back when gently touched. Sift powdered sugar in a 10×12 inch rectangle on a clean linen towel. Turn the cake out onto the sugar, lifting off the pan. Peel the paper off of the cake and roll cake jelly-roll fashion, starting with the short end, towel and all. Cool completely, seam side down, at least 30 minutes. Combine the filling ingredients except cherries and angelica and beat until thick. Refrigerate while cake is cooling. Unroll the cake, spread filling to within 1 inch from edges of cake. Re-roll the cake and place seam side down on serving plate. Cover loosely with foil and chill for 1 hour before serving. Cake may be frozen at this point. To serve, sprinkle with powdered sugar and decorate with cherries and angelica. Filling can also be doubled and used for a frosting for an even richer dessert. Cut off one end of roll and place on log for a wood-knot effect. Use the tines of a fork to create a wooden look down the log.
Cathy Carson

Quick Banana Pudding

YIELD: 8 servings
CALORIES: 343
CARBOHYDRATES: 43g

FAT: 16g
PROTEIN: 7g

3¾ ounces instant vanilla
   pudding mix
milk
8   ounces sour cream
8   ounces non-dairy whipped
   topping

½   of an 11 ounce box vanilla
   wafers
3   bananas, sliced in small
   pieces

Make pudding as directed on the box. Add sour cream and non dairy topping and beat well. Layer, starting with pudding, then wafers, bananas and then more pudding.

Jane Richardson

Husband and kid pleasing. Recipe from Mrs. Phillip Jacoby, Sonora, Tx.

Banana Pudding

YIELD: 6 servings
CALORIES: 344
CARBOHYDRATES: 60g

FAT: 9g
PROTEIN: 8g

½   cup sugar
3   tablespoons flour
¼   teaspoon salt
3   beaten egg yolks
2   cups milk

1   teaspoon vanilla
vanilla wafers
bananas
3   egg whites
¼   cup sugar

Mix dry ingredients, add eggs and 2 cups milk in top of double boiler. Cook over boiling water until thickened, stirring constantly. Add vanilla. Line baking pan bottom and sides with wafers. Cover with sliced bananas. Pour custard over bananas. Repeat layers. Beat egg whites, when stiff add sugar. Top pudding with meringue. Bake at 325 degrees for 20 minutes or until golden brown.

Jodie Sessom

Newfangled Bread Pudding

YIELD: 8 to 10 servings
CALORIES: 409
CARBOHYDRATES: 41g

FAT: 24g
PROTEIN: 10g

soft butter
6 slices bread
5 eggs
1 cup sugar
8 ounces cream cheese

1 teaspoon vanilla
dash of salt
3 cups milk
1 teaspoon cinnamon
raisins

Butter bread and cut into 1 inch squares using crusts. Place in lightly greased 11×7×1 inch pan. Slightly beat 4 eggs. Add ½ cup sugar, vanilla and salt and mix well. Heat milk and slowly add to egg mixture, mixing well. Add as many raisins as desired. Pour over bread squares. Sprinkle with cinnamon. Combine cream cheese and ½ cup sugar; blend until smooth. Add 1 egg, beating well and spread over soaked bread. Bake at 350 degrees for 45 minutes or until firm. Cool slightly.

Tammy Bunger

Jewell's Baked Custard

YIELD: 16 servings
CALORIES: 195
CARBOHYDRATES: 22g

FAT: 9g
PROTEIN: 7g

2½ cups milk
2 cups Half and Half
1 dozen eggs

1½ cups sugar
pinch of salt
4 teaspoons vanilla

Heat the milk and cream in a double boiler until hot. Remove scum from milk, if one forms. Beat the eggs in a large bowl until foamy. Add salt and sugar gradually to the eggs and beat until lemon colored. Add the vanilla to the egg mixture. Stir a small amount of the hot mixture into the egg mixture, then add the remaining hot mixture. Pour into a 2 quart glass baking dish. Place dish in a larger pan and add hot water halfway up the side of the custard dish. Bake at 325 degrees for 45 minutes or until firm in the center. Reduce heat to 300 degrees if the custard browns too fast. Cool completely on rack before refrigerating. Do not cover.

Camille Jones

Chocolate Sponge

YIELD: 10 servings
CALORIES: 241
CARBOHYDRATES: 29g

FAT: 16g
PROTEIN: 5g

1 package gelatin
1 cup coffee
1 cup water
1 cup sugar
2 tablespoons cocoa

4 eggs, separated
1 teaspoon salt
1 teaspoon vanilla
1 cup chopped pecans (if desired)

Dissolve gelatin in ½ cup cold water. Bring to a boil the coffee, ½ cup water, ½ cup sugar and cocoa. Pour ½ of coffee mixture into gelatin and the other ½ into 4 egg yolks. Pour the two mixtures together and boil, adding salt, vanilla and pecans. Let cool. Fold in 4 beaten egg whites with ½ cup sugar to coffee mixture. Refrigerate.

Susan Mertz Slaughter

Serve with whipped cream on top.

Bread Pudding And Vinegar Sauce

YIELD: 9 servings
CALORIES: 278
CARBOHYDRATES: 48g

FAT: 9g
PROTEIN: 4g

2¼ cups milk
2 slighty beaten eggs
2 cups day old bread cubes
½ cup brown sugar

1 teaspoon cinnamon
1 teaspoon vanilla
¼ teaspoon salt
½ cup raisins (optional)

Combine the milk and eggs and pour over the bread cubes. Add the remaining ingredients and toss lightly. Spread into an 8×8×2 inch greased baking pan. Set the pan in a shallow pan. Pour hot water to 1 inch depth in pan. Bake at 350 degrees for 35 minutes. Serve with vinegar sauce.

VINEGAR SAUCE
1 cup sugar
1 rounded tablespoon flour
1 cup water

3 tablespoons vinegar
4 tablespoons butter
nutmeg to taste

Mix the sugar, flour and water in a sauce pan and boil until thick, stirring constantly. Add the nutmeg, butter, and vinegar. Stir until well blended. Use more or less vinegar as desired.

Lou Deaton

French Eclair

YIELD: 12 servings
CALORIES: 389
CARBOHYDRATES: 60g

FAT: 14g
PROTEIN: 7g

1   box honey graham crackers
3   3 ounce boxes French
    vanilla instant pudding

4½ cups milk
1   8 ounce carton non-dairy
    topping

ICING
1   cup sugar
⅓   cup cocoa
¼   cup milk

4   tablespoons margarine
1   teaspoon vanilla

Butter a 9×13 inch pan. Layer bottom of pan with whole crackers. Mix pudding and milk and then fold in non-dairy topping. Pour half of the pudding mixture over the crackers, then another layer of crackers followed by the rest of the pudding mixture. Top with another layer of crackers and refrigerate. Combine ICING ingredients except margarine and vanilla in a saucepan and bring to a boil. Cook for 2 minutes. Remove from heat and add vanilla and margarine. Let it cool and then beat until thick. Spread on top of pudding/graham cracker dish. Chill before serving.

Marilyn Chalmers

Cherry Delight

YIELD: 12 servings
CALORIES: 381
CARBOHYDRATES: 44g

FAT: 22g
PROTEIN: 3g

½   cup margarine
24 graham crackers
1   8 ounce package cream
    cheese
2   tablespoons milk
½   cup sugar

1   box non-dairy whipped
    topping mix, or 2
    envelopes
1   can cherry pie filling
½   cup nuts

Crumble crackers and mix with the margarine. Pat into bottom of a 9×12 inch baking dish. Beat cream cheese, milk and sugar until well blended. Add whipped topping mixed as directed on box. Pour into prepared graham cracker crust. Top with cherry pie filling and sprinkle with nuts. Chill.

Jeannine Henderson

Zabaione

YIELD: 4-6 large dessert cups
CALORIES: 272
CARBOHYDRATES: 16g

FAT: 18g
PROTEIN: 2g

3 egg yolks
3 tablespoons sugar
½ cup dry Marsala or dry
   sherry

2 cups whipping cream
2 tablespoons sugar, heaping
1 teaspoon powdered sugar

Bring water to a boil in the bottom of a double boiler. Stir egg
yolks and sugar until yolks turn a lighter color. Add the Marsala
slowly. Mix well in top of double boiler. Stir over the boiling
water until mixture coats a wooden spoon. Do not allow to boil.
Remove from the heat and stir for 2 or 3 minutes more. Place in
crockery bowl to cool, about 1 hour. Whip cream and sugars in
chilled utensils until stiff. Gently fold in the cold zabaione. Mix
carefully and slowly with a wire whisk. Cover bowl with foil
and chill until ready to use. May be made several hours in
advance.

Cathy Carson, Camille Jones

Banana Split Dessert

YIELD: 12 servings
CALORIES: 342
CARBOHYDRATES: 71g

FAT: 19g
PROTEIN: 2g

2 cups graham cracker
   crumbs
½ cup margarine, melted
8 ounces cream cheese,
   softened
1 box powdered sugar
1 large can crushed
   pineapple, drained

5 bananas
8 ounces non-dairy whipped
   topping
1 small jar maraschino
   cherries
½ cup chopped pecans

Combine graham chracker crumbs and melted margarine. Press
into bottom of 9×13 inch cake pan. Place in freezer about 15
minutes. Beat cream cheese and powdered sugar until well
blended. Spread crumb crust with cream cheese mixture. Cover
cream cheese mixture with crushed pineapple. Slice bananas
onto crushed pineapple. Cover with non-dairy whipped topping. Decorate top with cherries and pecans. Refrigerate until
ready to serve. Keeps well for 4 or 5 days.

Barbara Malone, Teri Jackson

Imperial Chocolate Temptations

YIELD: 8 to 10 servings
CALORIES: 402
CARBOHYDRATES: 33g

FAT: 31g
PROTEIN: 6g

4	squares chocolate, unsweetened	¾	cup sugar
4	squares chocolate, sweetened	1	teaspoon vanilla
5	egg yolks	4	egg whites
		1¼	cups heavy cream, stiffly beaten

Melt chocolate in microwave at 30 second intervals until it stirs easily. Cool. Beat egg yolks with ½ cup sugar until light and thick; add chocolate and vanilla. Beat egg whites until foamy; add ¼ cup sugar slowly until stiff peaks form. Beat ¼ of meringue into chocolate mixture. Fold in whipped cream and remaining meringue. Spoon into serving dishes and chill.

Lou Deaton

Good company dessert.

Josephine's Vinegar Roll

YIELD: 10 to 12 servings
CALORIES: 574
CARBOHYDRATES: 76g

FAT: 30g
PROTEIN: 2g

1	pie crust dough for double crust pie	2½	cups water
½	cup vinegar(cider)	3	cups sugar
		1	cup margarine or butter

Mix together vinegar, water and 2 cups of sugar. Bring to a boil. Roll out pie dough thin and into a rectangle. Spread dough generously with part of softened margarine. Sprinkle with remaining 1 cup of sugar. Roll up as for a jelly roll, beginning on long side. Cut crosswise slices ½ inch thick and place cut side down in a 9×13 inch pan. Slice remaining butter over rolls. Pour hot sugar and vinegar mixture on rolls. Bake at 400 degrees until golden brown. Liquid will be creamy and thick.

Lou Deaton

This is an old family recipe. Men really like this.

Gingerbread

YIELD: 32 to 36 pieces
CALORIES: 136
CARBOHYDRATES: 19g

FAT: 1g
PROTEIN: 6g

1	cup vegetable shortening	1	teaspoon cinnamon
1	cup sugar	1	teaspoon vanilla
1	cup molasses	½	teaspoon nutmeg
1	egg	½	teaspoon cloves
2½	cups flour	½	teaspoon allspice
1	teaspoon ginger	1	cup hot water
1	teaspoon soda		

Cream shortening, sugar, syrup and egg. Add dry ingredients, then add hot water. Pour into greased 9×13 inch baking pan. Bake at 350 degrees for 25 to 30 minutes.

Susan McMullan

Strawberry Pizza

YIELD: 12 to 14 slices
CALORIES: 238
CARBOHYDRATES: 25g

FAT: 15g
PROTEIN: 3g

1	cup flour	½	cup sugar
¼	cup powdered sugar	4	teaspoons cornstarch
½	cup margarine, softened	4	tablespoons sugar
8	ounces cream cheese	2	cups strawberries

Mix first 3 ingredients to make crust. Pat onto pizza pan. Bake at 350 degrees for 6 minutes or until lightly browned. Cool. Mix cream cheese and sugar together and spread on crust. Chill while preparing topping. In blender, mix strawberries, (reserve some for garnish), sugar and cornstarch. Pour in saucepan and heat until thickened. Cool. Spread on top of cream cheese. Garnish with reserved berries. Chill completely before serving.

Susan McMullan

Mocha Cups

YIELD: 12-2 inch chocolate cups
CALORIES: 310
CARBOHYDRATES: 30g

FAT: 21g
PROTEIN: 3g

6   ounce package chocolate
    chips, semi-sweet
¼   cup water
¼   cup sugar
2   teaspoons instant coffee
    powder
dash of salt

1   egg
½   cup heavy cream
1   teaspoon vanilla
whipped cream, plain or
    flavored with liqueur or
    extract
12 2 inch chocolate cups

In blender, chop chocolate chips; add boiling water and whirl until chocolate melts. Whirl in sugar, coffee powder, salt, egg, cream and vanilla. Blend until smooth and turn into bowl. Chill until very thick (like mayonnaise). Spoon into chocolate cups and keep chilled until served. Top with a dab of whipped cream and a cherry or chocolate shavings.

Lockie Sue Bissett

Mama Baggett's Coffee Souffle

YIELD: 8 servings
CALORIES: 107
CARBOHYDRATES: 18g

FAT: 3g
PROTEIN: 4g

1½ cups cold coffee
⅔ cup sugar
1   tablespoon gelatin
½   cup milk

3   eggs, separated
¼   teaspoon salt
1   teaspoon vanilla

Heat coffee, ⅓ cup sugar, gelatin and milk over low heat. Add slightly beaten egg yolks, ⅓ cup sugar and salt and continue cooking, stirring often until mixture thickens slightly. Remove mixture from heat. Add vanilla and cool, stirring often. When souffle begins to set, fold in slightly beaten egg whites. Pour into mold and chill.

Sandy Baggett

A favorite holiday recipe of Mrs. E. B. Baggett, Jr. May sprinkle top of souffle with chocolate shavings.

Cream Puff Shells

YIELD: 16 puffs
CALORIES: 25
CARBOHYDRATES: 3g

FAT: 4g
PROTEIN: 2g

½ cup hot water
¼ cup butter
¼ teaspoon salt
¼ teaspoon sugar

½ cup flour
2 eggs
1 egg, beaten

Combine hot water, butter, sugar, and salt in saucepan. Bring to a boil, stirring occasionally. Reduce heat and add flour all at once, stirring vigorously until flour is absorbed and mixture leaves sides of pan and forms a ball. Remove from heat. Cool 5 minutes. With metal blade in place, pour batter into processor beaker and add 2 eggs. Process until smooth and shiny, about 30 seconds. The mixture will be very thick. Drop round tea-spoons of mixture on an ungreased cookie sheet, leaving 2 inches between puffs. Brush tops with the beaten egg and set aside for 5 minutes before baking. Bake in preheated 425 degree oven for 10 minutes. Reduce heat to 375 degrees and bake about 30 minutes longer. Remove from oven and make a 1 inch slit in the upper part of each puff. Cool on wire racks. Cut off tops; save. Fill just before serving. Replace tops at a slant.

Camille Jones

Ambrosia

YIELD: 8 cups
CALORIES: 520
CARBOHYDRATES: 126g

FAT: 2g
PROTEIN: 6g

2 dozen navel oranges
3 ruby red grapefruit
2 large cans pineapple tidbits
1 large jar maraschino
    cherries

2 cups miniature
    marshmallows
sugar to taste
fresh grated coconut

Section grapefruit and oranges, drain pineapple, and cherries and cut in half. Mix ingredients in large jar or bowl the day before serving and refrigerate. Serve with grated coconut.

Mary Jo Mason

Refreshing with a heavy meal. A traditional holiday dessert with fruitcake or cookies.

Chafing Dish Dessert

YIELD: 12 servings
CALORIES: 162
CARBOHYDRATES: 27g

FAT: 5g
PROTEIN: 2g

28½ ounce jar spiced peaches, whole
6 ounce jar maraschino cherries
16 ounce can pear halves, in syrup

cornstarch
almonds
brandy or rum(optional)

Drain fruits, reserving syrups. Heat fruits in chafing dish. Blend the syrups and cornstarch, using 1 tablespoon cornstarch to each cup of syrup. Stir into hot fruit and heat until thickened. Add a jigger of brandy or rum if desired. Serve in individual compotes. Sprinkle with roasted slivered almonds. Serve hot. May also be served over pound cake with a dollop of whipped cream.

Benny Gail Hunnicutt

Hot Fudge Sauce

YIELD: 2½ cups or 40 tablespoons
CALORIES: 177
CARBOHYDRATES: 26g

FAT: 9g
PROTEIN: 1g

4 squares unsweetened chocolate
½ cup butter
½ teaspoon salt

3 cups sugar
1 12 ounce can evaporated milk

Melt chocolate, butter and salt together over low heat. Add sugar ½ cup at a time, stirring after each addition. Begin adding milk gradually when the sauce thickens. After it is mixed well, cook for 5 to 8 minutes, stirring occasionally. The longer you cook it, the harder it will be when served over ice cream. Refrigerate and heat to serve as wanted.

Nancy Vannoy

Banana Nut Ice Cream

YIELD: 1 gallon or 16 cups
CALORIES: 455
CARBOHYDRATES: 57g

FAT: 23g
PROTEIN: 9g

6 eggs
2 cups sugar
1 can sweetened condensed milk
1 cup whipping cream

1 tablespoon vanilla
2 cups toasted, chopped pecans
4 cups mashed bananas
milk

Beat eggs. Add sugar and beat until creamy. Add sweetened condensed milk, whipping cream, and vanilla. Beat. Pour mixture into ice cream container. Add milk to the container until it reaches the ⅔ mark. Freeze in ice cream freezer. After 15 minutes, add 4 cups bananas and 2 cups toasted pecans. Continue to freeze.

Jeannine Henderson

Easy to prepare, smooth and tasty, can use any kind of fruit.

Butter Finger Ice Cream

YIELD: 1 gallon or 16 cups
CALORIES: 305
CARBOHYDRATES: 31g

FAT: 17g
PROTEIN: 9g

6 eggs
¾ cup sugar
1 can sweetened condensed milk
1 pint half and half

½ pint whipping cream
1 teaspoon vanilla
6 large butter finger candy bars, frozen
milk, enough to fill to line on freezer

Beat eggs and sugar until light yellow and thickened. Gradually beat in condensed milk, half and half, and whipping cream. Crush butter finger candy bars and stir into mixture along with the vanilla. Pour into freezer and add milk to fill line. Freeze.

Belinda Wilkins

No Icey Ice Cream

YIELD: 4 quarts (16 cups)
CALORIES: 394
CARBOHYDRATES: 64g

FAT: 11g
PROTEIN: 11g

5   eggs
2   cups sugar
2   small packages
    gelatin(flavor of chosen
    fruit)
½ cup boiling water

2   cans sweetened condensed
    milk
1   can evaporated milk
fresh fruit or 2 tablespoons
    vanilla
milk

Dissolve gelatin in boiling water. Put all ingredients (except sweet milk) in ice cream freezer bucket. Mix well. Fill bucket with milk. Freeze in crank or electric ice cream freezer.

Elizabeth Clark

You will need an ice cream freezer. This ice cream can be put in your home freezer and eaten the following day.

Rich Vanilla Ice Cream

YIELD: 1½ Gallons, 24 servings
CALORIES: 339
CARBOHYDRATES: 42g

FAT: 16g
PROTEIN: 9g

12 eggs
4   cups sugar
4   quarts whole milk
1   pint whipping cream

2   tablespoons flour
pinch salt
2   to 3 teaspoons vanilla

Beat eggs until light and fluffy. Beat in the sugar. Add the milk and cream, reserving some milk to blend with flour. Mix the reserved milk with the flour to form a smooth paste. Add to the custard mixture along with the salt. Cook over low heat, stirring constantly, until it begins to thicken and coats the spoon. Remove from heat, add vanilla. Cool completely and pour into electric ice cream freezer. Freeze according to manufacturer's instructions.

Jane Richardson

Fruit Sherbet

YIELD: 18 to 20 servings
CALORIES: 254
CARBOHYDRATES: 51g

FAT: 5g
PROTEIN: 4g

1   15¼ ounce can crushed
    pineapple
6   cans Orange Crush soda
    pop

3   bananas, mashed
2   14 ounce cans condensed
    milk
    juice of 1 lemon

Mix all ingredients and freeze in an ice cream freezer.

Tina Bean

Oatmeal Sundaes

YIELD: 12 servings
CALORIES: 533
CARBOHYDRATES: 53g

FAT: 36g
PROTEIN: 5g

½   cup oatmeal
½   cup brown sugar
1   cup butter

1½ cups pecans, chopped
½   gallon vanilla ice cream
1   jar caramel topping

Mix first 4 ingredients together and press into a pizza pan or cookie sheet. Cook at 350 degrees for 30 minutes. Cool. Crumble ½ of this mixture in a 9×13 inch pan. Slice ice cream and place over crumbs. Pour caramel topping over ice cream and freeze. Before serving, press or spoon reserved oatmeal crumbles over topping. Serve in squares.

Paula Bailey

Ice Box Cake

YIELD: 12 to 14 servings
CALORIES: 367
CARBOHYDRATES: 35g

FAT: 25g
PROTEIN: 3g

1 cup crushed pineapple and juice
1 cup grapenut cereal
1 cup pecans, toasted in small amount of butter
2 eggs, separated

½ cup butter
1 cup sugar
½ pound vanilla wafers
1 cup cream, whipped
maraschino cherries

Pour pineapple over grapenuts and pecans. Beat egg whites until stiff, set aside. Cream butter, sugar, and egg yolks. Mix in pineapple mixture. Fold in egg whites. Crush vanilla wafers. Put half crushed wafer crumbs in a serving bowl, top with pineapple mixture. Sprinkle other half crumbs over top. Chill. Serve in sherbet glasses topped with whipped cream with a cherry on top.

Marolyn Bean

A pretty dessert for Christmas Dinner.

Pineapple Frozen Cake

YIELD: 20
CALORIES: 262
CARBOHYDRATES: 34g

FAT: 14g
PROTEIN: 2g

2 cups sugar
1 cup margarine, softened
1 number 2 can crushed pineapple

1 cup chopped pecans
1 pound graham crackers, crushed

Cream sugar and margarine, add pineapple, nuts and crushed crackers. Mix thoroughly and pack into cracker box. Freeze. Remove from box. Cut in squares and serve frozen.

Katharine Russell

Bazaar

Bumpgate — unique to West Texas, an easy way to avoid
opening so many gates.

Cactus Jelly

YIELD: 8 pints

2 quarts cactus juice	3 boxes powdered pectin
½ cup lemon juice	5 pounds sugar

Singe spines off of cactus tunas over gas flame. Scrub with a stiff brush in cold water. Cover cactus with water in a large, heavy saucepan and cook for 15 minutes. Cut the cactus tunas in half and add more water and cook until tender. Strain juice through a cloth. Mix together cactus juice, lemon juice and pectin. Bring to a boil and add the sugar. Bring to a rolling boil for 1 to 3 minutes or until it slips off the spoon. Pour into hot, sterilized jars and seal.

Kay McMullan Stewart

Aunt Margaret's Cranberry Jelly

1 quart cranberries	2 cups sugar
1 cup water	

Combine the water and cranberries in a 3 quart pan. Cook until all of the cranberries have burst. Remove from the heat and press through a sieve. Put the pulp back into the pan and heat just to a boil. Remove from heat, add the sugar and stir until it is dissolved. Pour into serving dishes or jelly glasses and cover with plastic wrap. Refrigerate.

Elizabeth Upham

Fig Preserves

1 quart figs, not quite ripe	1 lemon, thinly sliced,
1 quart sugar	optional
	1 cup water

Peel and measure the figs. Put sugar in a saucepan and add the water. Bring to a boil and add the figs and lemon. Cook until clear. Remove from heat and put aside until the next day. Place back on the heat and bring to a full boil. Turn off the heat. Pour into sterilized jars and seal.

Lou Deaton

Peach Preserves

3 pounds peaches   2 pounds sugar

Blanche, peel and slice peaches. Cover peaches with the sugar and let them stand until syrupy. Boil as rapidly as possible without scorching the peaches. Cook until clear and syrup thickens, stirring frequently. Pour into hot, sterilized jars and seal immediately.

Lou Deaton

Prickly Pear Jelly

1 gallon prickly pear cactus   4 cups juice from fruit
   fruit, very ripe, deep   4 cups sugar
   garnet color   2 packages fruit pectin

Gather the fruit using tongs and gloves. Wash small stickers from the fruit with a brush. Place the fruit in a large enamel kettle, cover with water and boil gently until fruit is shriveled. Strain through several layers of cheesecloth. Place the juice and sugar in a kettle and bring to a boil. Add pectin and bring to a rolling boil for 2 to 3 minutes. Pour into jelly glasses and seal with paraffin.

Mary Jo Mason

You will need courage to gather the fruit.

Mo's Chow-Chow

YIELD: 12 to 18 pints

2 gallons green tomatoes
1 gallon cabbage, 2 heads
1 quart onions, more if desired
4 sweet bell peppers
4 or 5 hot peppers, more if desired
4 cups sugar
1 quart vinegar, to cover

2 teaspoons tumeric
2 teaspoons salt, more to taste
2 teaspoons cinnamon, more to taste
2 teaspoons ginger, more to taste
2 teaspoons cloves, more to taste

Grind together the first 5 ingredients. Put in a large enamel pan and add the sugar, vinegar and spices. Cook on low heat until thick, adding more salt, sugar or spices to taste. Pack in sterilized jars and process in boiling water bath for 5 minutes.

Mary Jo Mason

This was my Grandmother Ward's recipe.

Bread and Butter Pickles

8 quarts cucumbers, sliced
8 large onions, thinly sliced
5 large sweet peppers, sliced lengthwise
1 cup salt
2 quarts white vinegar

1 teaspoon tumeric
3 teaspoons powdered mustard
7 cups sugar
¼ teaspoon mustard seed

Combine cucumbers, onions, peppers and salt and let stand for 24 hours. Bring vinegar, sugar, tumeric, mustard and mustard seeds to a boil. Drain cucumbers and add to vinegar mixture. Bring back to boil, spoon into hot jars and seal.

Carmen Sutton and Sandra Childress

The food processor comes in handy here!

Edna's Dill Pickles

Small to medium sized
   cucumbers, washed and
   dried
dill seeds or stalk

3 quarts water
1 pint white vinegar
1 cup salt

Pack cucumbers in jars. Add dill seeds or stalk. Cook the remaining ingredients for one minute at the boiling point. Pour hot mixture over pickles in the jars. Let set for 1 minute and then put hot lids on the jars. Seal while hot. Invert jars. These pickles will be table ready in 6 weeks.

Jane Richardson

This recipe is from Mrs. Edna Schwartz, Priddy, Texas

Cocoa Mix

YIELD: 1 gallon dry mix or
48 cups of cocoa CALORIES: 143
CARBOHYDRATES: 28g

FAT: 5g
PROTEIN: 5g

1 24 ounce box of non-fat
   dry milk
2 pounds Nestle's Quick

1 pound powdered sugar
1 pound non-dairy creamer

Mix all the ingredients in a large bowl. Put the mix in air tight containers. To serve, mix ⅓ cup of the mix with 1 cup hot water.

Cathy Carson

This makes a great gift.

Cinnamon Rolls

YIELD: 5 to 6 dozen
CALORIES: 188
CARBOHYDRATES: 30g

FAT: 6g
PROTEIN: 3g

6½ cups flour
3 teaspoons baking powder
2 teaspoons salt
1 teaspoon soda
¼ cup sugar
½ cup vegetable shortening
1 package dry yeast in ½ cup warm water

2 cups buttermilk
6 tablespoons butter or margarine, melted
1 cup sugar
3 teaspoons cinnamon

Sift the first 5 ingredients together. Cut in the shortening. Add the dissolved yeast and buttermilk. Mix well. Roll the dough thin or to about ¼ inch. Spread with the melted butter or margarine. Mix the remaining sugar and cinnamon together. Sprinkle on dough, allowing the butter to absorb the mixture. Roll jelly-roll style and slice in 1 inch thick slices. May brush with melted butter and freeze at this point. Place with sides slightly touching in a greased baking pan. Bake at 350 degrees for 30 minutes. Glaze with powdered sugar and milk if desired.

Nancy Vannoy

Cinnamon Rolls

YIELD: 3 to 4 dozen
CALORIES: 160
CARBOHYDRATES: 23g

FAT: 6g
PROTEIN: 2g

1 package dry yeast
⅓ cup warm water
1 tablespoon sugar
1½ cups scalded milk
¾ cup vegetable shortening
2 eggs, beaten
¼ cup sugar

5 cups flour
¾ tablespoon salt
sugar
cinnamon
½ cup margarine, melted

Add the yeast and 1 tablespoon sugar to the water in a large bowl. Add the shortening to the milk and set aside. Beat the eggs with ¼ cup sugar and add milk mixture gradually and then mix into the yeast mixture. Beat in three cups of flour and the salt. Knead in the remaining 2 cups of flour. Cover and let rise in a warm place until doubled in size. Divide dough into halves and roll out each into a rectangle. Sprinkle with sugar and cinnamon and drizzle margarine over all. Roll jelly-roll style and cut into 1 inch slices with a sharp knife. Place in pans and let rise again until doubled. Bake in 425 degree oven for 8 to 10 minutes. Drizzle with a powdered sugar and milk glaze, if desired.

Lorelei McMullen

The best ever and worth the trouble!

Pumpkin Bread

YIELD: 2 loaves - 24 servings
CALORIES: 279
CARBOHYDRATES: 45g

FAT: 10g
PROTEIN: 3g

3½ cups sugar
3½ cups flour, sifted
2 teaspoons soda
2 teaspoons allspice

1 cup water
1 cup vegetable oil
4 eggs
1 can pumpkin

Mix the dry ingredients together and add the remaining ingredients and mix well. Pour into 2 greased and floured loaf pans. Bake at 350 degrees for 1 hour.

Jeannine Henderson

Julia's Pumpkin Nut Bread

YIELD: 1 9 inch loaf, 10 slices
CALORIES: 295
CARBOHYDRATES: 42g

FAT: 13g
PROTEIN: 5g

2 cups flour, sifted	1 cup solid pack pumpkin
2 teaspoons baking powder	1 cup sugar
½ teaspoon soda	½ cup milk
1 teaspoon salt	2 eggs
1 teaspoon cinnamon	¼ cup butter, softened
½ teaspoon nutmeg	1 cup chopped pecans or walnuts

Sift together the first 6 ingredients. Combine pumpkin, sugar, milk and eggs and mix well. Add the dry ingredients and the butter. Mix well. Stir in the nuts and spread into a well greased 9 inch loaf pan. Bake at 350 degrees for 45 to 55 minutes or until bread tests done with a toothpick or a cake tester. When doubling this recipe use 1 #303 can of pumpkin and double the remaining ingredients.

Cathy Carson

Freezes well.

Apricot Brandy Pound Cake

YIELD: 12 to 16 servings
CALORIES: 480
CARBOHYDRATES: 64g

FAT: 19g
PROTEIN: 6g

1 cup butter	½ cup apricot brandy
3 cups sugar	1 teaspoon vanilla
6 eggs	½ teaspoon rum extract
3 cups flour	½ teaspoon lemon extract
½ teaspoon salt	¼ teaspoon almond extract
¼ teaspoon baking soda	¼ teaspoon orange extract
1 cup sour cream	

Cream together butter and sugar. Add eggs one at a time. Combine flour, salt and soda. Then combine sour cream, brandy and extracts. Alternately add sour cream mixture and flour mixture into creamed mixture. Pour into a greased and floured 10 inch tube pan. Bake at 325 degrees for 70 minutes or until done.

Lou Deaton

Good for Christmas gift, cake sales or bazaar. Freezes well and also keeps several days tightly wrapped.

Carrot Cake

YIELD: 20 servings
CALORIES: 299
CARBOHYDRATES: 33g

FAT: 18g
PROTEIN: 3g

2½ cups flour
1   teaspoon baking powder
1   teaspoon soda
1   teaspoon cinnamon
1   teaspoon salt

1½ cups salad oil
2   cups sugar
4   eggs
2   cups finely grated carrots

Sift the first 5 ingredients together. Combine the oil and sugar and mix with the dry ingredients. Add the eggs and beat well. Gradually add the carrots until well mixed. Pour into 3 eight inch greased and floured cake pans. Bake at 350 degrees for 50 to 60 minutes. Cool layers to room temperature and then frost.

ICING
½   cup butter
8   ounces cream cheese
1   pound powdered sugar

1   teaspoon vanilla
1   cup chopped pecans

Combine the butter and cream cheese and beat well. Gradually add the powdered sugar and continue beating. Add vanilla and nuts, mix well and spread on cooled cake.

Jeannine Henderson

German Chocolate Cake

YIELD: 20 servings
CALORIES: 360
CARBOHYDRATES: 38g

FAT: 23g
PROTEIN: 4g

1 package German Sweet Chocolate
½ cup boiling water
1 cup butter
2 cups sugar
4 egg yolks

1 teaspoon vanilla
½ teaspoon salt
2½ cups cake flour
1 teaspoon baking soda
1 cup buttermilk
4 egg whites, stiffly beaten

Melt the chocolate in the water. This can be done in the microwave or on range top. Cream the butter and sugar until fluffy. Add the egg yolks, one at a time, beating well after each. Add the cooled, melted chocolate. Sift the dry ingredients and add alternately with the buttermilk to the chocolate batter. Beat until smooth. Fold in the beaten egg whites. Pour into three 9 inch layer pans, lined on the bottom with waxed paper. Bake at 350 degrees for 40 minutes. Cool before frosting.

ICING
1 cup evaporated milk
3 tablespoons flour
1 cup sugar
3 egg yolks

½ cup butter or margarine
1 teaspoon vanilla
1⅓ cups coconut
1 cup chopped pecans

Combine the milk, flour, sugar, egg yolks and butter. Cook over low heat, stirring constantly until thickened, about 12 minutes. Add the coconut and pecans. Beat until spreading consistency.

Cathy Carson and Janie Chandler

Italian Cream Cake

YIELD: 20 servings
CALORIES: 459
CARBOHYDRATES: 28g

FAT: 38g
PROTEIN: 6g

5   eggs, separated
½ cup margarine
2   cups sugar
½ cup vegetable shortening
1   cup buttermilk

2   cups flour, sifted
1   teaspoon soda
2   teaspoons vanilla
1   cup chopped nuts
2   cups shredded coconut

Beat the egg whites until stiff and set aside. Cream the margarine and shortening, add the sugar and beat well. Add the egg yolks, one at a time and beat well after each. Add the buttermilk alternately with the dry ingredients and beat well. Add the vanilla, nuts and coconut and mix well. Fold the egg whites into mixture and pour into three 8 inch greased and floured cake pans. Bake at 350 degrees for 25 to 30 minutes. Cool layers and frost.

ICING

12 ounces cream cheese,
       softened
¾ cup margarine
24 ounces powdered sugar

3   teaspoons vanilla
1½ cups nuts
milk, as needed

Beat the cream cheese and margarine until well blended. Add the powdered sugar, vanilla and nuts and mix well. Add milk 1 tablespoon at a time until icing is of spreading consistency.

Becky Childress

Can be frozen.

Lemon Buttermilk Pound Cake

YIELD: 20
CALORIES: 361
CARBOHYDRATES: 50g

FAT: 17g
PROTEIN: 4g

1½ cups butter or margarine
3 cups sugar
3 cups flour
½ teaspoon salt

½ teaspoon soda
6 eggs
1 cup buttermilk
2 teaspoons lemon extract

Cream the butter and sugar until light and fluffy. Add the eggs one at a time, beating well after each. Sift the dry ingredients and add to creamed mixture alternately with the buttermilk, beating well. Add the lemon extract and beat well. Pour into a 10 inch greased and floured tube pan or two 9 inch loaf pans. Bake at 325 degrees for 1 hour and 15 minutes. Cool in pan for 10 minutes, remove cake from pan and pour glaze over cake.

GLAZE
1½ tablespoons milk
1 tablespoon butter or margarine

1 cup powdered sugar
1½ tablespoons lemon juice

Heat the milk and butter and pour over the sugar. Stir until smooth. Add the lemon juice and stir. Pour over the warm cake.

Cathy Carson

Pumpkin Cake

YIELD: 20 servings
CALORIES: 390
CARBOHYDRATES: 45g

FAT: 23g
PROTEIN: 3g

2 cups sugar
1½ cups oil
4 eggs
2 cups flour

2 teaspoons soda
1 teaspoon salt
3 teaspoons cinnamon
1 can pumpkin

Combine the sugar and oil on low speed of an electric mixer. Add the eggs, one at a time, beating well after each. Combine the dry ingredients and add to the first mixture, a little at a time, mixing well. Add the pumpkin and mix well. Bake in a greased and floured tube pan at 350 degrees for one hour. Frost with cream cheese icing.

ICING
8 ounces cream cheese
¼ cup margarine

1 pound powdered sugar, sifted
2 teaspoons vanilla

Beat the cream cheese and margarine together. Add the powdered sugar and vanilla and beat well. Spread on cooled cake.

Elizabeth Upham

Waldorf Astoria Cake (Red Velvet)

YIELD: 20 servings
CALORIES: 303
CARBOHYDRATES: 38g

FAT: 16g
PROTEIN: 3g

½ cup shortening
1½ cups sugar
2 eggs
2 tablespoons cocoa
2 ounces red food coloring
1 teaspoon salt, scant

2¼ cups flour
1 teaspoon vanilla
1 cup buttermilk
1 teaspoon soda
1 tablespoon vinegar

Cream the shortening, sugar and eggs until fluffy. Make a paste of the cocoa and food coloring. Add the creamed mixture. Combine the flour and salt. Combine the buttermilk and vanilla. Add the flour and buttermilk mixtures alternately. beating well after each addition. Gently fold in the vinegar and soda, blending well. DO NOT BEAT. Pour into two greased and floured 9 inch layer pans or three 8 inch layer pans. Bake at 350 degrees for 30 minutes. Cool layers. The 9 inch layers can be split to make 4.

ICING
3 tablespoons flour
1 cup milk
1 cup margarine or butter,

1 teaspoon vanilla
1 cup sugar

Cook the milk and flour over medium heat until very thick, can use ¼ cup flour. Add a dash of salt if desired. Stir constantly. Cool in the refrigerator. Cream the butter and sugar until fluffy and white. You can use ½ cup of shortening and ½ cup butter instead of the 1 cup butter. Add the cooled flour mixture and vanilla. Beat until the consistency of whipped cream. Frost on the cooled cake layers.

Paula Bailey and Cathy Carson

Try making half the batter green and half red for a Christmas cake.

Marilyn's Spritz Cookies

YIELD: 36 cookies
CALORIES: 95
CARBOHYDRATES: 11g

FAT: 5g
PROTEIN: 1g

1 cup butter	2½ cups flour
¾ cup sugar	½ teaspoon baking powder
1 egg	pinch of salt
1 teaspoon vanilla	

Cream the butter and sugar. Add the egg and vanilla. Mix the dry ingredients and add to the first mixture. This dough can be rolled and cut, but it is best when used in a cookie press and baked in strips. Bake at 375 degrees for 8 to 10 minutes or until golden brown. Remove very quickly from ungreased cookie sheets. This recipe freezes well.

Lorelei McMullan

Divinity

YIELD: 48 pieces
CALORIES: 170
CARBOHYDRATES: 23g

FAT: 9g
PROTEIN: 1g

4 cups sugar	1 teaspoon vanilla
1 cup water	5 cups pecan halves
1 cup white corn syrup	4 egg whites, stiffly beaten

Put one cup of sugar and ½ cup of the water in a small pan. Put remaining sugar and water, along with the syrup, in a large pan. Put both pans on at the same time, using medium heat on the large pan and the small pan on high. Cook ingredients in the small pan until all the water is gone. Pour into the egg whites in a thin stream, beating constantly with an electric mixer. When the mixture in the large pan reaches 240 degrees (soft boil), pour into the egg mixture ⅓ at a time, setting the pan back on the stove each time to keep it warm. Add the vanilla and nuts. Drop by teaspoon on wax paper.

Benny Gail Hunnicutt

Susie Harrison's Microwave Fudge

YIELD: 20
CALORIES: 240g
CARBOHYDRATES: 24g

FAT: 17g
PROTEIN: 4g

1   12 ounce package chocolate
    chips

1   can Eagle Brand Milk
1¾ to 2 cups chopped pecans

Combine chips and milk, microwave on high for 20 to 30 seconds. Stir. Microwave again for 20 to 30 seconds. Stir in pecans and spread in a buttered 9 inch square pan.

1987 Day Care Board

The lower the wattage of the microwave oven, the more cooking time required.

Fudge

YIELD: 3 pounds 48 servings
CALORIES: 144
CARBOHYDRATES: 21g

FAT: 7g
PROTEIN: 1g

3   cups sugar
¾   cup butter
⅔   cup evaporated milk
1   12 ounce package semi-
    sweet chocolate pieces

1   7 ounce jar marshmallow
    cream
1   cup chopped nuts
1   teaspoon vanilla

Combine the sugar, butter and milk in a heavy 2½ quart saucepan. Bring to a full rolling boil, stirring constantly. Continue boiling for 5 minutes over medium heat or until candy thermometer reaches 234 degrees, stirring constantly. Remove from heat and stir in chocolate until melted. Add remaining ingredients and beat until blended. Pour into 9×13 inch pan. Cool to room temperature and cut into squares. To make peanut butter fudge, substitute 2 cups crunchy peanut butter for the chocolate and omit the nuts.

Belinda Wilkins

Mil's Peanut Brittle

YIELD: 24 servings
CALORIES: 213
CARBOHYDRATES: 30g

FAT: 10g
PROTEIN: 5g

2 cups sugar
1 cup corn syrup
1 cup water

2 cups unsalted, raw peanuts
2 teaspoons soda
2 tablespoons margarine

Combine the sugar, water and syrup in a heavy pan. Cook rapidly while stirring until the sugar is dissolved. Do not stir after this point is reached. Continue to boil until mixture spins a thread, about 3 to 6 minutes. Add the peanuts and cook until mixture is brown all over, 12 to 15 minutes. Add the soda and margarine. Stir with a wooden handled spoon until well dissolved. Pour out on a large sheet of heavy foil that has been greased with butter. Let it cool and break into serving pieces.

Jodie Sessom

Caramel Corn

YIELD: 24 servings
CALORIES: 241
CARBOHYDRATES: 27g

FAT: 14g
PROTEIN: 4g

2 cups popcorn, unpopped
½ cup light corn syrup
2 cups brown sugar
1 cup butter

½ teaspoon baking soda
1 tablespoon vanilla
1 pound can salted peanuts

Pop the popcorn. Stir together syrup, sugar and butter in a large saucepan. Cook on low heat for 5 minutes. Remove from heat and stir in the soda, vanilla and peanuts. Pour mixture over the popcorn and mix well. Bake at 250 degrees for 1 hour stirring every 15 minutes. Store in airtight containers.

Belinda Wilkins

Poppycock

YIELD: 4 quarts
CALORIES: 252
CARBOHYDRATES: 24G

FAT: 17G
PROTEIN: 4G

1 cup brown sugar	½ teaspoon soda
½ cup margarine	15 cups popped corn
¼ cup light corn syrup	1 to 2 cups pecans and/or
½ teaspoon salt	peanuts

Preheat the oven to 200 degrees. In a large saucepan, heat the sugar, margarine, syrup and salt, stirring occasionally until mixture is bubbly around the edges. Continue cooking on medium heat for 5 minutes. Remove from heat and stir in the soda until foamy. Place corn and nuts in a large flat pan with deep sides. Pour hot syrup mixture over all and stir to coat. Bake for 1 hour, stirring every 15 minutes. Store in airtight containers.

Sherry Scott

Pie Crust

YIELD: 2 pie crusts
CALORIES: 273
CARBOHYDRATES: 12g

FAT: 19g
PROTEIN: 2g

¾ cup Crisco	2 cups flour
1 tablespoon milk	1 teaspoon salt
¼ cup boiling water	2 sheets wax paper

Add milk to Crisco and blend with a fork. Add boiling water to first mixture and blend with a fork. Beat with a whisk until all moisture is absorbed. It should resemble whipping cream. Add the flour and salt and mix until the dough forms a ball. Divide in half. Moisten the counter top and place one sheet of wax paper on it. Place dough on paper and put the other sheet on top. Roll in a circle. Remove top sheet and place pie pan on dough. Run your hand under the bottom wax paper and flip the dough and plate together. If a baked pastry is needed, bake at 400 degrees for 10 minutes, pricking pastry with a fork to prevent bubbles.

Cathy Carson, Janie Chandler, Lockie Sue Bissett

This recipe doubles, even triples well. Freeze several for convenience.

Pecan Pie

YIELD: 8 servings
CALORIES: 570
CARBOHYDRATES: 68g

FAT: 32g
PROTEIN: 6g

4 eggs, beaten
1 cup sugar
½ teaspoon salt
4 tablespoons margarine

1 teaspoon vanilla
1 cup light corn syrup
1½ cups pecan halves

Beat together until blended the eggs, sugar, salt, vanilla, margarine and syrup. Stir in pecans. Pour into unbaked pie shell and bake at 325 degrees until center no longer shakes or until knife inserted into center comes out clean.

Janie Chandler

VARIATION: Preheat oven to 350 degrees. Use ¾ cup sugar, 1¼ cups light corn syrup, ¾ cup butter and 1¼ cups pecan halves. Continue mixing as above adding other ingredients listed. Pour into a 10 inch pie shell or 9 inch deep dish. Bake for 45 minutes until nicely browned. Filling sets as pie cools.

Cathy Carson

Pumpkin Pie

YIELD: 8 servings
CALORIES: 329
CARBOHYDRATES: 47g

FAT: 13g
PROTEIN: 7g

2   eggs, beaten
1   16 ounce can pumpkin
1   cup brown sugar, firmly
    packed
1   teaspoon cinnamon
½   teaspoon nutmeg
½   teaspoon ginger

¼   teaspoon cloves
1   tablespoon flour
½   teaspoon salt
1⅔ cup evaporated milk
1   10 inch pie shell or 9 inch
    deep dish

Combine eggs and pumpkin. Blend in the sugar, spices, flour and salt. Mix well. Add the milk and mix well. Pour into desired pastry shell and bake at 425 degrees for 15 minutes, reduce heat to 350 degrees and bake for 35 to 40 minutes or until a knife inserted into center of pie comes out clean.

Cathy Carson

VARIATION: Use only 1 egg and 2 tablespoons brown sugar. Omit the flour and cloves. Use 1 can Eagle Brand milk instead of evaporated milk. Continue mixing and adding ingredients as above. Bake at 375 degrees for 40 minutes or until pie tests done.

Helen Bean

Chicken Spaghetti

YIELD: 12 servings
CALORIES: 404
CARBOHYDRATES: 22g

FAT: 24g
PROTEIN: 27g

3   to 4 pound fryer, cooked,
    boned and cut-up
1   package long spaghetti
½   cup margarine
1   cup chopped celery
1   cup chopped onion

1   cup chopped bell pepper
2   cans tomato soup
2   cups chicken broth
salt, pepper and garlic powder,
    to taste
1   pound cheese, grated

Cook the spaghetti and drain. Saute the vegetables in the butter. Add the soup and 1 to 2 cans water. In a separate bowl, combine the chicken and chicken broth and set aside. Add seasonings and tomato soup and half of the cheese to the spaghetti. Stir in the chicken and broth. Pour into a casserole dish and bake at 350 degrees until bubbly. Top with remaining cheese and serve.

Karen Childress

Chicken Spaghetti

YIELD: 20 servings
CALORIES: 332
CARBOHYDRATES: 23g

FAT: 17g
PROTEIN: 23g

1 hen plus 2 chicken breasts,
   cooked, skinned, boned
   and cut-up
broth from cooking chicken
2 cups chopped celery
1 48 ounce package spaghetti
1½ cups onions, chopped

1 cup ripe chopped olives
1 cup green chopped olives
2 cans cream of chicken soup
1 pound American cheese,
   cubed
1 pound Velveeta cheese,
   cubed

Cook the broken spaghetti, celery, onions in broth until al dente. Drain, reserving broth. Stir in prepared chicken and olives. Heat the soup and cheeses in a saucepan until melted and mix into spaghetti. Thin with chicken broth if too thick. Bake, covered at 350 degrees until bubbly.

Cathy Dawn Davis Moore

Divide between 2 casseroles and freeze one for later.

Chicken Spaghetti

YIELD: 10 servings
CALORIES: 392
CARBOHYDRATES: 24g

FAT: 19g
PROTEIN: 32g

4 pounds chicken, cooked,
   boned, skinned and cut up
2 cups chicken broth
1 bell pepper, minced
5 celery stalks, chopped
¾ cup minced onion
1 clove garlic

1 box spaghetti, cooked
1 large can mushrooms
1 16 ounce can tomatoes,
   seived
salt and pepper
1 pound cheese, grated

To simmering chicken broth add pepper, celery, onion and garlic. Cook until tender. Add spaghetti, chicken and mushrooms and mushroom juice, tomatoes and salt and pepper to taste. Simmer slowly until blended and thick. Add cheese and serve. Add more broth if necessary.

Helen Bean

Lasagne

YIELD: 6 to 8 servings
CALORIES: 651
CARBOHYDRATES: 38g

FAT: 155g
PROTEIN: 48g

SAUCE
5   strips bacon
¼   cup chopped bell pepper
2   onions, chopped
3   pounds ground chuck
2   tablespoons oregano
2   teaspoons garlic salt
2   teaspoons salt
3   16 ounce cans tomatoes

3   10¾ ounce cans tomato puree
2   6 ounce cans tomato paste
2   10½ ounce cans tomato soup
3   4 ounce cans sliced mushrooms

Fry bacon in a large saucepan with lid. Remove, drain and crumble bacon. Brown the pepper, onion and meat in the bacon drippings. Add remaining ingredients including the crumbled bacon. Simmer for about 6 hours or until thick. Makes 16 cups of sauce.

CASSEROLE
4   to 6 cups sauce from recipe above
¾   pound lasagne noodles
1   cup grated Parmesan cheese

1   pound cottage cheese
1   pound sliced mozzarella cheese

Pre-heat the oven to 375 degrees. Grease a large baking dish. Cook the noodles according to package directions, drain and rinse. Make a layer of pasta noodles, mozzarella, cottage cheese and sauce. Second layer of pasta and sauce; third layer same as first layer; fourth layer same as second. Sprinkle with Parmesan cheese. Bake about 1 hour or until bubbly. You may need a cookie sheet under the casserole to prevent oven spills. Freezes well.   **Karen Childress**

Homemade Handcream

1   pound UniBase
1   cup glycerin

1   ounce non-foaming bath oil
3   cups distilled water

Mix above ingredients at low speed with an electric mixer until smooth. This should take about 30 minutes. It should be fluffy and thick. Pour into bottles or plastic containers. Store in a dry place.   **Shawn Mitchell**

UniBase and glycerin are available at drugstores. This makes a great gift.

Index

OZONA WOMAN'S LEAGUE
P. O. Box 1552
Ozona, Texas 76943

Send me _____ copies of *Diamonds in the Desert!* at $13.95 per copy plus $2.00 postage and handling. Texas residents add $.84 for sales tax.

Name: _____

Address: _____

City: _____ State: _____ Zip: _____

All proceeds from the sale of this book will be used for community service projects sponsored by Ozona Woman's League. Make checks payable to:

OZONA WOMAN'S LEAGUE

OZONA WOMAN'S LEAGUE
P. O. Box 1552
Ozona, Texas 76943

Send me _____ copies of *Diamonds in the Desert!* at $13.95 per copy plus $2.00 postage and handling. Texas residents add $.84 for sales tax.

Name: _____

Address: _____

City: _____ State: _____ Zip: _____

All proceeds from the sale of this book will be used for community service projects sponsored by Ozona Woman's League. Make checks payable to:

OZONA WOMAN'S LEAGUE